D0928456

NINE CITIES

THE ANATOMY OF DOWNTOWN RENEWAL

A Retrospective Review of Nine Cities In Which
Panel Studies Were Made by ULI — the Urban Land
Institute

by Leo Adde

DALLAS — DENVER — DETROIT — MIDLAND
NEWARK — PEORIA — PHILADELPHIA
PITTSFIELD — ST. LOUIS

The original preparation of this report was undertaken with
support from the Department of Housing and Urban Development under its Urban Renewal Demonstration Program. It is
being published with Urban Land Institute funds. ULI — the
Urban Land Institute — is solely responsible for its contents.

ULI — the Urban Land Institute — 1200 18th Street, N.W.
Washington, D.C. 20036

i

Statement of Objectives of ULI—the Urban Land Institute

ULI — the Urban Land Institute is an independent, nonprofit research organization incorporated in 1936 under the laws of the State of Illinois. Its interests and activities cover the entire field of urban planning, growth and development. Among the principal purposes of the Institute are to study and to interpret trends in urban development and land use and to seek their orientation in the changing economic, social and civic needs of the country; to study principles and methods by which urban land can be developed and improved most efficiently; and to act as a clearinghouse in this field for the dissemination of information in the form of case material, reference books, monographs, and technical journals.

This book is one of a series of research publications to further the objectives of the Institute and to make generally available authoritative information of assistance to those seeking knowledge in the urban field.

* * *

The opinions expressed in this book are those of the individual Panel Members, city officials and civic leaders so identified. The interpretations of fact and value judgments are by the author and do not necessarily reflect those of the Officers, Trustees and Staff of ULI — the Urban Land Institute.

Preface

Throughout this book, the author refers to the **Urban Land Institute Panel Study Service**. Therefore, a brief description of **ULI's Panel Study Service** will enhance the reader's understanding of the nine case histories which follow.

Over the past 22 years, ULI has conducted 75 separate Panel Studies, most of them sponsored by public or quasi-public agencies in the areas involved.

Several aspects of these studies make them unique. First of all, Panel Members serve without pay. ULI Panels are independent advisory groups comprised of men at the policy level who contribute their time and experience to communities where they do not live or have financial interests.

Although it may sound old-fashioned in today's context, the Panel members take their "compensation" in the satisfaction of giving their time and know-how to help bring about an improved urban environment and to assist the Urban Land Institute in its land use and development research. ULI Panel Studies are made only at the invitation of local sponsors who, in turn, contribute to the financial support of the Institute's research and educational programs.

Thus the conclusions and recommendations of ULI Panels are objective, impartial and constructive. These studies are neither consultant's reports nor technical studies, but rather a "look over the shoulder" by some of America's most widely-known, experienced practitioners and entrepreneurs. A major benefit of most ULI Panel Studies is that they frequently serve as catalysts for urban and economic development efforts in the communities in which they are conducted.

Since ULI Panels are comprised of men in the business of making things happen—men who use studies rather than prepare them— their services are usually not available, either individually or collectively, except through the ULI Panel Study Service. Each man is selected from the 100 nationally-recognized individuals who serve on the Executive Groups of the three ULI Councils: Central City,

Industrial and Community Builders. Their selection to serve on a particular Panel is based on the private or public background of each as it relates to the specific problems being considered.

The ULI members who served on each Central City Panel reviewed in this report are listed at the beginning of the chapter dealing with their respective study areas.

The ten ULI Panel Studies referred to in this volume range over nearly two decades, and the cities themselves cover three centuries of change.

Since June 29, 1967, when Leo Adde completed his work, many events in these nine cities, as well as hundreds of others, have transpired to push the focus of this volume from the desks of city officials, city planners, and private developers into the forefront of the nation's consciousness. "Cities" has become a headline synonym for discord.

Almost every day, one can read reports of mounting involvement of the public at large, the business community and the federal government in what were once considered local community problems to be resolved by local officials.

In this same two-year period, the literature on the subject of city renewal has increased perhaps a hundredfold. The recent voluminous reports of the National Commission on Urban Problems and those of the Advisory Commission on Intergovernmental Relations are cases in point.

The purpose of this report is to evaluate the impact of the Panel's recommendations and to identify the motivating factors involved in each of the nine cities studied. The observations and conclusions contained in this volume represent one man's evaluation of how community leadership, working with and guided by public officials, achieved various degrees of success in these nine cities.

Robert E. Boley
Executive Director
ULI — the Urban Land Institute
Washington, D.C.
April, 1969

Introduction and Acknowledgments

The report which follows sets forth the results of an intensive investigation and reporting on the experiences of nine American cities combating the decline of their downtown districts. These cities were chosen as among the most significant from a list of about 30 in which studies had been conducted by panels of the Central City Council of the Urban Land Institute since 1949, and where in each case specific recommendations had been made by the panel for central city improvement. Time, size and geographic location were also factors in the selection. The investigation covered:

(1) A thorough review and digest of the panels' findings, conclusions and recommendations for the cities in which panel studies had been made.

(2) Selection of the cities to be investigated in depth.

(3) Independent field investigation of these cities with extensive interviews with local public officials and others involved as well as with members of the respective study panels.

(4) Analysis and reporting on results and accomplishment, if any, including the validity of panel recommendations over time, factors contributing to action or lack of it, political and financial considerations and elements which have led to successful accomplishment.

In 1951, two ULI panels found Philadelphia on dead center in downtown renewal with respect to the "Chinese Wall" [1] and redevelopment of the Triangle area extending from City Hall to the Schuylkill River between Market Street and the Ben Franklin Parkway. The city was also at odds over rebuilding as opposed to relocating the city's wholesale produce market. Today, the wall is gone with Penn Center and in-town apartments occupying a substantial portion of the Triangle, and the Dock Street market is a memory. The forces which stimulated and actuated these dramatic changes are dealt with in Chapter Two of the report.

In 1964, Newark renewal efforts were found to be guided largely by one public official with reliance for survival being placed in large degree on extensive public housing efforts. Local leadership was

---

[1] "Chinese Wall" refers to the 16-tracks of the Pennsylvania Railroad built in 1881 above grade which connected the 30th Street Terminal with the Broad Street Terminal, next to Philadelphia's City Hall.

reluctant "to depart from a proven formula for limited success" in attacking central city development. The panel's recommendations for broadening the efforts to reverse the higher income exodus, emphasize rehabilitation, broaden the tax base, more coordinated planning, and creation of a dynamic community concept in the Colleges Expansion Area, among other things, has apparently met with a low degree of official enthusiasm. What long-term effects the July, 1967 riots will have in Newark's renewal efforts and economic life is at this time a matter of conjecture.

In 1950, a ULI panel found downtown Dallas struggling with the postwar surge of traffic and pedestrians on its downtown streets and with less blight than most cities of its size. Recommendations revolved around problems of congestion and retaining the vitality of the central core. Choosing the local and private approach to "renewal," Dallas has not only made notable progress in some areas but has gone far beyond what was then envisioned by the panel or the city in its dynamic growth. But despite its wealth and vitality, the city has not fully defined its goals or objectives or recognized the growing problems of blight, nor has it fully comprehended its situation as a hub in a rapidly growing metropolitan and regional complex.

Peoria, in 1956, was still a "river town" in the eyes of the downtown merchants and many of its leading citizens—the school plant was inadequate, planning was virtually nonexistent, air pollution was becoming a problem and water supply was becoming critical. The panel's focus on downtown Peoria revealed that, in failing to upgrade the area to serve its increased affluence, the city was missing the boat to the tune of some $25-million in yearly retail sales, 1,500 jobs and several hundred thousand dollars in tax revenue. The rapidity with which the Peoria leadership—public and private—attacked its problems, and the results evident a decade later, represent a unique story among smaller American cities. In doing so, it has set some precedents in downtown renewal and may be in the process of setting more in the legal sphere relating to the future of downtown vs. outlying retail-commercial development.

Downtown Midland, Texas, and Pittsfield, Massachusetts, in 1966 were found to have as many similarities as differences. While time has not yet accumulated sufficiently to draw conclusions, it appears that for Midland's atrophied Main Street retail district "time has run out"; this in the presence of a highly educated, high-income, but transient, population, unmotivated by the retail needs of the community, and with a civic wealth found in few urban areas of the nation. By contrast, Pittsfield's central decay was being attacked with an "eagerness for a renewal effort" that has resulted in a proliferation of plans and political competition for control.

Denver, in 1955, was experiencing the beginnings of its present downtown growth; a dynamic city with no major competition within 500 miles. The panel's recommendations helped to generate new downtown retail store and hotel development and the Skyline renewal project, and planted the concept of unified planning and renewal for the emerging elongated central business district anchored at one end in "skid row" and the void of a recently vacated department store. However, the momentum generated by the new retail and commercial development to the southeast, the lack of continuity in the effectiveness of the city's "mover" group, together with considerable political hassling over the Skyline project, to date has slowed full realization of Downtown Denver's potential.

In 1954, St. Louis was not only experiencing a marked decline and decrease in its central business district but, paradoxically, an increasingly congested inner core clogged with vehicular traffic. The panel study conducted October 12-15, 1954 evaluated a wide range of problem areas, recommending among other things drastic clearance and rebuilding of "great segments of the close-in city," rendering services on a regional basis, compressing the 16-year expressway plan into five years and sharply increasing downtown off-street parking. Raymond R. Tucker, then mayor, adopted the recommendations of the report as his "Blueprint for Action" in setting up task force committees. Behind the constructve efforts at the public level, however, was and still is the continuing and highly effective and influential private group, Civic Progress, which has been instrumental in quietly nurturing and smoothing the path for the relatively rapid advance St. Louis has made in the field of city rebuilding.

In 1955, Detroit's post-war hopes of ridding itself of its mid-town residential slums had bogged down in a welter of conflicting decisions while, at the same time, the city's monumental civic center was just beginning to rise on the Detroit River. The panel's advice helped to guide Detroit away from the then prevalent notion that the central city was destined to house only those who had neither the choice nor the means to live elsewhere. The city was advised on what was needed to again make the core an attractive and productive area.

The present report was nearing completion when the riots broke out across the country. The ferocity and magnitude of the Detroit riots surprised nearly everyone concerned. Detroit had made remarkable progress in central city renewal, using the valid premise that new mid-city accommodations should be provided for the increasing urban middle-income people of both races. Perhaps Detroit's very success in this program was an indirect cause of bitterness among those who had not succeeded in lifting themselves to this level. In any event, when the cause and effect relationships of this catastrophe are studied and analyzed, all large cities throughout the nation will have access to a grim but useful history.

From these investigations into downtown renewal in nine cities, with their many dissimilarities, there emerges a number of common ingredients of major importance. While the presence of these ingredients may not ensure the complete viability of the civic fabric, their absence will almost surely result in something less than success.

Simply stated, these ingredients include the following. Which are most or least important will depend on many variables.

(1) A strong sense of community direction and goals and wide citizen understanding and involvement in their realization, based on sound knowledge of the city's nature and realistic analysis of its deficiencies and potentials.

(2) Broad-based plans and programs delineating these goals within realizable limits.

(3) A moratorium on "politics" in the partisan sense.

(4) Recognition of the need to utilize all the resources of public and private effort, including those of eminent domain, to accomplish the goals.

(5) An organization composed of the "movers"—"The Power Structure" if you will—limited in size and representing business leaders and decision makers in the community who are personally dedicated to maintaining and restoring the health and vitality of their community, of which the central city areas are a vital part.

It is not now clear what long-term effect recent happenings in a number of cities, and notably two covered in this report, will have on their future. But as the report concludes, these and "other difficulties must be met and mastered simply because the failure to do so would be an admission that many national values have been spurious."

This report was undertaken by ULI—the Urban Land Institute under a grant from the Department of Housing and Urban Development, Urban Renewal Demonstration Program which released it for publication by ULI on May 28, 1968. Work on the study was actively started on June 23, 1966, and completed on June 29, 1967. The Institute sincerely appreciates the opportunity of conducting it.

In proceeding with this work, the Institute was fortunate in obtaining as investigator and writer the services of Leo Adde, whose instructions were to report it as he found it. His seventeen-year career in journalism, in both the newspaper and broadcast media, provided the type of independent and objective investigation and reporting talents desired.

Adde has functioned as government "beat man" for *The New Orleans Item* and *The Miami Herald,* where he was also assistant city editor and member of the editorial board. His career in Louisiana has included covering the many facets of state-city politics during the administration of New Orleans Mayor deLesseps S. Morrison and Governor Earl K. Long.

The Herald brought Adde to Miami during the early days of the Dade County Metro government where he covered Metro's struggles and successes and helped to dispel some of the public's misgivings about a new layer of local government. Other assignments during his five-year tour with *The Herald* included feature articles on the changing face of Miami Beach and the political and economic impact of the Cuban refugees. Returning to New Orleans, Adde produced a series of documentaries on the city's decaying central city which helped to revive its slum-eradication agency, and on the inequities in the distribution of state educational funds for which he received several press awards. Adde received his education at Louisiana Tech and Loyola University of the South, and served as a commissioned officer in the Navy in World War II and Korea.

In January, 1969, Leo Adde was appointed News Director of television station WTOP-TV, Washington, D.C., the CBS affiliate that is one of the five broadcast properties of the *Post-Newsweek* stations.

Assisting in preparation of this manuscript for publication were members of the ULI Publications staff: Robert E. Levine, Barbara G. Cavanaugh and Terry Drummond.

ix

The Institute wishes to express its sincere appreciation to all of the persons who gave freely of their time and knowledge of the local scene in each of the cities covered. These include, most importantly, the civic, business and political leaders and public officials who were and are directly involved in the renewal efforts of their city, as well as the chairmen and members of the ULI panels which studied these cities over a period of time ranging from the early 1950's to the present. Their recollections, together with the independent investigations of Leo Adde, have made this report possible.

MAX S. WEHRLY
Executive Director
(1951-1968)
Urban Land Institute

Table of Contents

Chapter Seven:

Chapter Eight:

Chapter Nine:

Chapter Ten:

Epilogue:

Index

Table of Illustrations

xv

Addendum

It is three years since work began on this project. If, as the ULI editors have intimated, the work is not hopelessly outdated at the time it goes to press, the reason is not any prescience on the part of the writer, but rather the agonizingly slow pace of central city renewal, in planning and execution.

The factors which complicate the problem are piling up faster than are the innovative devices for reconstructing the urban cores. Examples abound of the proper way to design and finance a redevelopment project, some of these examples emanating from cities covered in this study. It has been discovered, however painfully, that a new clutch of towers and stores rising in the center of town does not guarantee that the people will become peaceful toward their environment and each other. The *style* of urban life, in the most profound sense of human relationships, has become the crucial domestic problem.

In the most critical analysis, everything which has been tried has failed to meet its goal entirely. Neither urban renewal, model cities, privately-financed redevelopment, spontaneously triggered clearance caused by riots, militancy, appeasement, the ministrations of technology and sociology, nor the inter-action of all these things has produced a blueprint for reconstructing the cities. But in another sense, no technique has been proven inadequate as part of the solution *except* wanton, pointless destruction.

Clearly, we are capable of building anything we are capable of designing. The trouble is, nobody has a design for cities now which can attract and accommodate individuals across the whole spectrum —from Board Chairman to his company's skilled workers to the people at the far end of the welfare line. But we know how to begin.

Washington, D. C.
July 18, 1969

Leo Adde

CHAPTER ONE

THE PREVIEW

NEEDED: THREE "Ps": PARTICIPATION, PLANNING, POWER OF EMINENT DOMAIN

President Lyndon B. Johnson's 1965 message to Congress calling for the creation of the Department of Housing and Urban Development contained one statement that could sustain both the gravest fears and the most soaring hopes of persons concerned about the state of this highly urbanized Union.

"In the remainder of this century—in less than 40 years—urban population will double," said the President, "city land will double, and we will have to build in our cities as much as all that we have built since the first colonist arrived on these shores. It is as if we had 40 years to rebuild the entire urban United States."

The first reaction to a realization of the enormity of this job is likely to be trepidation. It is obvious that, in all the 300 or so years since these shores were graced, or marred, by the first cluster of colonists' cabins, America has not mastered the art of building cities. Some parts of a large number of cities have been conceived and constructed with a salutary regard for beauty and durability. Some cities have become adept enough in the techniques of "renewal" to rescue their most treasured sectors from encroaching blight. Many of these same cities have bulldozed their most disgraceful excrescences and filled the voids with excellence. But no cities have eliminated all slums, ugliness, traffic congestion, air pollution, and all the other affronts to the human spirit endemic to urban life in the Twentieth Century.

If the doubling of America's urban inventory in the next 40 years is not achieved with considerably more expertness in city building than has gone before, the result would be a disaster of more than national scope. The wealthiest and most technologically advanced nation on earth is under scrutiny by a world which probably attaches as much prestige to providing decent living conditions for the humblest humans as it does to feats in space, for example.

KEY TO OPTIMISM

The magnitude of the urban challenge holds the key to optimism. The national character of America was built upon a courageous response to crises. Two years after his historic housing message, in his 1967 State of the Union address, President Johnson said with optimism and within the permissible range of oratorical accuracy that "We have set out to rebuild our cities on a scale never before attempted." The President touched upon a factor which will determine at least the pace of the national effort to rebuild its cities:

"Federal energy is essential, but it is not enough," Mr. Johnson said. "Only a total working partnership among federal, state and local governments can succeed. The test of that partnership will be the concern of each public organization, each private institution, and each responsible citizen."

Demonstrably, there is room for everybody in the partnership and for every degree of constructive effort, down to making the wise decision on size and location of a downtown parking garage.

The notion that federal government had an interest in the condition of privately-owned urban property was first expressed in 1892, when the 52nd Congress appropriated $20,000 for the Department of Labor to investigate slums in cities with more than 200,000 population.

The urbanization of the United States is summarized in the 1960 U.S. Census of Housing. Of the 58.3 million housing units in the country, 40.7 million were in urban areas—and 14.7 per cent of this housing was found to be deteriorating or dilapidated. However, 85.3 per cent was "sound."

Charles Abrams, Chairman of the Division of Urban Planning, School of Architecture, Columbia University, wrote in his book *"The City Is the Frontier"*:

"Although urban renewal started as a measure to clear the city's slum towns, its emphasis has steadily veered toward rebuilding the city's downtowns. The growing need to salvage the city's threatened business centers coupled with the private developer's enthusiasm for the still-solvent downtown residential sites brought pressure on Congress to broaden its purpose. . ." [1]

"However imperfect the effort, the move by cities to revitalize their main streets is at least an acknowledgment that something more than new housing and slum clearance are needed to restore the city's health. And since regenerating a city's downtown is a vital part of its medication, this phase of the renewal program is one of its more important contributions." [2]

How is this regeneration achieved? Publicly-assisted programs as well as efforts which were accomplished solely by private enterprise have both scored remarkable successes. The odds on success improve when the city has planned its growth and rehabilitation with skill. Since 1936, the independent Washington-based research group, ULI—the Urban Land Institute, has provided practical advice for city planners, developers and others wishing to test their ideas on business and professional men having immense cumulative experience in their fields. Beginning in 1947 ULI has offered "Panel Study" services which have been utilized by nearly 70 cities.

ULI PANEL STUDIES DESCRIBED

Robert E. Boley, who became Executive Director of ULI on January 1, 1969 recently summarized the function of ULI panels:

"Urban Land Institute does not take the place of the professional land planner or the architect. ULI's principal contribution lies in its ability to assemble and utilize the talents of practitioners whose

---

[1] The City Is the Frontier, by Charles Abrams. Harper & Row, Publishers, New York, 1965, p. 167.

[2] *Ibid.*, p. 169.

accomplishments qualify them to test plans and theories in the crucible of a composite experience of hundreds of years."

These practitioners are Executive Group members of ULI's three Councils—the Central City, Industrial and Community Builders. As Boley put it, "these Councils are comprised predominantly of entrepreneurs and professional men who possess unique experience in the fields of land use, development, financing and marketing." When a sponsoring agency in a city contracts with ULI for a panel study, the Institute draws upon its Executive Group membership for men to volunteer their services. Several weeks in advance of their visit to the study city, these men receive information dossiers containing data on the city and a list of questions or problems from the sponsor intended to guide the panel toward the sources of concern within the city. Panel members convene for three or more days of first-hand investigation, interlaced with evenings of spirited discussion among panelists. On the final day a meeting of sponsors and interested townspeople is held at which an oral presentation is made by the panel, and more questions are asked and answered on the spot. Later a printed report containing the ULI recommendations and supporting information is prepared for the sponsor.

Occasionally these panel statements, which are free of the constricting format of master plans and feasibility reports, resort to pungent phraseology. The citizens of Pittsfield, Mass., for example, had their attention compellingly drawn to the constructive recommendations in a ULI report which also told them:

"You have let downtown just plain wear out. Walk down the sidewalks. They look miserable because they are patched with black tar and in some places have grass growing up through the concrete. Pittsfield looks like an old, worn-out city."

On balance, however, the ULI panel which studied Pittsfield's renewal problems in 1966 regarded it as a city with ample leadership and economic resources, awaiting only a prod along the right course. The city was inspired to alter and speed up the course of downtown renewal. This was one instance from many in which ULI's Central City Council had a hand in stimulating downtown redevelopment.

The purpose of this study has been to investigate and report on downtown decay and revitalization in nine cities which have been the scenes of ULI panel sessions. Reports on more than a score of cities were reviewed, and those used in this study were selected to present the broadest possible range of experience in renewal.

In time span, the ULI panels range from 1950 to 1966.
In size, the cities are as small as 60,000 population and as large
as two-million-plus.

In method, the study cities are spread over a broad spectrum
range from those placing complete reliance on private enterprise to
those depending largely on wholesale employment of governmental
programs, principally federally-assisted urban renewal and local tax
subsidies to redevelopers.

RENEWAL ACHIEVEMENTS

In degree of renewal achievement, the list of cities includes some
showing spectacular successes, and one which may never muster the
will to begin.

Cities covered in depth in this study and dates of the ULI panel
studies are: Dallas (1950), Philadelphia (1951), St. Louis (1954),
Detroit (1955), Denver (1955), Peoria (1956), Newark 1964-65),
Midland, Tex. (1966), and Pittsfield, Mass. (1966). Several other
cities were studied in less detail.

Anyone looking for a neat renewal formula of general application
is going to be disappointed. This is the most obvious and overwhelming conclusion from an investigation of American cities—and perhaps
it is the only finding which can be stated categorically.

The terms "slum" and "blight" have been variously used to describe
decadence in central city areas.[3] "Neglect" is a subjective word when
used in connection with slum-ridden, blighted cities, and this word
probes toward the heart of the matter. When cities have been
neglected so grossly that they are plunging into serious difficulty,
who is responsible? Elected officials may be guilty of incompetence,
or they may be able men constrained by the unfortunate political
realities. Civic leaders, the "Establishment," the power structure—
the choice of label is immaterial—may be apathetic or simply
greedy. The latter circumstance, not unknown, happens when those
persons who wield the most influence in a community believe it more
beneficial to their interests to maintain deplorable conditions than
to bring about their correction, and are unmotivated to choose the
more responsible course.

---

[3] The nature of this decadence might be more clearly expressed if the term
"slum" is applied only to the human aspects of the problem and "blight" to
the physical and environmental conditions. *Ed.*

Glenn McHugh, a New York investment counsel and ULI trustee, epitomized the situation when he said, "No two cities are alike."

However, there are, in the record of ULI central city studies and their aftermaths, certain indicators of an effective approach to *revivifying* a city.

Inertia or misdirection are frequent causes for bungled central efforts at city improvement. Direction and momentum can be generated most effectively by a compact organization of the genuine leaders in a city, usually corporation executives, bankers, educators and others of comparable prestige and talent. They do the work themselves. Merely lending prestigious names to organization letterheads and delegating the chores to subordinates does little good. The "movers and shakers," as they were known in Philadelphia, must be empowered to commit the prestige of their companies or institutions, and sometimes a bit of money, to a civic betterment effort.

The motivation of such organization is not obscure. An altruistic desire to make a community a better place for all its residents actually is a factor. Entwined with this is the realization one's own private interest benefits when worn out parts of a central city are renewed with high-tax-yield properties, and when increasing numbers of people are attracted to the core area to shop, work, and live.

Pittsburgh's Allegheny Conference provided a model for such "mover" groups. With variations to fit local situations, organizations of this type played formidable roles in the downtown transformations of Philadelphia, St. Louis, Detroit and Peoria.

Denver's leadership assembly gave itself a pre-set expiration date. When the downtown redevelopment plan was left to move forward under its own momentum, it faltered. Fortunately for the city, an anti-renewal political assault was mounted which was noisy enough to rouse the leaders but not, as it turned out, powerful enough to do any real harm.

In Dallas, the cliche "power elite" takes on fresh significance. Here, the men who represent financial power have assumed a proprietorship over local government and, despite the inherent dangers in such a system, have succeeded in placing some admirable figures in public office. Private fortunes and a widespread antipathy to publicly-assisted programs have set the tone and given substance to central city renewal, and it has been considerable.

Newark is a singular case. Its civic leadership dispersed by the overwhelming weight of the city's downtown problems, Newark was ready for a strong-man performance, and it got it from Housing Authority Director Louis Danzig. Aggressive and capable, he quickly dominated the remaining factor, the political.

Two Hunter College faculty members, Murray Hausknecht and Jewel Bellush, wrote in the Journal of the American Institute of Planners (September, 1966) that "Danzig assumed office with NHA in 1948 at a time when the politicos were threatened by an official investigation of charges of corruption in the Authority, which deterred them from continuing their usual control over the office." Once in command, Danzig was able to maintain his dominance. He has turned in a virtuoso 'performance in renewal direction.

In Philadelphia, the formerly tarnished attractions of mid-town living have been brightened to a degree perhaps unsurpassed in this country. At a 1966 conference on central city renewal co-sponsored by ULI and Princeton University, Edmund Bacon, executive director of the Philadelphia Planning Commission, declared exuberantly that "We are on the threshold of cracking the suburban ideal. The trend back to the central city will accelerate far beyond any current projections." And perhaps it will, if, as Chicago developer Arthur Rubloff said at the same conference, "Downtown is made stimulating —more than walled canyons of tall buildings deserted after 5 p.m."

The Director of the Center for Metropolitan Studies at Northwestern University, Scott Greer, undertook in his book *"Urban Renewal and American Cities"* to explain the "logic" of using renewal procedures in the central city. The logic, he wrote, "is based upon the fact that land-use may be frozen by multiple ownership and obsolete planning, which break land into too many fragments, each too small for contemporary demand. . . . The private redeveloper is at the mercy of the holdout."

The experience of cities included in this study shows that the private developer undertakes large-scale land assemblage at great peril. After a group of downtown redevelopers in Denver lost a large sum through jousting with a multitude of land-owners, that city turned to urban renewal, with its condemnation procedures, for renewing the surrounding area. In Peoria and Dallas, where large downtown tracts were assembled by private interests averse to publicly-aided renewal, they favored some assistance in dealing with holdouts.

In summary, then, the most effective aids to central-city renewal have been:

1. The active participation of a small group of the city's most influential citizens.

2. Planning which regards the entire central city as an entity.

3. Use of the power of eminent domain in land assemblage.

It became obvious, during this study of renewal experience, that no individual or organization has all the answers. One of the strengths of the ULI panel approach has been that the participants, with a background born of a vast accumulation of practical experience, offer no panaceas. Some of the ills besetting American cities are awesome, and attempts to cope with them are best launched from a position of humility. Two of these problems appear predominant— one concerned with physical characteristics, the other with the human factor:

1. There is yet no satisfactory method for transporting people within a central-city area and, particularly, within the Central Business District.

2. The harmonious mixing of white and non-white populations is still regarded realistically as a difficult social proposition.

CHALLENGE NUMBER ONE: METROPOLITAN TRANSPORTATION

Unless an urban dweller is clever enough to arrange his living quarters, his job, his preference in shopping and entertainment, all within walking distance of each other, he faces a bleak choice. He can ride transit, which he likely finds too time-consuming and inconvenient, or he can take a taxi or drive his own car, which he probably finds too expensive and inconvenient.

If there is any solace in realizing that the infrequent buses, clogged streets, and inadequate parking also cause inconvenience to the suburbanite who comes downtown, it certainly is not a potent enough balm to ease the widespread dissatisfaction with transportation within the core city. Thus, the new air-conditioned, enclosed-mall shopping center, the new headquarters office building on the outskirts of town, the industry relocated from city to pasture are welcomed by the mobile middle-class, with scant regard for the debilitating effect on the core city.

Transportation was called the most critical urban problem by former ULI president Boyd Barnard, speaking in 1960 before the

National Construction Industry Conference of the United States Chamber of Commerce. Barnard said the only feasible solution would involve a system of coordinated public transit subsidized by the community and perhaps by the federal government. Hunter Moss, who went from the Central City Council chairmanship to ULI presidency while this study was being prepared, noted with some dismay in 1966 that many local governments were still anachronistically extracting franchise and fuel taxes from withering public transit systems. Whenever a transit operator decides to cash in his dwindled stock of chips and look elsewhere for a higher return on his capital with fewer headaches, local government takes up the transit burden in the same spirit with which it regards a sudden increase in the welfare rolls.

When the Metropolitan Dade County government in Miami, Fla., purchased the major elements in that region's chaotic transit system, it was faced immediately with a drivers' walkout. Once that was settled, and the Metro government entered active proprietorship of a transit system, it was forced to concede that, if revenues did not cover payments on the purchase bonds, service would have to be curtailed on the least profitable routes. Elected officials responsible for the transit system purchase could seek solace in reassuring each other the action was inevitable, but they also knew that a government-owned busline presented many more ways to antagonize the public—that is, the voters—than to please them. The enthusiastic transit operator, in or out of government, is a rarity.

Aside from the question of ownership, there is also the matter of design to complicate the transit business. A bus is a bus, and it always exudes some kind of nauseous exhaust, impedes one lane of traffic, comes along too infrequently and packs together people who would associate so closely with one another on no other occasion. When a transit operator in a bold attempt at modernization buys some air-conditioned buses, he merely provides a comfort which people have come to take for granted in their office, home, and probably in their automobile.

Whence comes the research-and-development money for transit, to improve speed and convenience? Who pays for the rights-of-way and advanced equipment which will equip transit to fulfill its role in the revitalized city? The inevitability of federal subsidies becomes more and more apparent.

The modes of automobile travel may be as archaic as the present means of mass transportation. ULI past president Joseph Lund said that "in 50 years the huge expressways and interchanges we are building now may be considered as obsolete as the barge canals built between 1830 and 1850.

"The expressway program was not sufficiently thought through," he added. "If we had used the same amount of money and brains to provide some other means of transportation, we would have developed something else which was more efficient, and saved large areas of downtown." But Lund adds that "the freeway experiment had to be tried" because nobody had a better idea at the time.

The better idea for moving people in and around their city is still waiting to be conceived.

Funded with a sufficiently large sum of money and provided with enough man-hours of effort by topflight technicians, the transit dilemma could be conquered before too long. It is not possible to write a similar theorem on the question of establishing racial harmony in the big cities. However, it is possible to see the outlines of a solution, and these spring from economics as much as from the labyrinth of the social sciences.

CHALLENGE NUMBER TWO: HARMONIOUS MIXING: RICH AND POOR, BLACK AND WHITE

"Income, and not color, sets up the barriers to where people live," said ULI Central City Council member John W. Combs of Ontario, Canada, at the Princeton conference. Danzig, Newark's renewal leader, said, "You can mix races, but you can't mix rich people and poor people." Some participants at Princeton challenged these dicta as oversimplifications of the most complex problem of the day. Others cited instances of Negro and white families of similar economic status freely and successfully living as neighbors in high-rise and garden-type apartments in larger metropolises including Chicago, New York, Detroit, and others.

The continuing agony for cities springs from the multitudes of families locked into poverty. Their neighborhoods are unpleasant for others to look at, and their abjectness has a way of activating a large siphon tapped into municipal tax funds—all incentives for home-owners and industries to make the flight outside the suffering city's boundaries.

ULI elder statesman Barnard observed in his remarkable 1960 address that "the golden age of suburbs has passed. Taxes in the suburbs often surpass those within a city, and suburban problems are becoming the same as the city's problems of 25 years ago." One other concern of many large cities and their satellites for which there is no ready answer is the provision of metropolitan services. Among the cities in this study, St. Louis provides a prime example of a metropolitan hub constricted by outmoded political boundaries. It seemed a good idea to the burghers of the town in 1875 to create a compact "free city," a combination county and city. St. Louis concentrated its assets on developing parks and streets, while cutting off the pesky demands for services from the nearby semi-rural towns. But as those villages grew to become large suburbs competing with the central city in many respects, St. Louis realized it had set in motion its own decay.

The most ambitious metropolitan government experiment in this country, launched in Dade County (Miami) Florida in 1957, has been only partially successful. Political necessity required leaving intact the boundaries of 27 municipalities within metropolitan jurisdiction. Metro Miami bogged down on the intricate question of equitable taxation for the internal cities and the vast incorporated area containing a population larger than that of Miami proper.

Looking at his own Boston, Lund said that the region-wide crime wave might provide the overdue jolt which would persuade the conglomeration of suburban townships to merge their police forces with Boston's. "Suburban cities gradually will give up more and more powers to a metropolitan government as the hard facts dawn on them," Lund said.

Unified, cooperative regional planning offers an enormous potential for more efficiency and less wasteful duplication in urban services. The means to create such agencies, or to lend legal potency to the many ceremonial, advisory regional planning commissions now in existence, is not now forthcoming from state legislatures and town halls.

A third force is emerging to complicate the city-versus-suburb struggle. It is the "new town," the complete community planned and built from scratch. If the prototypes in Reston, Va., Columbia, Md., El Dorado Hills, Calif., and elsewhere are successful, they could siphon vitality from the closest major cities, particularly from the core areas.

During an interview in Philadelphia, Barnard said an alternative effect could be turned to the advantage of the large cities if it is planned and controlled. "As metropolitan areas continue to grow," he said, "it becomes increasingly difficult to provide services for physical plants which keep spreading out in all directions. Before commuting within the area, by highways or public transportation, becomes as difficult here as it did in London, we should be preparing incentives for diverting this growth." The new town concept, he said, overlooks the plight of an existing part of the urban scene— "the relatively small town, located perhaps 50 miles from a large, growing city which is sapping its strength."

"Everybody would be better served," he said, "if an existing town of 20,000 or 25,000 population, unable to compete with the large city nearby, is re-planned as a city of 75,000 people. The effort must be made to bolster such cities by providing incentives for people to move there. We can make better communities out of the declining small towns, while easing some of the pressures on the largest cities."

Barnard emphasized "action now." There is a sense of urgency in the statements of thoughtful men regarding the problems of cities of all sizes. Unrest is characteristic of the times in the urbanized United States. Dissatisfaction is intensified by the realization that urban renewal on any scale requires a distressingly large amount of time.

"I believe that in a generation we can reform even cities like New York and Los Angeles if we make the proper decisions now," city planner Constantinos Doxiadis told a magazine interviewer. "If we don't—well, I don't say man will die, but we may end up with a human animal deprived of his soul. If I am prevented from smelling flowers and am left to breathe only car exhaust, what will be left of me? I'm not sure—maybe a monster."

The correction of cities' shortcomings, one of the "now" problems of the late 1960's, developed as a recognized national concern in the years since World War II. Urban Land Institute has had a hand in what has been done so far, and this is recounted in part in the following chapters.

Park Towne Place Apartments, Philadelphia's North Triangle: "The effort must be made to bolster . . . cities by providing incentives for people to move there." *Boyd T. Barnard*

PHILADELPHIA, PA.

January 17, 1951. Report and Recommendations on the Redevelopment of the Triangle Area.

Panel Members Participating

Boyd T. Barnard, Jackson-Cross Co., Philadelphia —Chairman

David D. Bohannon, David D. Bohannon Organization, San Mateo

L. F. Eppich, Denver

Newton C. Farr, Farr & Co., Chicago

Ernest M. Fisher, Columbia Univ., Institute for Urban Land Use & Housing Studies, New York

Charles Fleetwood, Prudential Insurance Co. of America, Newark

John W. Galbreath, John W. Galbreath & Co., Columbus, Ohio

Robert P. Gerholz, Gerholz Community Homes, Inc., Flint, Michigan

Charles E. Joern, William Joern & Sons, LaGrange Park, Illinois

John McC. Mowbray, Roland Park Co., Baltimore

Hugh E. Prather, Sr., Highland Park Shopping Village, Dallas

Richard J. Seltzer, R. J. Seltzer, Philadelphia

Clarence M. Turley, Clarence M. Turley, Inc., St. Louis

F. Poche Waguespack, Waugespack, Pratt Co., New Orleans

Foster Winter, J. L. Hudson Co., Detroit

CHAPTER TWO

PHILADELPHIA

"COURAGEOUS LEADERSHIP COMBINED WITH SKILLED PLANNING"

Philadelphia, Pa., population (1950) 2,071,605, (1960) 2,002,-512, (1965) 2,030,000.

1951—ULI panels called in to advise on redevelopment of the key 200-acre downtown "Triangle" and on relocating the Dock Street produce market which cast a pall of decay over the most historic sections of the central city.

Panelists found "a sleepy, unprogressive city," its initiative dulled by years of political non-leadership which, at best, was merely lethargic. But the old order was changing.

The "Greater Philadelphia Movement" was arousing men who cared deeply about the future of their city and possessed the talent to conceive and execute a remarkable urban rejuvenation. ULI's guidelines for Triangle redevelopment and to produce-facility reloca-

PHILADELPHIA, PA.

January 18, 1951. The Dock Street Area: Report & Recommendations to the Dock Street Committee, Greater Philadelphia — South Jersey Council & Philadelphia Redevelopment Authority.

Panel Members Participating

Hugh Potter, River Oaks Corp., Houston—Chairman

William H. Ballard, William H. Ballard Co., Boston

Judson Bradway, Judson Bradway Co., Detroit

Walter K. Durham, Architect, Philadelphia

Philip W. Kniskern, First Mortgage Co., Philadelphia

Paul L. McCord, Paul L. McCord Co., Indianapolis

Henry S. Miller, Henry S. Miller Co., Dallas

Charles A. Newhall, Brookline, Mass.

E. L. Ostendorf, Ostendorf-Morris Co., Cleveland

Walter S. Schmidt, Frederick A. Schmidt, Inc., Cincinnati

A. J. Stewart, Citizens Fidelity Bank & Trust Co., Louisville, Ky.

Waverly Taylor, Waverly Taylor, Inc., Washington, D.C.

tion helped inspire the significant early successes in one of the nation's most successful efforts in central city rejuvenation.

Sleepy and unprogressive no longer, Philadelphia is proceeding with a difficult two-front campaign to eliminate residential slums while rebuilding its downtown retail focus, Market Street East.

1945: A WORN-OUT CITY

Philadelphia stood high on anyone's list of worn-out American cities in the 1940's. There was no choice except to make the massive, costly, agonizing effort necessary for renewal. Somehow the job had to be done, because the alternative was unthinkable. This historic city with more than two-million population, center of the fourth-largest metropolitan area in the United States, could not be allowed to atrophy. Philadelphia's renewal effort was begun in 1945, when this city established the first formal renewal agency in the nation. Now, after the passage of 22 years and the investment of more than $1 billion in renewal, Philadelphia stands foremost among the great rebuilt cities of America.

Currently, with its citizens better housed than ever before in the city's history and with its renowned universities expanding into former slum areas, Philadelphia is turning toward a unique rebuilding of its principal downtown commercial street. The Market Street East program envisions spending $200 million in public funds to raze much of the North side of Market Street between City Hall and Independence Mall and construct an underground rapid transit terminal, pedestrian mall and parking garage. The result would be what the Old Philadelphia Development Corporation, a key agency in renewal, calls "the new backbone for center city."

Philadelphia's purpose was to shore up the basic structure of a viable city when it established its Redevelopment Authority. There was no federal program to guide the renewal effort. Caught in the squeeze between a deterioration of its tax base though blight and the enormous demand on governmental services caused in part by the same blight, Philadelphia was confronted by a dilemma as acute as that facing any city in the nation. More than 60 percent of Philadelphia's industrial buildings were obsolete. About 30,000 parcels of real estate had been taken out of productivity, either vandalized, boarded up, or otherwise made unusable.

Philadelphia's proud old center-city residential areas were in shambles, and skid row was encroaching on one of the most historic buildings in the nation, Independence Hall. Private industry, freed of wartime restrictions, had not leapt to the job of renewal. Indeed when private enterprise was able to measure the urgent job of renewal against its own resources, the task was clearly beyond its capabilities.

1949: CIVIC LEADERSHIP: GREATER PHILADELPHIA MOVEMENT AND TITLE I

Philadelphia's fledgling Redevelopment Authority scratched at the surface of the problem for nearly four years. Then, in 1949, effective tools for the job began to appear. Twenty-four civic leaders, convinced that the city was at grips with a survival crisis and was in danger of losing the match, formed the Greater Philadelphia Movement to assist the public agencies.

In that same year, 1949, the first renewal-oriented Housing Act was passed in Washington, its provisions influenced by Philadelphia's frustrating experiences in self-help renewal during the first postwar years.

The Housing Act of 1949 was passed over some potent organized opposition. Real estate and business groups opposing the legislation called it socialistic, bureaucratic, undemocratic, and termed housing a local rather than a national problem.

Philadelphia, among other large cities, had already gained enough bitter experience to refute the latter argument. A particular boon to Philadelphia was Title I of the Housing Act of 1949, providing federal grants equal to two-thirds of the "write-down" of renewal land—the excess cost of acquisition and clearing over the purchase price obtained from the re-developer. The act provided $500 million in grants plus a $1 billion loan fund to finance renewal programs. A surface analysis might interpret the write-down as a public subsidy to private development. On closer analysis, however, it becomes evident that the public investment produces an adequate return. The investor pays as much as he would for development land elsewhere—perhaps in a suburb, where the dispersal of what should be central-city-type development only increases and aggravates the erosion of mid-town. Once the central-city redevelopment is completed, it pays taxes on an increased assessment precisely because it is located in a revitalized central area of rising property values.

However, the "profit" on a publicly-assisted redevelopment effort comes only after a period of heavy outlay and ledger imbalance. In Philadelphia, assembled, cleared mid-town slum land had cost around $300,000 an acre. A private developer, operating unassisted in a free and open market, was inexorably attracted to cheaper land outside the central city. The Housing Act of 1949 was the "equalizer." It put central city, in this case mid-town Philadelphia, firmly into the business of redevelopment.

Although renewal activity under Title I of the 1949 Act has accounted for most of Philadelphia's renewal (57 projects, involving $106 million in federal money) it has not been the only effective means of redevelopment.

Philadelphia pioneered in a program of "assistance other than money," and it has been the second most active phase of the redevelopment program. There are two sub-categories. The city uses its power of eminent domain (but no city money) to acquire land needed for industries and institutions when their activity is meshed with the over-all renewal program. Temple University and the University of Pennsylvania have been aided by this procedure.

Another form of city assistance takes the form of "certifying" an area for renewal, qualifying its residential development for special financing through the Federal Housing Administration.

In still another category of renewal activity, Philadelphia maintains an industrial land bank, with an inventory of about 1,000 acres available for resale to industry.

In a few cases in which a particular program could not wait for the procedures required by federally-assisted renewal, or in which federal aid was not available, Philadelphia has acquired land with its own funds, and sold it to developers.

The de facto start of central city renewal in Philadelphia sprang from a city-assisted program, in what was known as the North Triangle area. Impetus to this early renewal effort was provided by an Urban Land Institute Central City panel, invited to Philadelphia in January, 1951, to bring its expertise to bear on what was regarded as "the Triangle problem."

1951: SOLVING THE TRIANGLE PROBLEM

The Triangle is a 200-acre slice of the central city lying north of Market Street, its other sides being Benjamin Franklin Parkway and the Schuylkill River. At the time of the panel study, this land was recognized as crucial to the central city's well-being. The land had high intrinsic value, but development compatible with this high value was impeded by what Philadelphians scornfully called "the Chinese Wall," the elevated Pennsylvania commuter train tracks jutting across the base of the Triangle. Railroad management had discussed and promised the eventual removal of the tracks. Public agency officials thrashed over plans for area-wide redevelopment

Philadelphia's North Triangle Area, for years an un-developed wasteland in the heart of the city, became the city's first non-federal renewal project. North Tri-angle became Park Towne Place, a $15-million develop-ment of four high-rise apartment houses containing 971 units. (Aerial view see page 13)

covering the railroad's wide swath of land in the Triangle plus the larger area adjacent to it. The moment was ripe for redevelopment. However, the plans then current were beset by disputes and mis-givings.

Philadelphian Boyd T. Barnard, a real estate man who was a member of the ULI panel, recalled the setting for the conference. "The problems of the city were considerable, and they seemed to be centered on what to do with this Triangle area. Some of the symptoms of the city's overall problems were a declining population, and the number of business concerns moving out which we were not replacing," Bernard recalled. "Something had to be done."

Downtown renewal was actually tied to a series of interlocking problems. The elevated tracks were blighting an area which Barnard says was "ripe for development." As long as this renewal was delayed, the city was losing potential tax revenues which would contribute to renewal in other areas.

Hasty or misguided redevelopment, on the other hand, would mere-ly serve to replace old problems with new ones. Even worse would have been politically-motivated redevelopment plans, which are tradi-tionally aimed at enriching a few individuals rather than curing an ailing central city.

In a recent interview, Barnard, who is still active in both the real estate business and civic affairs in his city, described how Philadelphia avoided the most common major pitfalls in renewal—lethargy, ineptitude and political finagling:

"Between Market Street, which was the boundary of the Pennsylvania Railroad land, and beautiful Benjamin Franklin Parkway, which had been created some years before, was this Triangle area which was ripe for development," he said. "The potential was great for modernizing, building up and beautifying all of that area between Market Street and the Parkway. But as long as the railroad tracks were there, the area was bogged down in a blighted condition.

"Philadelphia, like nearly all other cities that I have observed, needed and still does need to provide good accommodations, both commercial and residential, in areas within walking distance of the center of the city in order to offset, to some extent, the tendency to move to the suburbs. There had to be some way found to make city living more attractive, which, of course, has been one objective of the renewal program. This has been very necessary to Philadelphia. In this particular Triangle area so close to center city with so much

The Triangle is a 200-acre slice of Philadelphia's central city lying north of Market Street, its other sides being Benjamin Franklin Parkway and the Schuylkill River. (Also see page 13)

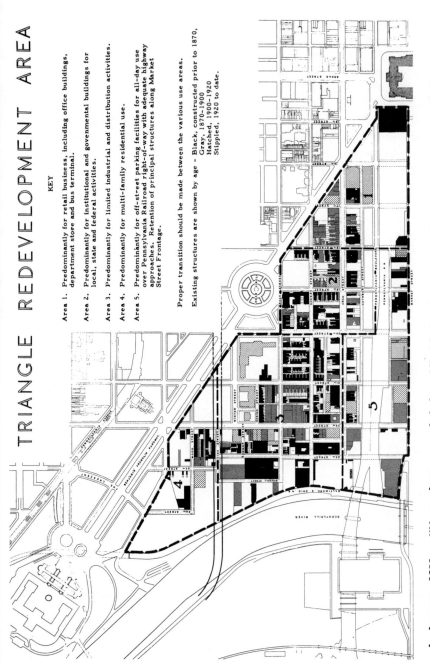

TRIANGLE REDEVELOPMENT AREA

KEY

Area 1. Predominantly for retail business, including office buildings, department store and bus terminal.

Area 2. Predominantly for institutional and governmental buildings for local, state and federal activities.

Area 3. Predominantly for limited industrial and distribution activities.

Area 4. Predominantly for multi-family residential use.

Area 5. Predominantly for off-street parking facilities for all-day use over Pennsylvania Railroad right-of-way with adequate highway approaches. Retention of principal structures along Market Street Frontage.

Proper transition should be made between the various use areas.

Existing structures are shown by age – Black, constructed prior to 1870, Gray, 1870–1900.
Hatched, 1900–1920
Stippled, 1920 to date.

In January, 1951, a ULI panel recommended that Philadelphia's Triangle Area be subdivided into five districts as shown by the above map.

land available, where there was no requirement for moving people out and demolishing either fair or even poor structures, there existed the most logical place to start renewal."

Barnard recalled the 1951 obstacles, economic, political or otherwise, which the ULI panel demonstrated a means of overcoming.

"I think the crucial thing in Philadelphia's experience was a changed political climate when the city's Republican administration, which had been entrenched in power for so many, many years, was finally dislodged by a young, active group headed by Joseph Clark, who became Mayor and who is now a United States Senator, and by Richardson Dillworth, who later became Mayor," Barnard said. "They got themselves into power, put through a new city charter which was along modern lines, and they were able to rally around themselves all the most substantial business and financial interests to move Philadelphia ahead.

"Various types of organizations came out of that political renewal, including the Citizen's Council for City Planning, which has been used as a model in other places.

"Other valuable organizations were The Greater Philadelphia Movement, which has the very best citizens behind it, and Old Philadelphia Development Corporation, which has a very fine Board of Directors and our best management civic leaders," Barnard said. "This organization has been responsible for the planning and execution of the development of the old city downtown known as the Society Hill area. Later, the West Philadelphia Corporation, also made up of our best citizens, prepared a planned program for the redevelopment of West Philadelphia around the University area. More recently, we have organized a North Philadelphia Corporation along the same general lines.

"That organization has a pretty tough job because it's operating in that area of the city which is largely non-white and where we've had serious racial disturbances. All these organizations are volunteer groups representing the most capable civic-minded people in the city, and I would attribute the progress we've made principally to the work and vision of these various organizations through these civic leaders," Barnard concluded.

The ULI Central City Council was invited to Philadelphia primarily to study the strategically-located 200-acre Triangle area and recommend a development plan.

This area's potential as a high-investment, highly-productive part of the Philadelphia central business district was inhibited by the absence of a river bridge at Vine Street and by the "Chinese Wall" railroad right-of-way paralleling Market Street at Broad Street, among other factors. Most of the buildings in the area were built before 1920, many, in fact, before 1870.

The panel concluded that the Triangle Area could be developed successfully, in a "gradual and orderly" manner which would avoid draining off property values in other areas.

1951: FIVE RENEWAL RECOMMENDATIONS

Specifically, the ULI panel recommended that the Triangle be subdivided into five distinct use-areas:

Area 1—bounded by Franklin Parkway, Market Street and 18th Street. Predominantly for retail business, including a major department store, office buildings and a bus terminal.

Area 2—between 18th and 20th Streets, Pennsylvania Boulevard and Race Street. Predominantly for institutional and governmental buildings.

Area 3 (the largest)—bounded by the B&O railroad right-of-way along the Schuylkill River, Vine Street, Franklin Parkway, 20th Street and Arch Street. Predominantly for light industrial and distribution activity.

Area 4—About 12 acres at the northern end of the Triangle, above Vine Street. For multi-family residential use.

Area 5—An irregularly-shaped area at the southwest corner of the Triangle, lying south of Arch Street and west of 18th and 20th Streets. Predominantly for all-day off-street parking, built using air rights over the Pennsylvania Railroad right-of-way.

These recommendations came from a group chaired by Barnard and drawing on the experience of 14 members from many sections of the country, including Denver, Chicago, Dallas, Detroit and New Orleans.

The panel's finding that a successful development would be feasible was qualified by several conditions: elimination of the Broad Street station and the Chinese Wall, completion of the Vine Street Bridge, the Philadelphia Redevelopment Authority's acquisition of some privately-owned property for rezoning and resale to private developers at "prices which will permit a fair return after development."

What type of developer would be both most capable and most likely to take over large parts of the Triangle? Panelist Charles Fleetwood, then a vice president of the Prudential Life Insurance Company, said every effort should be made to interest institutional developers, insurance companies, savings banks and the like. But as a practical matter, he pointed out, the development of "unproven real estate" involves risks which are more readily undertaken by private interests using their own or borrowed capital.

Fleetwood pointed out that the large developer has certain built-in advantages. In residential portions, for example, there can be uniformity of planning and the "characterization" of neighborhoods. But he said that smaller developers should not be overlooked, despite the dangers that piecemeal development could cause land values on the final phases to soar to the point of precluding development.

Local law would prevent the Redevelopment Authority from assembling a large tract of land and selling it part-by-part as small developers turned up. The panel called this phase-by-phase procedure desirable, but conceded that "we are dealing with the actual facts that exist, now."

The panel attached great importance to securing an overall design which had harmony, but which avoided monotony, for the Triangle, which was called the most important gateway to the central city.

A recommendation was made for creation of an architectural committee to pass on all design for the area—a group with broader scope than the existing "art jury" which was concerned only with structures fronting on Franklin Parkway.

For enhancing the "character" of the Triangle, the panel recommended "employment of the most able and distinguished designers available to study and report on possibilities of landscaping and developing the approaches to the area."

Area 2 was selected as the ideal location for a modern city hall, courts and county building, and possibly state and federal buildings. If the existing city hall and county building were moved, to permit opening of Market and Broad as through-streets, another desirable result would be encouraged—a major new department store on Market Street between 15th and 18th. A major new hotel was regarded as feasible in the general area, possibly on Market Street, but the panel rejected the suggestion for a large-scale "amusement area" centered around a sports arena.

The panel cautioned against permitting "unreasonably high" office buildings. It set as criteria for the ideal building 15 to 20 stories, covering about 60 per cent of the site area, and with parking close by.

In Section One, east of 18th Street, a theoretical limit of 5 million square feet was placed on new office building construction, sufficient, it was said, for at least 20 years. Higher buildings would "create intolerable congestion" and excess new space would generate a vacancy problem.

PARKING: KEY TO REDEVELOPMENT

Parking was termed a "most important factor in the entire redevelopment program." The panel saw no problem in allocating parking space in the residential area of the Triangle. The recommended allotment was one parking space for two families, a lower than normal ratio made possible by the convenience of public transit nearby.

However, it was foreseen that commercial-area parking would require extensive planning and engineering analysis. In the office and hotel area, parking could be incorporated in the same buildings as the parent activities, some of it below street surface. In addition, larger-scale parking could be located within 1500-feet of the activity served (for all-day parking). Large, concentrated parking areas were recommended only if the promise of adequate access roads were met. The panel's thinking on parking was kept "fluid," as one member phrased it, to permit the scattering of parking garages and development of underground car storage areas.

For truck loading and deliveries, it was recommended that all such activity be conducted off-street, in rear alleys, courts or basements.

The panel's conclusions on the location and extent of housing development inside the Triangle was the most provocative and perhaps controversial portion of the entire ULI report.

The Philadelphia Planning Commission had projected a huge residential complex between 20th Street and the River. While conceding that the "area lends itself to (such a) housing development, the panel took the stand that such use was "neither the highest nor the best for this entire area."

The panel's stand was based on three factors:

Land acquisition at $125,000 an acre plus the public costs of providing neighborhood schools, playgrounds and other neighborhood amenities presented formidable financial difficulties.

The competition from Triangle housing on such a large scale might harm another contemporary housing effort, rehabilitation and new construction in the Rittenhouse Square area.

Finally, a sounder economic use for the area seemed indicated to the panel.

It was recommended that housing be confined to the 12-acre Area 4 north of Vine Street. The major portion of land between 20th Street and the river was earmarked by the panel for small, modern two and three-story buildings combining office space, facilities for laboratory research and light manufacturing, together with distribution and servicing functions.

Panelist Fleetwood pointed out that the demand for such facilities was high, that financing was no problem, since long-term leases to strong tenants were the rule, and added that this type of land usage would be compatible with and acceptable to the neighboring residential sector.

The panel's thinking on the timing and phasing of the Triangle development was necessarily inconclusive, because of the Korean War crisis at that time. However, it was considered desirable to develop a unified project, as far as possible, with related units completed at one time.

The panel concluded on the optimistic note that a redevelopment plan "worthy of the great 200-acre Triangle Area . . . will excite and challenge the interest and support of all Philadelphia."

Judged on foresight, the eventually-proven soundness of its recommendations, and service to the study city, ULI's Philadelphia panel compiled an enviable record.

A Chicago realtor on the panel, Newton Farr, recalled that "the initial benefit to Philadelphia was that we brought together all the disputants. The Pennsylvania Railroad's owners had not made up their minds about removing the Chinese Wall and the Broad Street station. The general public seemed preoccupied with the inconvenience which they thought would result from eliminating the station.

"We simply pointed out the obvious necessity for eliminating the Chinese Wall and pointed out the best land uses," Farr said. "We helped the planning officials in Philadelphia to firm up their views.

They were floundering over plans for land usage even after redevelopment began. I believe we gave them some highly useful ideas and firmed up their courage."

SETTLING THE HOUSING CONTROVERSY

The focus of controversy had been housing versus general commercial use of the Triangle. The City Planning Commission envisioned devoting most of the entire Triangle, the western two-thirds between 20th Street and the river to apartment housing. Philadelphia planners were entirely correct in their broad thesis (as proven in their own city and others) that an infusion of new middle and upper income residents is a marvelous core revitalizer.

However, the panel was a major factor in discouraging what would have been a monumental blunder, as demonstrated by later residential development in mid-town Philadelphia. The panel asserted firmly that housing was not "the most appropriate use" for the major Triangle sector.

It was conceded that a vast housing project might succeed, if the city were willing and able to bear the burden of the nearly-prohibitive write-down cost in land acquisition and could provide the schools and other amenities of neighborhood life. Such an onerous course appeared ill-advised to the panel when there already existed other central city residential areas, then largely blighted but potentially renewable at feasible costs. The panel said, "A significant fact, which must not escape us, is the rehabilitation, restoration and construction of housing units in the Rittenhouse Square area, which might be seriously affected by a large housing development in the Triangle."

The panel "strongly recommended" that housing be limited to the small Triangle area north of Vine Street—probably the most important recommendation made by the ULI panel.

In 1951 North Triangle was a dilapidated 12 acres of shabby industrial buildings and run-down housing. Two-thirds of the residences had no heat. More than half had no hot water, and nearly half had outside toilets. This unsavory patch of blight had frontage on one of the city's foremost boulevards, Benjamin Franklin Parkway. The site was to become one of the gateways to central city, via the Schuylkill Expressway. But as it existed during the pre-renewal ferment, North Triangle was a blot on the city's face and an underproducer of real estate taxes, considering its location and potential.

PARK TOWNE PLACE, CITY'S FIRST NON-FEDERAL PROJECT

The Redevelopment Authority, bolstered by an $800,000 loan from the city government, acquired North Triangle at a cost of $1.7 million. North Triangle became the city's first non-federal renewal project. The land was leased to a developer for $75,000 a year. North Triangle became Park Towne Place, a $15-million development of four high-rise apartment houses containing 971 units. Financed through a Federal Housing Administration commitment, Park Towne became the first such development in the United States to qualify for federal aid under Section 220 of the 1956 Housing Act. Park Towne Place was completed and occupied during 1959. The development now produces for Philadelphia $300,000 more a year in property taxes than the area did formerly, a nine-to-one gain.

The panel's effectiveness in dealing with the remainder of the Triangle was hampered by local indecision over the future of City Hall—whether to abandon the ornate structure at the foot of Market Street and relocate the seat of city government somewhere near the base of the Triangle. Wisely, City Hall was preserved. Architecturally and esthetically, it is a bridge between the stark colonial simplicity of early historic buildings in the city, and the modernity of the newest buildings, such as those of Penn Center. This center is a handsome cluster of office space and shops, including an underground mall, which the railroad inserted in place of the old "Wall" and downtown depot. The investment in Penn Center, all private, is more than $123 million. Before the transition, the Pennsylvania Railroad paid $324,000 in real estate taxes on the property. Now the redeveloped 17 acres produce about $1.8 million in municipal revenues.

In 1963 a South Triangle redevelopment area plan was published, covering the area between the river and three streets, 20th, Vine and Arch. However, this plan for a new riverside park abutting row and apartment houses has not been given a sufficiently high priority to bring about a start of renewal.

The southwest corner of the Triangle is included in a larger renewal project area of 111 acres, Schuylkill River Park. Scheduled for completion during the 1971-75 period, this project's uses would be residential, commercial, public, institutional and an extension of Fairmount Park. Also inside the Triangle, Franklin Institute redeveloped seven-tenths of an acre with a $5-million research center and laboratory at 20th and Race Streets. This project gives a good example of the interplay between government and private agencies. The Redevelopment Authority acquired the property, with the re-developer agreeing to reimburse all costs. The cleared land was delivered by the Redevelopment Authority to the Philadelphia Indus-trial Development Corporation, which is leasing the completed five-story laboratory to Franklin Institute.

No governmental financial subsidy was required, and the city receives an eventual net gain because of the Institute's upgrading effect on surrounding property.

Veteran ULI members regard the Philadelphia panel as one of the most meaningful ever held by the Central City Council. Mr. Farr summed up some of the results of the Triangle study:

"We found that the planners had decided on so much housing in the Triangle because they never believed the downtown area could absorb that much new land in other uses. Our panel brought to Philadelphia men who had experience and fresh ideas about the evolution of downtown districts.

"No one had thought of the feasibility of a new hotel in the Penn-sylvania Railroad area. When the panel suggested this, there was concern about locating a hotel many blocks away from existing hotels. But with the encouragement we gave them, the developers went ahead with the new Sheraton Hotel, near Penn Center, which anyone will concede has been successful from all viewpoints.

"TOTAL PROGRAM" RENEWAL

"At the time the use of air rights was a revolutionary concept," Farr continued. "We had seen it work in Chicago, where Marshall Field had built the Merchandise Mart over the Chicago and North-western Railroad right-of-way. This idea was incorporated into the two-level shopping development in Penn Center.

"Although I was part of it, I still must contend that ULI did a stupendous job in Philadelphia," Farr concluded.

In any review of the remarkable renewal which is revitalizing the Philadelphia core, it is difficult to draw a boundary delineating renewal directly tied in to the central city. Eventually it becomes clear that there is no need for a theoretical boundary, that to create one would be arbitrary and superfluous. Philadelphia was the first city to awaken to the fact that urban renewal was more than slum clearance.

This city developed the "total program" concept. Re-housing slum dwellers was related to the need for industrial renewal, to provide more and better jobs for the residents. Full-spectrum renewal included provision for public institutions, educational and cultural, to equip the population for more productive lives. As a whole city begins to undergo revitalization, it becomes better equipped to cope with its remaining problems.

Under this broad concept, the plight of the food-handling industry, crowded into a squalid, uneconomical Dock Street Market on the eastern fringe of the central area, became a concern for metropolitan area residents, Market Street merchants, and everyone concerned with bettering the well-being of the entire city.

"RAZE THE DOCK STREET MARKET"

A second Urban Land Institute panel in 1951 urged that the Dock Street Market be razed and the food distribution center relocated. Food tradesmen had been operating in the Dock Street area since the 1690's, and the section became the food wholesaling headquarters around 1870. But as the city grew, expansion was choked off and improvements inside the area were negligible. Any type of food wholesaling activity was obviously not the best use of this valuable and strategically-located tract situated just east of historic Independence Hall, only a few minutes travel time from the retail center.

The Dock Street problem became the concern of a ULI panel on which Hugh Potter, an attorney and long-time real estate developer in Houston, played a major role. In a recent interview Mr. Potter recalled the state of the old market when the ULI panel saw it in 1951 and the events which led up to its relocation.

Potter said that "There was a strong feeling in Philadelphia that the old market should be moved, and this was at once apparent to the members of the panel. It was badly run down. The buildings were old and the facilities obsolete. Even the loading docks were not of a height adapted to trucks which brought the produce in, and there had to be a sliding metal plate put on the dock platform to the truck that was being unloaded. Sometimes those plates were at an angle so acute that it was tedious and burdensome to truck the stuff up or down hill to and from the trucks to the storage space.

"There had been so much complaint about the dirtiness in and about the market that many people with sensibilities knew that this

Based on a ULI panel recommendation, the Dock Street food distribution center—in operation since the 1690's—was moved to a new location. Dock Street has since been redeveloped as a high-grade residential area. The area became the Washington Square East urban renewal, 43.4 acres popularly known, once more, by the historic name *Society Hill*.

thing should be removed from the very center of Philadelphia," Potter said. "The place was infested with rats, and there were just two or three lavatories in the whole area. It was antiquated, dilapidated, worn out and filthy."

The question which inevitably arises is: Why did it take so long for the city to insist that something be done?

"You might as well ask what causes any city to permit itself to deteriorate and to delay so long in rehabilitating," Potter said. "This just happens. It is the nature of people. They have to have impressed on them the fact that it costs them more if they let the deterioration go far enough than to correct it."

Potter provided a further insight:

"In Philadelphia, the problem was exaggerated and emphasized by the fact that it had become known as an unprogressive town. Philadephia was regarded as the sleepiest town in America and among the most unprogressive. These criticisms finally commenced to impress the people who owned property in Philadelphia, and so they got a man like Edmund Bacon as the city planner, very able, very well informed, and one of the best I've ever run across. Bacon convinced the persons who owned property in the downtown district that the Dock Street Market should be rooted out and moved to the suburbs where it belonged."

"When this was finally drummed into the people of Philadelphia and they realized that they could do it," Potter said, "and after the market removal had been recommended to them by some outside agency which had no political interest in the matter—like the Urban Land Institute, I think they were then stimulated to act. They've done it in a very magnificent way."

In 1954, a plan for relocation of the food district was germinated within the Greater Philadelphia Movement, a voluntary group of business leaders. A new site was found, 388 acres in South Philadelphia in the general area recommended by ULI. It had been used as a garbage dump. Although this site was accessible by throughways, a Delaware River Bridge and three railroads, it was lying fallow and producing a mere $29,000 a year in real estate taxes. Land for the center was acquired by the Redevelopment Authority, some $7.5 million of city funds being spent for this purpose between 1956 and 1963. The city also invested about $7 million for streets and utilities and appropriated another $3 million for construction from its Industrial Development Fund. These expenses are being recouped through use charges on the utilities and through 5 per cent bonds from the users. Private financing outstripped even the public underwriting of facilities. At the end of 1965 private investment in the food center was $72 million, with another $23 million anticipated by the time the facility is in complete use.

SOCIETY HILL, INCREASED TAX REVENUES

In tax revenues, Philadelphia has benefitted in many ways. The property tax gain in the new food distribution center is 50 to one. More tax increment came from industrial land around the former dump, which with values increasing from a former 25 cents a square-foot to about one dollar a foot.

The old Dock Street Market site was redeveloped as a high-grade residential area, also with a pyramiding increase in real estate tax revenues. The area became the Washington Square East urban renewal, 43.4 acres popularly known once more by the historic name Society Hill. Twenty million dollars has been invested in the area for three apartment towers, new town houses and some commercial facilities, shops, restaurants and theaters. More than 700 historic old homes were rehabilitated.

The gain in property tax revenues in Society Hill has been roughly three to one.

In retrospect, it is evident that Philadelphia's aspirations in renewal ran ahead of enabling legislation in the years immediately after World War II, and in fact the pressures building within the city for renewal influenced the shape of federal legislation. The momentum which placed Philadelphia in the forefront of renewal methods has continued, establishing several national "firsts" in the process.

Philadelphia was the first city to set up a coordinator for local, state and federal renewal efforts. The city was first to start and first to complete a renewal program, the four-acre Penn Towne section of 138 new apartments and 36 rehabilitated units north of the central city at a cost of $2.36 million, including a $659,700 state subsidy. Perhaps the city's most far-reaching accomplishment in the field was the broad concept of total-program renewal, in which commercial, industrial and institutional revitalization increased the capacity for slum eradication.

The key reason why renewal efforts based on similar laws floundered in some cities and flourished in Philadelphia was the competence of its civic leadership and the willingness to follow up nobly-phrased intentions with sustained effort. The Greater Philadelphia Movement was formed in 1949 because existing civic organizations were stagnating at a time when the need for "do'ers" was escalating. *The New York Herald Tribune* once commented editorially that its home city suffered because "one of our problems has always been that quality leadership didn't organize effectively and demand that the city be kept in order." Philadelphia fortunately had such leadership. The Greater Philadelphia Movement's membership is limited to 35, an elite group of "movers" including executives of six leading banks, heads of six large industries and two ranking insurance companies, and partners in eight influential law firms. Pennsylvania's U.S. Senator Joseph S. Clark, who became mayor in 1952, at a time when GPM was emerging as a major shaper of the city, described the organization as "predominantly a group of conservative but intelligent businessmen of integrity who have the interest of their city very much at heart." Clark offered another comment which is indicative of the reason why urban renewal has never been used as a political trampoline by ambitious Philadelphians. He said GPM "is suspicious of politicians, be they at the local, state or national level."

GPM has shown prowess in the field of political accomplishment, however. It was the moving force behind securing Philadelphia's Home Rule Charter in 1951. The Food Distribution Center, fraught with opportunities for politicking if mishandled, was conceived and executed smoothly by GPM.

1957: NEW CIVIC LEADERSHIP—OLD PHILADELPHIA DEVELOPMENT CORPORATION

There is much overlapping membership between GPM and the Old Philadelphia Development Corporation, a blue-ribbon, non-profit group formed in 1957 to spur the revitalization of the central city. Nominally no more than a citizens' advisory committee, OPDC has provided the necessary element of enterprise in civic leadership. This group's efforts have been the single most important element in successful center-city renewal.

OPDC president in 1966 was William L. Day, board chairman of The First Pennsylvania Banking and Trust Company. A reason for the prominence of so many bankers in Philadelphia's legion of

Philadelphians called the commuter train tracks jutting across the base of the Triangle the "Chinese Wall."

"movers" is offered by the former First Pennsylvania president, the late William F. Kelly. He said, "The future of our companies, all of them, is tied to the growth of our city. When I spend time on civic affairs I'm in effect working on the bank's business, too.

"The growth of our bank, its well-being in the years to come," continued Kelly, "depends upon what is done here in Philadelphia."

In many cities, Central Business District renewal has gone on independent of, at times in spite of, being ringed by ramshackle residential neighborhoods, the characteristic slum belt around metropolitan commercial centers. In Philadelphia, the drab Market Street retail core had such surroundings before the renewal of the Society Hill neighborhood and the Independence Hall sector.

The Old Philadelphia Development Corporation, in its role as official consultant to the Redevelopment Authority, concentrated its considerable influence on the historic but rundown mid-town neighborhoods. Society Hill was scheduled to be certified by the City Planning Commission as a renewal project in 1948, but the project languished for lack of the type of rehabilitation and conservation assistance which was finally passed by Congress in 1954. When the Redevelopment Authority got moving in the area, it acted rapidly, first acquiring 31 acres in the Dock Street district between 1957 and 1959.

The project became briefly a political issue, to the detriment of the man who raised it. In the 1959 mayoralty race, candidate Harold E. Stassen called "old city" renewal something conceived for the wealthy and well-born—a barb hurled at opponent Richardson Dilworth, a member of OPDC. The reaction of Philadelphia's power structure was evident in a venting of wrath upon the unfortunate Stassen. After Dilworth became mayor, he constructed a colonial-style home on Society Hill.

In April, 1966, OPDC President Day made a significant observation on the state of affairs in "old city" followed by an announcement of major importance.

Day said: "Restoring Market Street to a position of preeminence as an urban shopping center certainly can be regarded as one of the most significant renewal projects ever undertaken by a large American city. . . . It is our conviction that Market Street must be saved, otherwise the restoration of Society Hill and the Independence Mall area will have no permanence or meaning. The whole must be considered as integral to our plans."

Philadelphia's vigorous rehabilitation and redevelopment program saw city eyesores, such as the railroad track maze to the left, replaced by Penn Center, one of the most successful environmental changes of the century.

Day announced that OPDC was expanding its sphere of interest. "One project has led to another," he said, "and OPDC now believes it is logical and necessary to turn its attention to the vital commercial, institutional and cultural environments which reach westward from city hall and Broad Street to the Schuylkill River"—into the base of the Triangle. Meanwhile OPDC was stepping up its efforts in the renewal of the commercial hub, Market Street East, and Day reported "there now seems to be general agreement on a plan which will be a prototype for many cities across the country."

Thereafter, center city, the vital area within the historic section where the Schuylkill and Delaware Rivers are at closest proximity, would be viewed and renewed as an entity. It was a seemingly simple concept, but painstakingly reached, and a milestone in city renewal.

Underlying the priority given to revitalizing Market Street was a base of solid research.

One of the basic source documents behind the decision to undertake the massive Market Street East development pointed out graphically that this prime commercial area was in a period of slow but significant decline while the rest of Philadelphia prospered.

1958: LAND ABSORPTION ANALYSIS

This study was the market capacity and land absorption analysis prepared by a Washington, D.C. economic consulting firm, Larry Smith and Company. Central Business District retail sales, which stood at $639.8-million in 1958, went into a slow downward glide. By 1963, retail sales were down to $568-million.

The central business district's share of total metropolitan area retail sales was about 15 per cent in 1954, 13.7 per cent in 1958, and 10.3 per cent in 1963. During this period of decline, one of the five major downtown department stores, Snellenburg's, went out of business, and the building stood vacant as a warning that matters would get worse unless there was a concerted effort to make them better.

Further statistical evidence: the central district's share of department store space in the metropolitan area declined from 88 per cent in 1954 to 49 per cent in 1963. Downtown department stores handled 71 per cent of regional sales in that category in 1954, but only 34 per cent in 1963.

While this downslide was taking place, Philadelphians were acquiring more and more spendable income. Per capita income rose from $1,130 in 1949 to about $2,310 in 1966. "Comparison goods" retail sales, called by the researchers "good indicators of the purchasing strength and standard of living," was $1.2-billion in 1954 and $1.6-billion in 1963. This was a 34 per cent rate of increase, which was about double the rate of population growth.

The central district's decline was attributable partly to the flight to the suburbs of the population, followed by merchants in pursuit of their business. These trends were accelerated by what the Smith survey termed "functional obsolescence" of the central shopping district. Its attractiveness deteriorated. A first-hand survey of Market Street East in 1966 showed an unattractive jumble of cut-rate shops lying like a crumbling five-block bridge between the four major department stores, two at each end of the major retail strip.

These four stores contain 4-million square feet of floor area. The Smith study found a potential need for another 500,000 square feet of "additional prime retail area at the core of downtown"—provided that downtown renewal is undertaken vigorously on a sweeping scale. This study said, "If skillfully exploited, potential future demand for retail space (in the core area) can provide a real opportunity for a successful redevelopment of this major portion of the central business district." There was a warning against attempting anything less than full-scale renewal: "In a city the size of Philadelphia, no partial retail project on a small scale in any part of the central business district is believed to create conditions strong enough to provide the necessary climate for a successful CBD revitalization."

Large-scale redevelopment would take time, both for the physical rejuvenation and for the re-attraction of the shopper who had become accustomed to heading for suburban centers instead of downtown. The Smith survey forecast a declining share of metropolitan area sales for the central business district, but a slowing rate of decrease leading to an increase in downtown sales after 1970.

By 1970, the first effects of the renewal effort would be felt. It was predicted that sales would creep upward until they reached a constant level plateau by 1985, the year in which the maximum impact of the renewal program would come.

In summary, the Smith report lent impetus to the Market Street East renewal effort, and additionally laid a documented base for optimism over the future of the street as a commercial center.

After outlining statistically the tribulations of Market Street, the report went on to state that, "It has been generally recognized that problems of this magnitude are not beyond solution, and with the aid of urban renewal and rehabilitation efforts, improvements in the economic climate can be brought about.

"It is therefore believed that the present under-utilization of (Market Street East) land is a full justification for the action of urban renewal."

1966: PLANNERS' PROPOSALS: MARKET STREET EAST

Market Street East had been under study for four years, but actual planning had not begun by the end of the summer of 1966. However, staff members of the Redevelopment Authority developed some ideas about features they wanted to see in the planning. These included:

Removing all buildings on the north side of Market Street for five and a half blocks east of 9th Street.

Providing an underground shopping mall which would link up to the Penn Center concourse, culminating in a continuous walkway from 18th to 6th Streets with access to all retail, office, governmental and transportation facilities.

Building a 4,000-car underground parking garage.

One staffer believed the total cost of Market Street, from all sources, will reach $200 million.

Philadelphia, a 5-million-person metropolis and the hub of a 19-county area, is a rapid-transit-oriented city. Therefore, the present situation, in which the Pennsylvania Railroad service terminates at the west side of the core, without direct connection to the Reading Line's terminus on the east, exercises a restraining influence on downtown commerce. One apparently certain feature of the Market Street East plan would break through the transit barrier, and make the entire retail core accessible to all transit riders. Additional access could come from the new Kirkwood subway route to New Jersey. Above-ground transportation would be directed over ramps from the Vine Street Expressway.

OPDC took the position that "The concept for Market Street East is centered around a unified mass transportation system on a scale heretofore unknown."

The Redevelopment Authority's official listing of renewal projects put a net cost of $16.5 million for Market Street East, with $11 million coming from a federal grant, $3.2 million city and state cash, and $2.3 million local contribution other than cash.

Another major project, this one with an indirect beneficial influence on mid-town vitality, is a proposed $50 million science research center on Market Street between 34th and 40th Streets. One Greater Philadelphia Movement member, the late Harry A. Batten, said, "I'm convinced that the only thing which will save Philadelphia is more jobs, and I'm convinced that we will not get them unless we have a research center that will attract new industries, electronics and space and the like."

But the Market Street East redevelopment, more than any other project, would epitomize Philadelphia's success with urban renewal.

A city crippled by the customary slum-ring around the downtown core, losing its most productive taxpayers in a suburban exodus, and losing the battle with residential and industrial blight, would have neither the mind nor the money for rebuilding the main shopping street.

Philadelphia has not conquered the problem of blight, to be sure. *The Philadelphia Bulletin* recently commented, "Philadelphia has problems yet unsolved. It has vast seas of slums. It still has deteriorated commercial areas. It still has about 15-million square feet of obsolete industrial space."

CONCLUSION: PLANNED RENEWAL IS A SUCCESSFUL INVESTMENT

However, Philadelphia may face this formidable remaining renewal challenge confidently, because the city has used renewal prudently in the past. During the two postwar decades the city has invested in renewal close to $50-million in tax revenues.

It has been a spectacularly successful investment.

Renewal projects have taken about $100-million in assessed valuation off the tax rolls. The measure of renewal's success is gauged by the fact that some $350-million in tax ratables has gone back onto the tax rolls as a direct result of renewal. The indirect benefits are not precisely calculable, but they are massive. Land at the south end of the Triangle which was valued at $10 a square foot in the early 1950's now goes for $50 a square foot. Sales records show that Arch Street property bordering on a renewal area has tripled in value.

The best estimates available indicate that private investment in renewal areas has been around $300-million annually.

Every dollar invested by the city in renewal has been matched several-fold by the state and federal funds, and this sum in turn has generated a roughly 7-to-1 private investment.

Philadelphia has wrought its transformation on an investment of just two per cent of its municipal revenues. The non-monetary investment, in human resources, was incalculable.

This city provides a challenge and inspiration to cities which are aghast at their own decay but are restrained from corrective action by fear. It is all too easy to see urban problems in terms of an insuperable dilemma, in which either rampant blight or the corrective process would lead to municipal bankruptcy.

Philadelphia has proven otherwise, demonstrating that through courageous leadership and skilled planning the great, ailing cities of America can find new life.

Philadelphia's downtown renewal programs have successfully blended the old and the new in *Society Hill*.

NEWARK, NEW JERSEY

November 30-December 3, 1964. (A Preliminary Report to the Newark Housing Authority) Land Use and Marketability Aspects of the Tentatively Proposed Community Renewal Program.

Panel Members Participating

Hunter Moss, Hunter Moss & Co., Miami—Chairman

William J. Campbell, Herbert V. Jones & Co., Kansas City, Missouri

Andrew R. Evans, Westinghouse Electric Corp., Pittsburgh

R. John Griefen, Cabot, Cabot & Forbes Co., Boston

Earl D. Hollinshead, John W. Galbreath & Co., Pittsburgh

Joseph W. Lund, R. M. Bradley & Co., Inc., Boston

Larry P. Smith, Larry Smith & Co., New York

Walter Sondheim, Jr., Hochschild, Kohn & Co., Baltimore

(See Page 46)

CHAPTER THREE

NEWARK

TO SURVIVE: "PLAN BIG, ACT BOLDLY"

Newark, N.J., population (1950) 438,776, (1960) 405,220, (1965) 395,000.

1964-5—ULI panels convened on successive years in a city with a common problem, the flight of the middle class from the blighted central city. The setting of the problem was unique—a city all but engulfed as an urban entity by its massive neighbor, New York, but kept afloat by its key location in one of the world's most highly industrialized regions.

Newark had provided itself a grip on survival through extensive public housing and urban renewal development designed for the needs of its growing lower-income population.

"Think and plan boldly," ULI advised, "and become once again a variegated city with attractions for all types and classes of population."

NEWARK, NEW JERSEY

September 20-23, 1965. (Report to the Newark Housing Authority: Findings and Recommendations, Second Session.) Land Use and Marketability of the Community Renewal Program.

Panel Members Participating (in addition to those listed on Page 44):

Boyd T. Barnard, Jackson-Cross Co., Philadelphia

Glenn McHugh, Equitable Life Assurance Society of the U.S., New York

However, fearful of attempting too much and risking costly failure, Newark's leaders were reluctant to depart from a proven formula for limited success in central city redevelopment.

Few cities in the United States have existed long enough to observe the 300th anniversary of their founding. Newark is one of the few, and its unfurling of tri-centennial banners in 1966 was carried out with an air redolent of more than conventional civic pride.

An anniversary booklet published by the Housing Authority of Newark, which is also the urban renewal agency, was titled "City Alive!" The exclamation point was perhaps the most significant element in the title. Although the United States is not old enough as a nation to have known the decline and disappearance of any major city, Newark at times has appeared to be skidding toward oblivion as a viable city.

Newark has made almost heroic efforts in slum and blight eradication. These have not been enough to bring the large catalogue of its urban woes under full control of the forces dedicated to preserving the city. But at least sufficient progress has been made to lift Newark to a point where the city can regain a front-rank status among American cities its size.

"Although the United States is not old enough as a nation to have known the decline and disappearance of any major city, *Newark* at times has appeared to be skidding toward oblivion as a viable city." *Leo Adde*

"CITY ALIVE!" vs. "GRIMY URBAN CANYON"

And so, the exclamatory element in the "City Alive!" slogan is an admixture of garden-variety civic pride plus an element of wonderment at survival, embellished with an air of defiance directed at a critical outside world.

Newark's people are touchy about the stock criticisms of their city, and at times their objections are well taken. During the political campaign of 1966, President Lyndon Johnson made an appearance in downtown Newark's Military Square on behalf of a Senate candidate. A national news magazine described the setting for this rally as "one of the grimiest urban canyons in the nation." Newark does indeed contain many sloughs of grimy blight, but Military Park is decidedly not one of them. The park itself is a pleasingly landscaped topping for a large parking garage, which was financed by three of the city's large commercial banks. The park is ringed by the city's major hotels. The largest of these, the Robert Treat, includes a large new section financed by a syndicate of local banks and insurance companies. Nearby, within the line of sight of anyone standing in Military Park, are the new headquarters of two major insurance companies, Prudential and Mutual Benefit.

This section of Newark, labeled as a "grimy canyon," is in fact a vibrant core which would be a credit to any city of 400,000 population. If the entire city were comparably suited as this area to its role in the urban complex, Newark would be a model for other middle-sized industrial cities. The flinging around of catch-phrase criticisms overlooks the city's formidable list of real problems, and obscures Newark's successes in the fight to revitalize.

The ULI panel which studied Newark twice, in 1964 and 1965. in connection with the city's Community Renewal Program, seemed to probe into the sources of the city's difficulties with these observations:

"For a city its size, Newark has very few neighborhoods which are attractive to higher income groups. To an even greater extent than other central cities, Newark has been drained of much of its leadership, from the standpoints of both income level and civic responsibility, through the long-term flight to the suburbs. Attempts to reverse this trend have been made by the creation of large, modern apartment complexes. It seems unlikely to the panel, however, that there will be a major return of higher income people from the suburbs unless certain drastic measures are taken to provide attractive *total* environment for the upper income groups."

On taxes: "The panel is of the opinion that Newark is suffering acutely from the problems of excessive taxation on real and personal property. It is paramount that immediate and continuing attention be given to determining ways to broaden the tax base so that the burden on real property can be reduced. . . . It is imperative that a broader tax base be enacted."

On housing: The panel found "an imperative need for a vigorous program of code enforcement and conservation" to avoid, as renewal projects are carried through to conclusion, "a mere shift of deterioration from one location to another."

Calling again for an exercise of more concerted leadership filtering down from the top echelons of the community, the panel said "A community organization job in the neighborhood areas is absolutely basic. Indigenous leadership in the areas must be developed . . ." The panel went on to state that "A widespread, intensive, well-maintained conservation and code enforcement program could well reduce dramatically the percentage of future clearance required when these areas reach the 'project' stage five, ten or fifteen years from now. It might prove to be Newark's most profitable investment in the renewal field."

On planning: The panel noted that renewal had been planned and executed in a disjointed, piecemeal fashion, with insufficient regard for the cumulative effect on the entire city and for the opportunities in inter-related planning. The panel observed, "The only solution for Newark's ills and problems will be realized by taking the broad view of the city as a whole. The industrial, commercial and residential aspects of the city's economy are intimately entwined. They represent both problems and opportunities. The panel feels that the greatest single opportunity lies in the aggressive planning, development and execution of a dramatic central core project . . ."

HOUSING OVER-EMPHASIS, INDUSTRIAL DEVELOPMENT NOW NEEDED

Although Newark's prime reason for existence centers on industry, the panel concluded that housing had been over-emphasized in renewal efforts, in relation to the necessity for commercial and industrial expansion.

At one point the ULI observers noted that "Newark is in the center of one of the best skilled labor markets existing anywhere (and) will continue to be attractive to industry if additional land can be made available at competitive prices."

Panelists seemed surprised to learn, as recorded in the report, that "the housing program of the City of Newark has in the past required many small industries to relocate outside the city." That was not the path of wisdom for a city in Newark's predicament, according to the ULI group. Instead, "It is felt that, ideally, industrial development should precede rather than follow residential and other types of development."

The cause-effect relationship seemed clear. More industry meant increased taxes and payrolls, and an expanded home market for employment, superior housing, goods and services.

Investigation in Newark showed that with a few notable exceptions those persons who function as the movers of the community reacted to the ULI's challenge to undertake a bold, dramatic transformation of the city's core with either polite and restrained nods of interest, or else with offhand rejection.

If the ULI group was correct in its analysis, then Newark required a dramatic raising of its goals, or faced an uninspiring future as a mediocrity among cities.

The slopes leading both upward and downhill from Newark's modest peak as an American city have been long and gradual. It is the third-oldest large city in the nation. Newark built a solid burgher prosperity, based on manufacturing, throughout the 19th century and earliest part of this one. Measured by population, the city's peak came in 1930, when it had 442,000 residents. "And then a decline began," notes the 300th anniversary pamphlet.

The mere loss of a few thousand numbers in net population (a roughly 40,000 drop in the past 30 years) in itself meant little. In theory a city could benefit by a minor exodus of its least productive residents while its solid citizens stayed put, rebuilding when signs of time-induced decay appeared, and contributing their vision and energies toward the common weal.

Newark's population decrease is symptomatic of a far different situation. A massive population turnover denuded the city of much of its middle-income, higher-taxpaying population. The economic status of Newark's residents in the late 1960's was about 20 per cent below that of the next-lowest Essex County communities, including

Orange and Irvington. The most affluent neighboring towns, South Orange and Maplewood, had living standards about 50 per cent higher than Newark's.

Newark is a city of just 23.6 square miles. The "flight to the suburbs" here required less geographic dislocation than in most other cities. But once a political boundary is crossed, be it 12 or 50 miles from the parent city's central business district, the psychological effect on the urban emigrant seems to be the same. ULI Panel Chairman Hunter Moss put it this way: "If you don't vote and pay taxes in a city, its problems immediately seem remote."

The non-white population in Newark increased from about 12 per cent of the total in 1940 to about 50 per cent in 1966.

The character of residential neighborhoods changed radically. One-tenth of the population now lives in public housing. Only seven per cent of the dwellings are owner-occupied, single-family houses. In 1960, an estimated 42,000 units of private housing rented for less than $60 a month, which put the occupants within the range of rentals for public housing.

For a balanced understanding of Newark's character as a city, it should be noted that the housing situation was not unrelievedly bleak. ULI's look at the city left the panel "impressed with the generally satisfactory condition of Newark's housing. It is obvious that much of the worst slum housing has been eliminated through total clearance . . . or will shortly be demolished. . . . Judging from external appearance, the remaining older housing is generally above slum level, although there are numerous pockets in a condition of advanced neglect . . ."

19TH CENTURY MIXED LAND USES— INEFFICIENCY—BLIGHT

A few close-knit neighborhoods tenaciously resisted change or marked deterioration. ULI discovered the "Ironbound" blue-collar district, termed a modern-day expression of "the 19th century American working-class city par excellence. . . . The corner saloon is a prominent feature of the area, and industrial activities compete with residential." This description was not meant to be unmixed praise, panelists said.

ULI regarded Newark as "a prime example of mixed industrial, commercial, residential land uses, with the resultant inefficiency of operations, and blight."

One example of Newark's urban renewal program is the new Newark *Star-Ledger* building (left), which replaced older, deteriorating structures (below) on Washington Street.

As the attractions of suburban living drained off the Newark middle class in the decades after World War II, the homes they left behind, and the replacements for these homes, were filled by the impoverished. Forty-four per cent of all households had incomes below $5,000 (compared with 26 per cent for the entire Newark standard metropolitan area).

Industry, the wellspring of Newark's prosperity, found the city less attractive as a location. Between 1952 and 1962, the number of manufacturing establishments dropped from 1,751 to 1,556, and jobs in manufacturing fell from 96,530 to 77,044. Newark still contains manufacturing establishments in about 300 different industrial classifications, but no major new industry entered Newark after the Anheuser-Busch brewery in the late 1940's.

Inevitably, the volume of retail trade in the Central Business District dropped—but not as much as might be surmised from a casual analysis of statistics. ULI found in 1965 that the decline had even then levelled off, and observed that "in comparison with cities of similar size, the downtown core retail area of Newark is in relatively healthy condition."

The apparent anomaly is explainable when Newark is viewed in the light of its unique advantages as well as its unusually acute problems. This is no moribund metropolis becoming a ward of its ever-spreading, wealthy surburbs. Rather, Newark is, as the ULI report observed, part of "the world's largest center of economic and financial activity," and a sub-center of New York City. In its own right, Newark is the core city for a North Jersey metropolitan area of 1.8-million population. Many persons who feel they have good reasons for not living in Newark can't escape the fact that it is still the place where they earn the means to support their ranch-style retreat in, for example, South Orange.

Milford A. Vieser, one of Newark's ranking business executives, noted that "for many years Newark has had a greater day-night shift of population than any other city." By day, the number of persons going to Newark to work and shop is estimated to be as great as the total permanent residential population.

Vieser's company, the Mutual Benefit Life Insurance Company, reached a close decision against abandoning Newark as its headquarters city in 1955, and gave impetus to considerable private renewal activity by this and other firms, notably another insurance company, Prudential.

"IF THERE HAD BEEN NO URBAN RENEWAL IN NEWARK, THIS WOULD BE A DEAD TOWN," LOUIS DANZIG

Alongside this activity has occurred some of the most energetic publicly-financed renewal in the nation. Louis Danzig, executive director of the Newark Public Housing Authority, said that "we have the largest per capita expenditure on public housing and urban renewal in the nation." Danzig added "If there had been no urban renewal in Newark, this would be a dead town."

The life-giving infusion of federal and local money into renewal projects is staggering. By Newark Housing Authority (NHA) figures, the public cost of renewal projects programmed by the end of 1966 was $200-million. Lumping highway construction into the renewal category, NHA estimates that by 1975, public investment in new construction will be $500-million, and predicts that private enterprise will spend another $500-million in Newark.

The urban renewal emphasis has been on housing, mostly low-rent. Slum clearance efforts and the projected expressway program are eliminating 18,000 units. New residential construction amounts to 23,485 units. More than 13,000 are being financed under FHA's 221(d)(3) program, and another 1,270 are public housing units.

By the end of 1966, NHA was able to announce that, in its opinion, the city was well over the hump in slum clearance, and "the total clearance phase of urban renewal in Newark is now coming to an end." Thereafter, the emphasis in housing work would be on fixing up salvageable structures, with a strong companion effort aimed at wiping out the comparatively small pockets of blight which had been found and noted by ULI field teams.

All told, about 2,500 acres of Newark's 15,000-acre total area were included in urban renewal projects.

In compact Newark, nearly all the major renewal projects either abut the central business district or are near enough to have a major effect on the CBD's vitality.

In Newark as elsewhere, those residents for whom downtown is the nearest major shopping center are usually not the most solvent citizens in the entire metropolitan area, but cumulatively they add up to an impressive reservoir of purchasing power.

When there is added to this number the residents of the closer-in suburbs (for whom the CBD may be closer than the nearest regional shopping center) and the several hundred thousand commuters who work in Newark, it is not surprising that the ULI panel found the Newark CBD in surprisingly healthy condition and predicted a mild upswing in the volume of retail trade.

While proclaiming that its battle against slums has been carried through to a fairly decisive victory, the Housing Authority made a candid admission that urban renewal would be directed toward upgrading the use of real estate which is not dilapidated but is "blighted" in the loose sense of not being put to its most productive possible use. NHA stated officially, "The main purpose of urban renewal is to convert badly used land to higher and better uses. Then the whole city benefits from new construction, more employment, more (tax) ratables and the elimination of slums and blight."

The direction which Newark renewal is taking, and apparently will take for several years to come, is guided by the strong hand of the energetic Danzig, an attorney-turned-public official who has been executive director of NHA since 1948.

Danzig has shown remarkable skill in building for himself a role as the consensus-taker who could keep the city's politicians and civic leadership reasonably satisfied with the way renewal was going and generally willing to support NHA through its crises.

In Newark the ranking civic groups have formed a fairly tight coalition operating out of a single office under one director. Harry W. Connor is the executive director of the Bureau of Municipal Research and of the Great Newark Development Council, whose letterhead supplies a comprehensive rundown of the city's leading bankers, insurance company executives and industrial chiefs.

TIGHT CIVIC COALITION

In the early days of Newark renewal, during the late 1940's and early 1950's, these civic groups opposed the city ordinance designating the Danzig-led Housing Authority as the redevelopment agency, on grounds that NHA overemphasized housing and neglected redevelopment which would directly improve the central business district. Danzig rallied his political backing at city hall and won the issue. This confilict has apparently receded into the dimly-remembered lore of Newark public life, as all antagonists found that Danzig's program had something for everybody concerned—and hobbling him seemed impossible anyway.

Civic group spokesman Connor said that reports of early conflicts among the political and business hierarchies over renewal were over-blown and at any rate peace and unity of purpose reigns now. For illustration, Connor cited the fact that he and Danzig are both board members of the National Housing Conference.

Insurance executive Vieser, who served for seven years as finance chairman of the Newark Economic Development Committee, con-tended that the city has come as far as it has principally because of cooperation among the elements of the power structure.

Vieser said that for 30 years Newark's commissioner form of government was unable and unwilling to do anything to halt "the steep downgrade" of the city.

"We had a most inefficient, ineffective city government," Vieser recalled, "and there was a spirit among the people that Newark was through." It was during the last days of this form of government that Mutual Benefit Life, a major downtown employer, shopped around for a new suburban site and indeed took options on some land out-side the city. The new city charter in 1954 changed the government to the strong-mayor form. Business leaders, men like Vieser, found that they could co-exist with city hall.

"NO OLD AMERICAN CITY CAN REBUILD WITHOUT BUSINESS LEADERSHIP"

"Here we have a unique cooperation and pooling of energies among government, business and community leaders," Vieser says. "We probably have more of this cooperation than any other American city."

Vieser added that "no old American city can rebuild without busi-ness leadership. Unless business puts forth its time and money, you just can't rebuild a city."

One close student of public affairs in Newark, Dr. Harold Kaplan, reported a different analysis of the leadership situation. He wrote in his book *"Urban Renewal Politics"* that "the single most significant characteristic of Newark politics in the last quarter-century has been the alienation of the city's business and professional groups." Kaplan said the reservoir of leadership came close to drying up during the middle-class exodus. "Behind the facade of civic leader participation were a few activists and the civic groups' professional staffs, whose major problem was to keep the organizations alive from year to year."

A new Western Union Building and a Broad National Bank Building replaced a street ...nt which consisted of a hodgepodge of single-use structures as part of Newark's urban ...ewal program.

No matter which estimate is more accurate—Kaplan's or the more sanguine appraisals of Newark civic leaders—the civic groups combined have not been able to equal the energy, resourcefulness and success of one strong-willed individual, Danzig, in shaping the city's renewal.

Danzig, in turn, has managed workable alliance with several strong mayors. One mayor, former Congressman Hugh Addonizio, had been a member of the Housing Subcommittee of the House Banking and Currency Committee. In his first successful campaign for mayor, Addonizio effectively used the charge that his opponent, the incumbent, had been moving too slowly on urban renewal. In Addonizio, Danzig had his most compatible ally at city hall so far.

Urban renewal in Newark bears the Danzig stamp more clearly than any other.

The ULI panel brought to Newark the analytical eyes of non-aligned, experienced outsiders. ULI's Walter Sondheim, a department store executive from Baltimore, saw the Newark renewal situation this way:

"Newark has had too much renewal on a project-by-project basis, and not enough based on a plan for the city as a whole," Sondheim told this reporter. "I am not singling out Newark for criticism, because the same thing has happened in a tremendous number of other cities.

"Newark is a striking example of what happens when urban renewal projects are pushed forward too aggressively.

"The result is what appears to be a crazy-quilt of projects," Sondheim charged.

Sondheim and other panel members foresaw a good potential for top-quality redevelopment in Newark's Community Renewal Program—*provided* the city forsook its piece-meal approach to renewal, and made the difficult commitment to a comprehensive concept.

The ULI panel urged the Newark Housing Authority to combine several of its disjointed CRP project areas into a "total environment" which might attract more middle and upper-income residents back to the central city.

ULI panelists conceded that, as matters stood in 1965, "there appears to be little market for any extension of the upper income housing market." On that point, ULI and Danzig saw eye-to-eye. However, the Newark Housing Authority accepted a limited potential for its renewal effort as inescapable. Its specifications for the key

CRP projects ringing the central business district featured the "safe" components—extensive new office building construction and more lower-income housing.

ULI advised that, by this approach, Newark would sell itself short. The panel urged a "big and bold" approach to planning a vast redevelopment area around the expanding college campuses (Rutgers in Newark and the Newark College of Engineering) in the heart of the downtown area.

NEW DIMENSION: COLLEGES EXPANSION AREA

The panel called for "a bold, dynamic, self-contained planned community around the Colleges Expansion Area (CRP Project 4) which could instill a new dimension for living in Newark." This approach would involve combining seven renewal projects, and, the panel advised "would provide sufficient land area to make possible the imaginative planning and use of such land to provide for upper middle income housing, college housing and probably some commercial development"—all within walking distance of the central business core.

Panelist Sondheim said in a later interview that "Newark seems resigned to its present role, a city without a middle class. But if Newark wants to become once again a viable, livable city, it has to do what any other city must do. That is, get a good mixture of population, become the kind of city people dream about as an attractive place to live."

Newark's daytime role was established. It is an enormously important industrial center. Its business district thrives largely because it houses the headquarters buildings for two major insurance companies. But when the workday is over, and between 300,000 and 400,000 in-migrant workers desert Newark for their suburban sanctuaries, the city becomes a place bereft of culture and interest.

Lying within sight of incomparably varied but troubled New York City, Newark was challenged to develop its own image and unique role in the Eastern Seaboard megalopolis, as a cultured city, offering the amenities of urban life to all strata of population. The Panel summed up its advice in this regard with the observation that "Newark's greatest single opportunity lies in the aggressive planning, development and execution of a dramatic central core project."

Danzig's immediate reaction, during the Panel session, was colorful but negative. "Most people in the town think our plans are already so big and so great that they will never come off. They think I am crazy now. If I go for your scheme they will surely put me away."

More than one year later, a planning consultant in the Housing Authority gave a somewhat more hopeful reaction of the recommendation. Dr. Ibrahim Elsammack said, "This idea has had a great deal of appeal among some community leaders. But any action on how it may be implemented is a long way off. We are unable to organize anyone yet to develop a detailed plan. As it is, we are committed to the hilt. Perhaps this (ULI plan) can be incorporated in the federal demonstration cities program."

The outlook for Newark, in the fall of 1966, was for continued limited success along its established pattern of renewal, unless a new factor was injected to upset its painstakingly worked-out formula. The formula is based on the pragmatic, expedient approach to renewal developed by the indefatigable Danzig. Inclusion of Newark in a demonstration cities program might cause the city's redevelopers, both public and private interests, to raise their goals for Newark.

It is not difficult to understand the bristling reaction by various Newark figures over the ULI exhortation to think and act "big and bold." There have been periods during the last two decades when a dedication just to survival required big, bold applications of civic courage. The fact that the ULI panelists, men whose careers have been founded on achieving the achievable, exhorted Newark to demand a more attractive future for itself must be regarded as indicative of latent opportunities in this city.

INSURANCE COMPANIES CHANGE OF HEART

Although Newark has availed itself unstintingly of publicly subsidized and underwritten renewal ventures, its most significant progress has come in the private sector of the economy. Two large insurance companies, Prudential and Mutual Benefit, maintain headquarters offices in Newark. In the early 1950's, each considered abandoning the decaying central city. Of incalculable importance to Newark was the insurance companies' change of heart. The ULI panel called the firms' decisions to remain in downtown Newark "perhaps the most important which have been made insofar as the effect on the economic stability and future redevelopment program of the city are concerned."

Prudential and an adjoining bank on Broad Street, Newark's principal commercial street, were growing restive after World War II in their headquarters buildings constructed in the 1890's—not merely because of the obsolesence of the structures but also because of the deterioration of the central city. If Prudential had pulled out, it would have taken with it about 8,000 office workers, and undoubtedly precipitated a further calamitous decline in the stable downtown population which contributed daily to the CBD's economy. Prudential executive James B. Murray, Jr. observed, correctly, that "our people give impetus to downtown if they do no more than go out at noon."

Prudential decided to remain and rebuild in central Newark, and as part of its redevelopment erected a new building for Fidelity Bank, largest in the state. Completed six years ago, the complex includes an enclosed mall with specialty shops. Prudential reasoned, in the deliberations leading up to its decision to rebuild, that Newark retained assets which made it salvageable from the morass of its liabilities.

"Newark was still the center of business and commerce for the state of New Jersey," said Murray, the executive director of Prudential's department handling mortgage loans within the city. Murray cited further advantages—the abundant labor market which benefitted Prudential as well as other major employers, and the concentration of transportation facilities.

Mutual Benefit's finance committee chairman, Milford Vieser, gave his company's reasons for its decision in 1955 to remain in the central city: "The overwhelming opinion was that our company would benefit by being in a city with a good labor market and excellent transportation." In addition to having an excellent local transit system, Newark, because of its proximity to New York, is a rail and airline hub.

There was another less tangible factor, according to Vieser: "We felt that working in the heart of the city would sharpen the wits of our people, as they took part in such activities as luncheon clubs. Being in the city gives the flavor of competition to business life, and this is lost in the solitude of the suburbs."

High-rise, multiuse buildings replace a series of deteriorating downtown structures in Newark's urban renewal.

Mutual Benefit's old headquarters was outside the central business district. Its new location at Washington Square effected an enlargement of the CBD. The Square itself is a tasteful triangle of greenery with its base on Broad Street, but there was nothing tasteful about its surroundings before Mutual Benefit moved in. "This area was one of the ugliest, grimiest slums in the world," Vieser recalled. The 35 acres which eventually were acquired by Mutual Benefit contained typically blighted buildings more than 100 years old, plus some 40 taverns and political clubs. Some of the property was off the tax rolls, being used for a police and a fire station.

DOWNTOWN BLIGHT BEFORE REDEVELOPMENT: $100,000 IN TAX REVENUES TO PAY $200,000 IN COSTS

The debilitating effect of this downtown blight left its mark on more than the city's esthetics. According to Vieser's figures, the Washington Square area was producing something less than $100,000 a year in property taxes before redevelopment, but required city government services which cost around $200,000 annually. Redeveloped by the insurance company, the same area will produce an estimated $1.5-million to $1.75-million in ad valorem revenues a year.

Mutual Benefit erected a 20-story home office building abutted by a 100-car garage; an 18-floor office and bank building; and three other buildings, with two more planned. "We had to acquire a large area to protect our initial investment in our home office building," Vieser said. "The result has been good for the city as a whole, and for our own company this investment has been successful beyond our dreams."

Vieser's firm carried out its redevelopment without any assistance from eminent domain powers, land-cost write-down, or any of the other aids of publicly-assisted urban renewal. Vieser recalled that, in assembling the land, the company sometimes had to pay more than the property was worth and "ran into two difficult situations involving leases." However, he concluded that "our problems were not too great and the overall cost of the land was not of material significance."

It is interesting to note that Vieser's obvious pride in stating Washington Square renewal's private-enterprise history does not mean that this ranking Newark civic and business leader stands in opposition to publicly-subsidized renewal.

Vieser made clear his position in a 1964 speech before the United States Chamber of Commerce, which was meeting in Washington.

"It is time that the American businessman recognized that the federal urban renewal program is, above all, a program for him. The basic purpose of urban renewal is not to compete with private enterprise; it is to clear the way for private enterprise," Vieser said. He even conceded that, under certain circumstances, public housing—which is usually anathema to most businessmen—has an acceptable role in renewal.

Vieser said that if a city's deterioration has reached an advanced state, public housing should be a part of a broad renewal program. "I know that in Newark public housing prevented living conditions from declining to the point where no one would have invested a dime of private capital in a renewal effort, with or without government participation."

Vieser summed up: "To those who think that the job of urban renewal can be accomplished by private enterprise alone, without the assistance of government, I can only say that it is time we stopped deluding outselves. The plain, indisputable fact is that most blighted urban areas are far too expensive to acquire and clear to allow any private developer to take on this obligation and still hope to make a profit."

COLONNADE—A MUTUAL BENEFIT SUCCESS STORY

Mutual Benefit lent the necessary impetus to Newark's first urban renewal project, which cleaned out a patch of blight within walking distance of the downtown core. In place of the blight the city got Colonnade Apartments, which has become a successful venture after surmounting early difficulties in attracting tenants. Colonnade is a 1,240-unit project renting at $50 a room—a rental which ULI in 1965 called "the top of the current market in Newark."

The public investment in the three Colonnade towers was $5.27-million federal funds and $2.64-million city. Originally developed by Metropolitan Structures, the apartment complex was later acquired by General Dynamics Corporation. Mutual Benefit Life is credited with persuading the builder and the architect, Mies van der Rohe, that this venture was worth the risk.

A Newark Housing Authority spokesman recounted that "There was considerable anxiety and head-shaking when Colonnade opened its doors." Because of the rent scale "skeptics predicted that the towers would never fill. But they did, and the striking fact was that three-fourths of the tenants came from the suburbs or from out of state, including New York City."

Twenty-two per cent of Colonnade's occupants have been former New York City dwellers, many of them attracted by the half-hour commute from downtown Newark to Manhattan.

Inexplicably, the type of venture proven feasible by Colonnade has not been repeated in Newark.

This reporter found that Newark's de facto leaders are basing their plans for the city's future on two premises. The first is that existing, entrenched industry and the huge downtown office centers will provide a tax base at least minimally adequate for the local cost of redevelopment. Secondly, Newark's hope of ever again becoming home to a sizeable middle class depends on elevating the status of the Negro population, which is now an estimated (by Danzig) 50 per cent of the total.

NEWARK'S FUTURE REQUIRES:
1) ADEQUATE TAX BASE
2) ELEVATING STATUS OF NEGRO MIDDLE CLASS

"What has happened in this city is not so mystifying or distressing when it is viewed in the light of the history of American cities," said Danzig. "Since the times of the great immigration waves of the past century, the cycle has repeated itself. Masses of underprivileged people flock into the city, work their way up from poverty, and then disperse, leaving the old neighborhoods and older sections of the city to the next wave. This happened with the Germans, Irish, Italians, and now it is happening with Negroes.

"The differences in this case are that these immigrants do not come from outside the country but from the rural South, and these new urban immigrants can't meld with the general population easily because they are black."

The average age of Newark's Negroes, according to Danzig, is 25 years, while the average age of white residents is 45 to 50. Those figures alone make understandable the prevalent thinking in Newark that the inheritors of the city will be a Negro middle class.

"Our Negroes are improving, in living standard, in purchasing power, in their overall skills as a work force," Danzig said. "Our goal is to do what we can do to improve them further, through better housing. And, who knows? Of all the urban immigrants, these may be the stay-in-town people."

Another figure cited with some pride by Newark leaders is the income level of Negro families, approximately $1,000 a year more than the national average.

"We are developing a fine Negro middle class," said civic leader Vieser in 1966. "The problems are not brushed under the table. Good communications are maintained between the racial groups, and the potential difficulties are recognized, met and usually worked out."

TAX STRUCTURE OPPRESSIVE

This city has taken upon itself an immense social responsibility, one which makes stringent demands on public finances. The ULI panel found serious fault with the tax structure, which places almost total reliance on ad valorem property taxes. Only 5,320 of Newark's 15,104 acres are developed and taxable. Newark's $115-million annual municipal budget is supported 90 per cent by real estate taxes.

The ULI panel found the tax rate oppressive. Its report said, "Newark is suffering acutely from the problems of excessive taxation on real and personal property. It is paramount that immediate and continuing attention be given to determining ways to broaden the tax base so that the burden on real property can be reduced." The panel pointed out Newark's big stake in creating new industrial and commercial jobs, and warned that "it is highly unlikely that new ventures would select a Newark site with major tax disadvantages.

An attempt to lighten some of the tax burden resulted in passage by the New Jersey legislature of a tax-abatement measure, the Fox-Lance law.

Under this law, developments in urban renewal areas pay taxes which are equal to 15 per cent of gross rents or two per cent of construction costs, for a 15-year period. The ULI panel acknowledged that Fox-Lance "tends to neutralize the real estate tax disadvantage." However, one ULI panelist, in a later interview, directed sharp criticism at the law.

"I think this is a poor way to stimulate development," said Walter Sondheim. "It discriminates against non-users of Fox-Lance, by placing a disproportionate share of the tax load on other taxpayers. Fox-Lance is a poor law, and the Newark tax picture is deplorable."

Sondheim viewed Fox-Lance as a regrettable expedient which skirts the basic issue of tax reform. "Tax concession programs are not the wise way to stimulate development of a city," he said. "If they are successful and are used extensively, they create a serious tax inequity. Good planning in renewal can attract developers without tax abatement schemes. Land write-down is a tremendous concession in itself, and use of eminent domain in assembling gives an advantage which no private developer could hope to achieve in downtown areas."

The ULI group, however, was not unanimous in disparaging the tax-abatement law. Panel Chairman Hunter Moss said, "I agree with Walter Sondheim when he says that Fox-Lance places a disproportionate share of the tax load on other taxpayers. But I still think it is the right answer to do something immediately about getting new industries into the Newark area.

"Taxes are never equitable under any circumstance," Moss continued. "The unfortunate point is that Fox-Lance has done away with the immediate need for overall tax reform!"

ULI members and Newark leaders were in unanimous agreement that there is no obvious, much less easy, solution to the city's tax dilemma.

Some limited relief from excessive reliance on ad valorem tax revenues is in sight. A new state sales tax will return an estimated $8 million a year to Newark, much of it earmarked for school purposes. A city sales tax was ruled out as "unrealistic" by Connor, and was regarded by Danzig as "suicidal."

The state property tax code was modified, effective January 1, 1967, to exclude most personal property, but this tax remains on machinery and equipment, thus limiting its effect on industry.

Cities which are ringed by thriving suburbs inhabited by the core's middle-class former residents often look toward a payroll tax as a means of extracting some income from the users of its central-city facilities. In Newark, so far, there has been only casual consideration of this measure, with no prospect of a serious push in that direction. Fox-Lance has served as a relief valve against pressure for comprehensive tax reform. The thorough overhaul which ULI urged is not discernible even on the far horizon.

Meanwhile, within the context of Newark's reality, ULI attempted to bring about a modification of Newark's major downtown renewal plans. Principally, ULI cautioned that the Newark Housing Authority's projected demand for new office space was grossly over-inflated. The agency allocated 8.43-million square feet of office space in future renewal projects, to be constructed by 1978. In its recommendation, ULI scaled this down to 4.3-million square feet. ULI noted that the anticipated normal requirement would be about 3-million square feet, but recommended exceeding the anticipated demand because "availability of first class office space, can, by itself, enhance the demand."

Potential developers' plans for downtown renewal projects were so nebulous at the end of 1966 that it was not possible to report on the effect of the ULI recommendations.

Newark Plaza, a 50.7-acre renewal project at the foot of Broad Street facing the Pennsylvania Railroad station, was called by ULI "the prime location in the redevelopment program for major office use." The panel urged full speed ahead on plans including 1.95-million square feet of office space, 500,000 square feet of retail space, and a 200-room hotel. Construction in Newark Plaza would define a firmly-anchored central business district, with Mutual Benefit's Washington Square complex a reasonable distance away at the other end. Excellent local transit would nullify the shortcomings of an elongated main street.

Intermediate projects, the same ones which ULI envisioned as the "big and bold" new apartment center, are also heavily laden with office space in Newark Housing Authority plans. For example, Essex Heights, nearly 90 acres to be developed in three stages, has a projected 2.5-million square feet of office space. ULI warned that there was every expectation of glutting the market with office space, and detracting from the optimum development of Newark Plaza and South Broad, another major downtown renewal project. Plans for South Broad include an "Autorama," a concentration of automobile dealerships—a plan which had not inspired stampede of interested businessmen by late 1966.

SO FAR, SO GOOD, BUT WHAT NEXT?

In summary, Newark had won the battle for survival, through the sometimes heroic efforts of public and private groups dedicated to renewing the city. But its future as a fully-dimensioned urban entity is in doubt. ULI's principal contribution has been a call to plan big and act boldly. The onus, to some extent, is on those who live and work in Newark, and to a greater degree on those persons who lay claim to being its leaders.

DALLAS, TEXAS

May 6-8, 1950. Panel of the Central Business District Council.

Panel Members Participating

Boyd T. Barnard, Jackson-Cross Co., Philadelphia —Chairman

Richard J. Seltzer, R. J. Seltzer, Philadelphia— President, ULI

Hobart Brady, Swope-Brady, Inc., Wichita

Newton C. Farr, Farr, Chinnock & Sampson, Chicago

Ward C. Gifford, Ward C. Gifford Realty Co., Kansas City

Paul L. McCord, Paul L. McCord Co., Indianapolis

Henry S. Miller, Sr., Henry S. Miller Co., Dallas

Hugh Potter, River Oaks Corp., Houston

Walter S. Schmidt, Frederick A. Schmidt, Inc., Cincinnati

A. J. Stewart, Citizens Fidelity Bank & Trust Co., Louisville, Ky.

Howard J. Tobin, Northwestern Mutual Life Insurance Co., Milwaukee

Foster Winter, J. L. Hudson Co., Detroit

CHAPTER FOUR

DALLAS

AN EXERCISE IN GROWTH

Dallas, Tex., population (1950) 434,462, (1960) 679,684, (1965) 790,000.

1950—One of the early post-war ULI Central City Panels studied a city beginning to cope with the surge of traffic and pedestrians onto its downtown streets. ULI recommendations on such matters as traffic circulation and parking, advanced for their day, have become standard procedures.

Dallas has found, however, that mastering the logistics of downtown movement and seeing the central city sprout shining new towers do not guarantee a complete feeling of civic satisfaction. Mayor Erik Jonsson touched a sensitive spot in public consciousness with his "Goals for Dallas" program, an explicit attempt to improve the quality of life in his city.

A SOARING SELF-RELIANT CITY

Where improvement means steel-and-stone construction, Dallas functions as a self-reliant city, disdaining aids such as federally-assisted urban renewal. But some thoughtful Dallas-ites believe this attitude will change as Dallas totals up its requirements and its resources.

Dallas might have been designed and built to the specifications of the outside world's conception of wealthy, glittering America, in particular that part of it called Texas.

The city's brilliant towers soar over the west-central Texas plains in a profusion which signifies an abundance of ambition and healthy civic pride among its well-endowed residents.

Dallas loses little of its first-impression grandeur when the visitor stands at the bases of the proud new downtown towers and surveys the streets of an exceptionally vibrant central business district, a clean, generally well-ordered 930 acres. About 133,000 people work in the area and another 100,000 or more enter it daily for shopping and business reasons. The people are brisk, friendly, well-dressed, confident. Dallas seems in control of its destiny.

And yet there are problems, areas of physical and human blight which the city's leaders are attempting to define and eradicate. Many aspects of these problems are beyond the scope of this report. However, these aspects will be dealt with as they touch upon the economic health of the core city and as they influence plans for renewal.

An observation from the Urban Land Institute panel study, 16 years before the writing of this report is still valid: "The Dallas downtown area is more free of the ravages of blight than most cities its size. So far this (blight) problem does not seem to be serious, but if unchecked may grow to dangerous proportions."

The massive Main Place development, a 10-acre, office and retail store complex, will cast its shadow on several squares of tacky one-story stores. On another downtown corner about a half mile away, an entrance of the renowned Neiman-Marcas store for years faced a dismal row of vacant quick-lunch stands and tawdry stores. (In 1967, construction was begun on a multi-story parking garage on this site.)

The Dallas city government's rehabilitation agency finds that it is incapable of compelling owners to de-blight their property through present legal powers, and is seeking stronger statutory authority.

Downtown stores draw most of their customers from persons who work in the central area and from the sizable convention trade. Still the central district must fill a role as the nearest shopping center for residents from the close-in residential areas, which are deteriorating at an alarming rate. Dallas is singularly lacking in high-density apartment-house neighborhoods inhabited by relatively high-income families—and is unsure whether it wants or needs this type of development. What Dallas does have, ringing the central area on the south and west, is its slums.

Dallas slums, in appearance, are low on shock-producing attributes. Compared to the dank tenements and sprawling shacktowns of many older cities, the Dallas slums are mild, indeed. There are almost no unpaved streets with litter-strewn gutters, so common in other cities. The present slum streets were paved many years ago, when their sturdy, spacious structures housed some of the thriving middle class between the two World Wars. The trees lining the streets are luxuriant in their 30 to 40 year growth, but the same time span has left its mark on many of the houses, which are costly-to-maintain structures designed and built for owners whose tastes have changed, or who long ago set out to pioneer in ranch-style, air-conditioned suburbia.

LACK OF GOALS:
"DAYS OF DECISION"—1966

The crisis of Dallas's slums is not in structural decay, but rather in the ghetto-like atmosphere. Most of the city's 130,000 Negroes and 25,000 citizens of Mexican descent see only faces like their own looking back at them when they greet their neighbors. On the surface, at least, there is no expressed concern that Dallas may be infected with a potential "Watts." However, the minorities have not been absorbed into the broader community life.

This 12 to 15 per cent of the population has not joined the brisk economic mainstream of the city as affluent customers of downtown stores, and habitues of its restaurants. The existence of the nearby slum population impedes the health of the central business district.

What Dallas eventually will do about its slum problem awaits the outcome of a two-phased civic debate, revolving first around the question of whether a community renewal program is indeed necessary and desirable, and secondly over whether to finance it through local resources alone.

Mayor Erick Jonsson started this public debate in February, 1966, during a speech titled "Days of Decision." He said, "As I have worked to fulfill my responsibilities as mayor of Dallas, I have become increasingly aware of the lack of goals and plans for our city. I consider this a grave condition, for I believe it results in expedient and injudicious decisions." Jonsson had first proposed developing formalized "goals for Dallas" in a November, 1964, speech before a civic club. For the next year, he worked on specific procedures for developing an apparatus to translate into workable programs this lofty definition of a city's purpose: "To serve people as they apply their efforts, divide their work, and use their talents and skills so as to maximize their value and to secure themselves and their families against the hazards of nature and those created by man—to grow in stature, to improve their way of life, physical, mental, spiritual."

This visionary concept of how political leadership should be used came from a man with a background of notable achievement in industry. Jonsson, now retired, had been board chairman of Texas Instruments, which at the time of the ULI panel was a tiny enterprise venturing into the uncertain new field of electronics. Under Jonsson's leadership, Texas Instruments developed the transistor, and the firm is now the world's largest manufacturer of circuitry based on transistor use. Jonsson was, in effect, recruited for politics by the Dallas Citizens Council. This organization was formed in 1936 among some 250 key executives to set up a pipeline for feeding the city's best administrative talent into city government. The council recruits candidates for mayor and the city council, and they seldom lose elections. The magazine *U. S. News and World Report* reported in February, 1964, that the Council serves as a "benevolent oligarchy" for Dallas. Whatever the fair and correct description of this type of supra-government influence may be, in Jonsson's hands it is now attempting an intriguing experiment in leadership.

Jonsson's Goals for Dallas movement led to formation of a planning committee, and later to an 87-member citizens group drawn from all sections of the city and stations in life. This group met in June, 1966, at Salado, Texas, to work at weaving a practical program from the idealistically-conceived goals.

The next step was to hold a series of neighborhood and community meetings, in order for all interested residents of the city to participate in shaping the design for the Dallas of the future. Thirty-three such meetings were held, attended by 6,380 persons. Their suggestions were the working material for another meeting of the executive group at a conference in February, 1967.

Jonsson's program had its critics. It has been shunned by some of the wealthier Dallas-ites, such as H. L. Hunt and Clint Murchison, Jr. Murchison called the mayor naive, and termed Goals for Dallas "really nothing new, but just a convening of people who have been wedded to pet ideas for years and were looking for new forums." A milder critic was Elgin Crull, who was city manager for 16 years and stepped down in June, 1966, partly because of philosophical disagreements with the Jonsson administration over the extent to which city government should assert itself into all phases of the city's life.

Nonetheless, the Jonsson approach was geared up for a concerted attempt at executing a consciously-idealistic urban redevelopment and future development effort. The thrust of Jonsson's effort is best epitomized by a paragraph in his "Days of Decision" address: "Our American cities, as they grow (and I'm glad they grow for many reasons), usually are quite disorganized. They have a life cycle of their own, and sometimes when they begin really to live, they begin also to die. If they are to have a worthwhile life and to realize a worthwhile destiny, they obviously stand a better chance to succeed if they have clearly established goals and plans."

If Mayor Jonsson succeeds at no more than steering Dallas in the general direction of a set of comprehensive goals for civic betterment, Dallas will have achieved another distinction which makes it atypical among American cities.

HEALTHY ECONOMIC BASE

The sheer wealth of Dallas citizens is staggering. A sizeable share of this wealth has been channelled into central business district development. Lloyd Braff, the former city traffic engineer who is executive director of the Dallas Central Business District Association, calculated that more than a half-billion dollars has been used to finance 65 separate construction and rehabilitation projects in the central area since 1950.

This downtown development surge has been fed by vigorous industrial growth. *U. S. News* reported that Dallas has more business firms allied with the oil industry than any other American city—112 such firms having a net worth of more than $1 million each. Dallas has been one of the leading international cotton markets, with an annual volume in trade of more than $500-million. The city has more than 100 aerospace and electronic companies. To attract and retain this type of industry, the city council raised $5-million in "seed money" for a graduate research center, a training ground for aero-scientists.

If there are indeed any "average" Dallas-ites in this almost larger-than-life community, they, too, have shared in the prosperity which has swirled around so spiritedly at the top economic echelons. Since 1950, employment in the metropolitan Dallas area—the number of jobs—increased from 264,495 to a 1965 high of 579,860. During the same period, effective buying income per family rose from $5,537 to $7,919. Retail sales more than doubled to a high of $1.8-billion.

Local government has, on principle, worked to improve the entire city with what *U. S. News* terms "a business tradition combined with a residue of Texas frontier individualism." Former City Manager Crull, who has taken up an executive position in the huge Republic National Bank (April, 1965, resources of nearly $1.5-billion, greatest among Dallas's 44 banks), stated that "In Dallas, businessmen have confidence in local government, and business takes part in the government. In other cities businessmen and government stand apart, at odds. But here businessmen don't want favors from government. They are concerned with what happens at city hall, and they take part in public affairs. When I needed help in getting something done as city manager, I could get on the phone and call most of the important businessmen in town and get the help I needed, with no strings attached."

These advantages in finance and politics might seem hopelessly unattainable to some less well-endowed city having greater problems and fewer resources, and looking around the country for a successful example to emulate. Nevertheless, Dallas has its value as a generalized example. So much has happened so fast that studying Dallas since 1950 is like looking at a study in time-lapse photography, in which the speeded-up action aids an evaluation of what has happened, good and bad; of successes, and of opportunities missed, efforts mis-directed.

LONG-RANGE REGIONAL PLANNING

One of Dallas's seeming successes has been in long-range planning, at which the city was one of the pioneers. In 1908, when it was a city of about 90,000 persons, Dallas hired George E. Kessler to develop a master plan for development. Three more plans evolved during the era in which Dallas's official thinking was keyed to a limited city-wide rather than metropolitan concept.

More recently, Dallas began to regard itself as the hub of a 10-county urbanized complex which will have an expected population of 3.6-million by 1985, with 2.3-million in Dallas County alone. From this concept have evolved the Dallas-Fort Worth Regional Transportation Study, undertaken by the Texas Highway Department, and the Economic Base Analysis prepared by the Bureau of Business Research of the University of Texas. The ten counties have since established the Northern Central Texas Regional Planning Commission.

In February, 1961, the Department of City Planning issued its "Dallas Central District" blueprint to the sponsor of this study, the Dallas Area Master Plan Committee. Much of the same ground was covered, and findings updated, in a July, 1965 report, the "Long-Range Transportation Plan for the Central Business District," prepared by De Leuw, Cather and Company, consulting engineers. These plans will be examined in detail later in this report.

When the Urban Land Institute Central City group convened in Dallas during May, 1950, the 12 panel members turned their attention to a city beginning to feel the surge of a notable post-World War II growth. It was evident that the metropolitan Dallas area was building on a healthy economic base.

The number of employed persons in the area was 264,500. Effective buying income was $5,537 per family. Other indices demonstrated the vitality of the economy. Bank debits were $15.2-billion, retail sales more than $704-million. Building permits issued in Dallas County in 1950 totaled $144.3-million.

However, there were signs that the heart of the city, the central business district, might have some of its own vitality buffeted into

As these before and after pictures suggest, Dallas has found that rehabilitation of single-family dwellings is one workable solution in the war against residential blight.

extinction by the dual forces being felt by all expanding cities of the era. One force was the strain of the mounting daily influx of people and vehicles into the central area. The other force was the counter-balancing and accompanying movement of people and their spendable incomes, of investors and their commercial activities, to suburban areas.

The Greater Dallas Planning Council, the Dallas Citizens Council, the Chamber of Commerce and the two daily newspapers—the *Times Herald* and *Morning News*—sponsored the panel. Its mission was to suggest some of the directions which Dallas should follow as it entered the second half of the 20th century. The panel was headed by two Philadelphians, the late Richard J. Seltzer, then president of the Urban Land Institute, and Boyd T. Barnard, board chairman of the Jackson-Cross Company and chairman of the ULI panel.

At the start of the session Barnard summarized the general impression which panel members had gained of the city. He said, "There is a certain small-town vitality about this community . . . and when I say 'small town' I don't say that in anything but the most complimentary terms, because those of us who live in older, larger communities realize that they can become bogged down by reason of their own weight."

GROWTH ESTIMATES OUTSTRIPPED

Panel members, of course, made no claims to clairvoyance or omniscience. Although they brought considerable experience in business and finance into the Dallas study, they were unable to foresee the extent to which Dallas's growth would outstrip most of the thoughtful estimates of the early 1950's. Nor could the panelists foresee how some of the pressing concerns of the day would be swept aside—and in the process be solved—by the rush of technological progress in the 1950's and 1960's.

There was, for illustration, a spirited discussion of what the panel called "a relatively new phenomenon with which cities have to contend, and that is the subject of air conditioning." To its credit, the panel regarded the technical problems as solvable, and air conditioning as inevitable and desirable. Panelist A. J. Stewart of Louisville commented, "We have reached the point where I don't believe any new buildings are planned that do not include all-year-around conditioning of air."

Less predictable was a determination of how much new mid-town hotel construction was needed. The panel stated, "We doubt the existence of a proven formula for accurately measuring the number of hotel rooms needed in Dallas . . . (But) considering the rapid growth of population and commercial activities, there is an impressive need for an increase of dormitory hotel facilities. (These facilities) have not kept pace with Dallas's growth. The unique importance of Dallas as a jobbing, retail and banking center emphasizes the great need for downtown hotel facilities."

Panelist Hugh Potter of Houston called motel development "far superior" to that in any other southwestern city, but added that motels would not have flourished "were it not for the fact that there is a dearth of first class downtown hotel rooms."

Walter S. Schmidt of Cincinnati warned that Dallas was losing trade and convention business because of inadequate hotel accommodations. Schmidt observed that hotel construction might well be economically infeasible because of construction costs and the competition with established older hotels. Public subscription of new hotel investment was suggested as one avenue of relief, although such ventures had proven unprofitable for investors in the past, as was the case with the Adolphus Hotel in Dallas.

The panel's concern over new downtown hotel facilities, as in the case of its wrestling with the "problem" of air conditioning, would have been less acute if panelists had had some inkling of the future. However, when the panel confronted the question of rehabilitating blighted areas in the central business district, it dealt with a problem which have defied the efforts of Dallas and many other cities, then and now.

1950: DOWNTOWN REHABILITATION

The panel advised that rehabilitation of downtown buildings would be encouraged by facilitating access to the central business district and by providing more off-street parking.

Panelist Howard Tobin of Milwaukee outlined further action: "We urge vigilance on the part of the downtown property owner and street association groups which have as their objective the rehabilitation of deteriorated and obsolescent properties. Rehabilitation is difficult to achieve on an individual basis."

Standardizing signs and eliminating overhanging signs was advanced as a task the property owners could undertake for and among themselves. One panel participant commented that if all signs in Dallas were eliminated "we'd have an awful howl from the merchants, but it ought to be done in every American city that expects to be a beautiful city." It was pointed out that shopping centers are designed as a unit and their appearance can be regulated by the developer. The central area can place itself at a competitive disadvantage when merchants try to compete with one another for the shopper's attention through ever-larger and more garish signs: "If the housewives of Dallas had never known Highland Park shopping village or any of those organized, well-developed centers, they would not be conscious so much of the heterogeneous nature of unplanned downtown business development."

Housewives and shoppers seldom would bring themselves within viewing distance of the downtown hodgepodge, or of a tastefully laid-out downtown either, if there were no convenient parking after they got there.

The panel said it would be necessary for Dallas "to provide adequate parking in order to stabilize the downtown district," and called this task "so difficult of accomplishment that it justifies use of the power of eminent domain in those spots within the (central business) area that must be preserved for parking service." Dallas businessmen and city officials were urged to make a joint effort to secure state legislative approval for a public parking agency.

The recommendation said further that the property, force-bought for parking, should remain in public ownership, and the public agency should control parking rates. But operation of the garages should be turned over to private enterprise. "The panel knows of no other method by which the solution of this problem can be attacked effectively on a permanent basis."

It was noted that Dallas in 1950 had about 13,000 off-street parking spaces in the central district. The panel stated that, even then, Dallas needed two and a half to three times more off-street parking space, and added this comment: "There is no danger of over-providing parking to serve the downtown area of Dallas within the foreseeable future."

One admonition for caution: conduct an origin-and-destination traffic survey, and use it to pick garage locations, to minimize congesting central business district streets.

Experience had shown that shopper-parkers demand that they be permitted to leave their cars within 500 feet of their final destination. However, all-day parking for downtown workers should be located as far away as 1,500 feet from the main central area streets, such as Elm and Commerce. Further dispersion of long-term parking could be gained by using city-owned land well removed from the central area for fringe parking, connected to the central business district by shuttle buses.

The panel acquiesed in the inevitability of some parking meters, but advised one-hour limits. "Anything beyond an hour would be parking for revenue rather than solving the parking problem."

TRAFFIC FLOW

Hand-in-hand with parking, as a downtown concern, is traffic flow.

The panel recommended:

Ban parking during peak hours on the most heavily-traveled CBD streets.

Eliminate left turns wherever possible on these same streets.

Use traffic patrolmen at the most critical intersections to increase the usefulness of signalization.

Do not widen any central area streets except as a last resort— that is, after curb parking has been eliminated and all turns prohibited; and after a comprehensive one-way street plan has been developed for the entire central business district.

Work to eliminate street jogs resulting from the uncoordinated street layouts made in Dallas's earliest days.

Panelist Stewart said the suggestions were realistic, stating that the panel was not distracted with concern over congestion. He said, "I don't think you are going to have a successful downtown Dallas without congestion . . . (the idea is not to) cure congestion but to try to accommodate some more."

Asked to advise the city on the effect decentralization of commercial enterprises will have on downtown property values, the panel gave this advice:

Decentralization in the sense of removing important businesses from downtown and re-locating them in outlying areas was not taking place in Dallas (in 1950). Suburban development was a healthy and proper manifestation of a growing city. Downtown stores, banks and other institutions had established suburban branches, but this was expansion then and not decentralization.

The panel commended Dallas for being "alert to the necessity of preserving and protecting its downtown district." A warning was added that depreciation of downtown values would increase the tax burden on every other taxpayer in Dallas.

However, Dallas was told by panelist Hobart Brady that it had not then reached the size at which decentralization could be viewed a major problem. He said cities with less than a million population are "less exposed to the decentralization problem." Mere size could generate a decentralization problem, as suburbs grow so large that they develop their own "tributary merchandising areas that permit them to offer" the diversified merchandising and commercial services now offered only in the central business district.

On the subject of mass transit, the panel could only view with alarm some statistical evidence and offer general advice. It was noted that half the persons entering the central area did so by transit. But in the four years preceding the panel, transit patronage decreased 12 per cent while mileage traveled was increasing 7 per cent—evidence of a growing city but a circumstance which creates financial problems for the transit company. The panel recommended traffic regulations which gave transit a "break"—such as a through curb lane at peak hours. Transit fare should be high enough to permit the company to buy equipment and offer service which made transit competitive with private automobiles.

The transit system management was advised to do some earnest market research, to learn whether the riding public wanted better service at higher fares, or poorer service at less cost. After the marketing should come a public relations effort, to "sell" transit to as many automobile riders as possible.

In the final part of its discusssion, the panel looked ahead into the then uncharted area of expressway construction. The panel limited itself to "general suggestions," notably two: That the expressway avoid breaking through the heavily congested central district; and, that it avoid walling-in the central district on the directions of its natural growth, to the north and east.

Chairman Barnard summed up: "We will have accomplished our purpose in coming here if we have created within the minds of these people a consciousness of the necessity of coordinating all the various interests in this community toward a better Dallas and toward a healthy downtown district."

ULI—the Urban Land Institute's 1950 seminar apparently served as an incubator of ideas on dealing with the specific questions of downtown traffic flow, parking, transit, hotel accommodations and blight eradication. All these are categories in which Dallas has made noteworthy progress.

HOW TO BECOME AN URBAN CENTER

But despite the profusion of planning, there was in 1966 concern among some key figures in the city's public life that Dallas had not yet fully comprehended or reacted to the responsibility of being the center of a vast urban sprawl. Crull, the former city manager, said recently, "The thing that worries me about Dallas is that we haven't yet realized we've quit being just a city and have become the center of an urban area. There are 28 incorporated municipalities in Dallas County alone. We need a study for metropolitan government. This is one area of planning that has been neglected. There is a regional Planning Council just starting, but I don't think it will be enough. The situation we have here is not a case of city leaders studying the 'Metro' idea and rejecting it. It hasn't come to that. The full force of the problem just has not hit the leaders yet."

Another significant view came from Avery Mays, a building contractor who heads the revitalized Greater Dallas Planning Council, which Mays describes as "the civilian front for achieving legislation needed for development of the city."

Mays said, "The city planning department needs strengthening. We have never had a strong enough one." He conceded that "if there were no master-planning of any sort or any form of officially programmed redevelopment, and private enterprise were allowed to run free, Dallas would not be so bad off, not nearly as bad off as some less fortunate cities that do have comprehensive planning. However, we would have to get used to living with blight." He added that private enterprise alone should not be expected to undertake all the tasks which are high in social-benefit returns but low on profit realization. Mays put it this way: "Dallas is not blessed with an abundance of charitable attitudes. Possibly it is too new a community."

He cited what he called some failures of the city's leadership and the rank-and-file citizenry:

"Slums are a genuine cause for concern. We've had city clean-up, fix-up programs which were good as far as they went. But there was nothing which could be done about neighborhoods where lot sizes and street widths are inadequate. These are areas where slum-breeding conditions cannot be overcome except by a redevelopment program." Mays said he believes that, with energetic leadership, a successful campaign could be launched to secure public support for re-location of slum dwellers with public financial aid.

Such public acceptance would represent a marked change of attitude for Dallas, which has a long history of local self-reliance and antipathy to governmental aid, particularly federal.

Mays said government assistance in renewal is the necessary alternative because effective strictly-private efforts have, in effect, been rejected. He explained it this way: "Some problems cannot be solved without joint federal assistance. Primarily, we need some agency with eminent domain to assemble land in blocks. And then there is the aspect of financing—local taxes are as high as people want them."

In the summer of 1965, Mays recalled, there was an effort to create a private foundation with a revolving fund for use in renewal. "But this program could not generate sufficient interest or gain enough public acceptance. Perhaps the people here have had it too good and are complacent."

Another similar effort was dropped in March, 1966. This concerned what Mays described as "low-cost, sweat-equity housing" under Section 312 of the 1965 housing act. "Lack of interest" was cited by Mays as the reasons for failure of this effort.

CHANGING RENEWAL ATTITUDES

However, Dallas attitudes toward government-assisted renewal appear to be changing, veering toward acceptance. Crull gave this summation:

"We have had no urban renewal, to consider one form of federal assistance, for purely emotional reasons, and not because Dallas has been capable financially of taking care of its own renewal problems. However, this emotional resistance will be overcome by pressures already building up. People here are beginning to take the attitude that the federal government takes their dollars away, and the only way to get them back is to put the noose (of federal aid) around their own necks and go down the same road as most other cities. Dallas is perhaps late in coming around to this way of thinking. In older cities, the costs of renewal have been so horrifying that federal aid was quickly accepted as the only sane method to proceed. Dallas will reach the point where its redevelopment costs are too heavy to bear alone."

The Dallas city government operated in fiscal 1965-66 on a budget of $98.33-million, an increase of $3.77-million over the year before. To support this scale of expenditure, the tax rate had to be raised from $1.60 to $1.70 for each $100 of assessed valuation. (Total assessed value of property for taxation was $2.95-billion for 1965-66). Ad valorem taxes represent by far the largest share of city revenues, $48.56-million. If businessman, civic-leader Mays, for one, read the public mind correctly, Dallas-ites do not want to pay any more taxes. But the voters may face the necessity of a tax increase even before their confrontation with the costs of renewal, in order to support a heavier bonded debt. *The Dallas Morning News* reported on June 28, 1966, that estimated costs of the new city hall had been revised upward to a new ceiling of $30-million (up from earlier estimates of $18-million to $20-million). The city may face a referendum on increasing its statutory limit of $135-million on general obligation bonds.

By contrast, Dallas's Office of Urban Rehabilitation had for 1966 an annual budget of a mere $110,000. Headed by William McClintock, this department has relied on persuasion backed up when necessary by "maximum enforcement powers" of the city's various codes—building, zoning, electric, plumbing and the rest. With a staff of 19, this agency has been credited with causing the demolition of 3,315 unsound structures in three slum areas, and the repairing of 5,118 dwellings. McClintock said his agency's next effort will be to set up a code enforcement program, which receives federal assistance under the 89-117 312 section of the 1965 housing act but does not require eminent domain.

Meanwhile, McClintock hoped for a program which would cut across Dallas's long-standing hands-off attitude toward governmental action against commercial area blight. With the aid of the city attorney, the rehabilitation agency head began drafting a "minimum non-residential standards ordinance." McClintock said he hopes to take his task force of inspectors into blighted areas of the central

Main Place, a soaring 10-acre development now underway in Dallas, covers the three main downtown streets, Main, Elm and Commerce. The site will be bisected by a tri-level Main Street and by Griffin Street and a new six-lane connector to the downtown freeway loop.

business district, compelling fix-up where it is practical, but ordering demolition where necessary.

Whether this or related efforts will result eventually in federal urban renewal in the classic sense, with condemnation of property and re-sale to private developers, is unpredictable. Central Business District spokesman Braff believes that it will. He notes "a weakening in Dallas's attitudes on this point." Braff said also that the slum-border on two sides of the central area has been harmful to downtown business. He concluded that "as time goes on and urbanization becomes more complex, there will be many areas in which urban renewal must be used."

Texas law permits urban renewal by local option, based on approval of a city council and of the voters in a referendum. Section Eight of the state renewal law requires that cities offer "encouragement to private enterprise," and says "a city shall afford maximum opportunity, consistent with sound needs of the city as a whole, to the rehabilitation or redevelopment of the urban renewal area by private enterprise."

Dallas has had a workable program approved by the Housing and Home Finance Agency begun in March, 1956. But the city has never had an urban renewal referendum.

Henry Miller, Jr., a Dallas real estate man and an Urban Land Institute trustee, was a member of a citizens committee which sponsored the urban renewal enabling act in the legislature at Austin a decade ago. Later, Miller became chairman of the Citizens Committee for Urban Renewal and organized a seminar to stimulate interest in renewal.

After that promising start, the project bogged down and eventually died. Miller recalled how it happened:

"Just about that time the Congressman from Dallas, who was the only Republican Congressman from Texas, seized on this as a political opportunity and started issuing blasts about urban renewal, especially the federal variety.

"Our citizens' committee had already requested the Dallas City Council to hold a referendum as required by the state act. But the Congressman and his supporters created such a stir that we postponed any action and never did bring it up again."

Miller said the slum problem, particularly, has not been corrected in the seven years since Dallas's abortive renewal effort, and that another effort should be made soon. "The Congressman was finally defeated, and with time there has been a change in attitude among Dallas people," Miller said. "In addition we seem to have an enlightened city government, and some forms of federal assistance have been accepted in Dallas since that time."

GO-IT-ALONE RENEWAL EFFORTS

Dallas's small-scale self-help rehabilitation effort was launched in 1957 in the 60-acre Little Mexico area, in which only 11 per cent of the 335 structures were found to meet Dallas housing and sanitation codes. The area was brought up to a reasonable level of habitability without federal assistance. But it is in this area that the inadequate lot sizes and street widths cited by Mays as renewal handicaps abound. By today's higher standards of what constitutes adequate housing, Little Mexico and the south and west Dallas areas eventually will face a more stringent renewal effort.

Dallas will be observing how its nearby sister city, Fort Worth, fares with a go-it-alone renewal effort. As Fort Worth headed into an April, 1966, referendum on urban renewal, there were—as reported by *The Dallas Times-Herald*—"pleadings from civic leaders that the city's growth and prosperity hinged on passage of the issue." The voters rejected urban renewal by 39,397 votes to 9,248. The opposition was led by the "Citizens Committee for the Protection of Property Rights." Mayor Willard Barr, who had urged passage of the urban renewal measure, said afterwards "the people have spoken. This is the American way." This vote was cast on a clear-cut issue. The question on the Fort Worth ballot was "Shall the city council be authorized to use the power of condemnation to acquire land in areas where more than half the buildings are destroyed or blighted beyond repair?" The answer was a resounding "No." How successful Fort Worth is in developing a workable alternative to the rejected proposition obviously will affect the course of events in Dallas a few miles away.

ULI member Miller said he believes the vote in Fort Worth is no reason for discouragement among pro-urban renewal civic leaders in Dallas.

"Although these two cities are close in miles, they are sometimes pretty far apart in thinking," Miller said. "The result of the Fort

Worth referendum should not rule out another effort for public approval in Dallas."

This crisis of decision was many years off when the Urban Land Institute panel met in the Baker Hotel in 1950 to consider problems with much less ideological content than urban renewal, but which had immense practical application for that day and this.

AREA-WIDE MASS TRANSIT PLANS

Mass transportation was a subject which the panel regarded as a vital element in central city development. Panel chairman Boyd Barnard said that "the central business district is, without question, as dependent upon a healthy, virile transit system as upon any other single factor."

Difficult times were ahead for Dallas transit. The "Dallas Central District" study reported in 1961 that "the total number of persons entering the core area during a day increased about 10 per cent in the 12-year period 1946-1958. The number of persons entering by automobile increased nearly 70 per cent, but those coming by transit decreased by more than 40 per cent." Nineteen fifty-eight was the year in which the auto replaced transit as the principal means of entry into the central business district.

The system had hit an all-time peak of 104-million passenger fares in 1946. The following year transit was divorced from its partnership with the electric utility, Dallas Power and Light. At that time the transit system was operating at a profit, but the typical decline in transit ridership which became prevalent nationwide about that time was soon felt in Dallas. By 1949 ridership was down to 88-million fares. Ten years later the figure was 40-million. In 1960 a Baltimore investor, Harry Weinberg, bought the system.

Ellis H. Watkins, the current administrative assistant to the Dallas Transit System superintendent, worked with the company in the balmy days of wartime auto shortages, then stepped out during a dispute over operational policies. Watkins recalled that the system's mileage was cut by the operator as an economy measure after he signed a union contract granting a 33 cent hourly wage increase. Equipment deteriorated and few replacements were purchased.

Watkins recalled that the city council held a show-cause hearing for Weinberg to demonstrate why he should not improve service. "The outcome was that the City of Dallas purchased the transit system. The purchase price was probably more than the system was worth, but the city still came out better than it would have through litigation." This was in 1964, after a disastrous year in which ridership declined to 31.6-million fares. In the first year of municipal operation, ridership actually increased for the first time in 18 years— a mere 241,000-fare increase, but significant nonetheless.

The city-owned system has made a concerted effort to win back a substantial share of the traffic into the central business district. One aid has been the indirect subsidy the system receives through its use of city departments including purchasing, auditing and legal.

In mid-1964 the city bought 95 new air conditioned buses for $2.8-million through a revenue bond issue. Later another 35 buses were bought. The most dramatic improvement has been a $12-million program which included an additional 310 new air conditioned buses. This massive modernization was made possible through an $8-million grant from the Department of Housing and Urban Development, in the form of two-thirds matching funds. The city's $4-million share was approved in a bond election. When the last of the new buses arrived in September, 1966, Dallas was ready to claim the most modern transportation system in the United States.

If and as the Dallas city government becomes involved in area-wide transportation planning, transit should be equipped to take part. Watkins said there is serious consideration for creating a multi-county transit authority, with sufficient revenue resources to develop long-distance rapid transit, new conceptions of short-haul service within the central business district, and all the other components of a transit system geared to the exacting demands of the 1970's and later. Dallas has placed itself, at no small public cost, in the position of keeping public transit capable of rendering as high a grade of service as a healthy central business district demands.

The De Leuw-Cather long-range transportation plan offered a calculated prediction of what role transit will play in the future. This study estimated that as many as 160,000 person-trips a day will be made by transit into the central business district by 1980, and 200,000 on a normal week-day by the year 2,000. The report said "Express buses will probably use the freeways and then distribute their passengers along the surface streets or use terminals within walking distance of many major destinations."

This same report stated that "no new type of person-conveyance appears urgently needed in the Dallas central business district," but some innovations, possibly a moving sidewalk device or the less revolutionary mini-bus might be desirable after 1980, when the most heavily traveled route through the core area will be used by 5,000 persons an hour in each direction at midday. The most likely highest-use route would be along Main Street between the new governmental building complex on the west and a proposed parking garage and bus terminal on the east. However, the central area would be served principally by conventional buses on most major streets.

Transit's role of augmenting the major means of transportation, the automobile, is established in Dallas as it is in all except a few of the largest cities in the country. At the time of the 1950 panel, Urban Land Institute members found consternation among Dallas's leaders at the prospect of accommodating the daily avalanche of automobiles into the central business district. The panel helped assuage some of these fears through reassurances such as this from panel chairman Barnard: "We are not looking at congestion as something to be afraid of in itself. We all recognize that people like to be where there are people, and if you make it possible for people to move so there is going to be nobody else around them, you defeat the thing you are trying to accomplish. Rather, the objective is making the central city accessible in such a way that it will attract people with a minimum of inconvenience and annoyance."

Dallas has achieved a high degree of success in holding to a minimum the inconveniences of downtown traffic movement and in parking. Dallas is particularly well-advanced in freeway construction. De Leuw-Cather found that "Dallas's system is far advanced both in actual construction and in planning for the future."

Central Expressway was begun in 1946. This super-road connects downtown with the northern portions of the city, and stimulated high-grade post-war residential development in this direction, while indirectly contributing to the surrendering of much of South Dallas to the encroachment of blight. However, the Dallas freeway system is more than sufficiently well-balanced now to afford all sections of the city and surburbs ready access to the core area. A freeway loop, when completed, will connect with six major arteries radiating from the central business district.

Braff, the Central Business District Association director, said that easy access "has been of immense importance in persuading private entrepreneurs to risk their money on central district streets which, as now planned, will be adequate through 1980, a significant statement since present CBD traffic is expected to double by that year. As expressway segments are completed, these will divert from the CBD streets the through-traffic, which runs as high as 60 per cent on certain mid-town streets. The engineers gave a strong recommendation to transportation terminals along the freeway loop with direct ramp connections. A proposed transportation-and-parking terminal between Peal and Central Expressways, Pacific Avenue and Commerce streets would accommodate an estimated 3,000 automobiles, whose riders would switch to transit for the last leg of their trips into downtown.

Dallas's achievements in traffic-movement planning could be studied with benefit by other cities of comparable population and terrain.

PARKING GARAGES NOW PLENTIFUL

The supply of parking space has kept abreast of the needs of auto-users without resort to the use of eminent domain, which appeared so necessary from the 1950 panel's vantage point. Braff and others underscored the obvious reason for this situation—that, so far, parking garages have been attractive, successful investments. There is no guarantee this state of affairs will continue, and Braff stated "it may be necessary in the future for government to get into the parking business."

ULI trustee Miller, referring to the same topic, the possibility of government involvement in parking garages, commented, "I don't think it will come to that."

The 1950 panel's recommendation for eminent domain in acquiring parking garage sites apparently had a shock effect among self-reliant Dallas-ites, with the consequence that investors set out to prove that the panel had underestimated private initiative.

Miller said, "I think it was the panel's suggestion which stimulated the building of parking garages by private investors. In fact, I know it was, because (my firm) had a part in acquiring the land for the first post-war, privately-financed garage. This was right after the ULI panel, and several Dallas investors wanted to prove that it could be done by private investors.

"They built this first one, which was successful, and within another year they built two more. Then other private investors started building garages."

The long-range transportation study found that "parking capacity should be doubled from the present 43,000 spaces in the entire business district to 90,000 by 1980." The engineers recommend that no more than 20,000 spaces should exist in the central core area bounded by Lamar, Commerce, Pacific and Harwood streets. So far, parking garage investors have been able to find attractively-priced land at sites where garages are convenient from the motorists' point of view. The transportation engineers warned that, in the future, parking will be needed at locations of extremely high land cost, either in separate garages or in parking space set aside in multi-purpose buildings.

In the broad view, all the planning and investment in transit, roads, parking facilities served as no more than an appendage to the central area itself, to the jobs and services available in the city's heart, of course, but to much more as well. A central business district which fulfills its role to the utmost has a symbolic function. It provides civic identity.

Measured against this latter criterion, the Dallas central business district has many supporters, but also some thoughtful critics. For illustration, one of the basic documents of the Goals for Dallas program makes this observation:

"The characteristic symbol of Dallas is the skyline of the core area—vigorous, aggressive, assertive. The contrast of towers with the prairie line is dramatic and compelling. The aspect of the core center at ground level, however, the central core lacks interest in form and embellishment. Aside from the need to transact business, there is little to attract people and, once there, little to secure their enthusiastic response or engage their loyalty.

"Many people are indifferent to downtown, perhaps because it does not offer the drama, variety and zest that one instinctively expects of the number one place. . . . As one moves through the central district, the center of town is never found. There is no spot that speaks out for the entire city to say, 'This is Dallas,' nor do any of the current public or private proposals contain the idea for such a central place or places."

This same essay goes on to say, by way of balance for its criticism, that "the central district is young and not yet so stratified as to resist change."

MAIN PLACE DEVELOPMENT

"Change has been a daily fact of life for the central business district. However much it might have given short shrift to esthetics, the transformation of the CBD has been impressive in volume. Since 1950 the amount of office space has increased 250 per cent. New office space has been added at the rate of 3-million square feet every five years."

The soaring, 10-acre Main Place development now underway may yet provide Dallas with its civic identity, although one participant in Goals for Dallas lumps it with the other "current proposals" which are dismissed as lacking in those qualities which would inspire the feeling that "This is Dallas."

Main Place is strategically located. It is spread out over the three main downtown streets, Main, Elm and Commerce. The site will be bisected by a tri-level Main Street and by Griffin Street, a new six-lane connector to the downtown freeway loop.

The Main Place developers have consciously set out to construct a new heart of the city. A half-acre sunken plaza is the hub of the development. Their brochure states that "open spaces will be programmed daily with activities for people to insure Main Place as the 'people place' of Dallas—an exciting urban environment comparable to Rockefeller Center in New York and the best of the European cities."

The three buildings in Main Place will cover only about one-third of the total acreage. Under construction is a 30-floor office building containing a million square feet of floor space. A second office building, 50 stories and 1.4-million square feet, will come later. The third structure will be a combined-use building with a 300,000 square foot department store topped by a 400-room hotel. The central and smaller plazas will be bordered by 225,000 square feet of commercial and, hopefully, recreational space. Beneath it all will be a 3,000-car garage. *Business Week* magazine called the development "a sunken superblock." The same magazine reported, without attribution, a note of concern—"What this much new office space will do to the Dallas real estate market worries some Eastern realtors. . . . Office vacancies in Dallas now run to 12 per cent of available space."

Assembling the 10 acres for Main Place was a 10-year job. One of the developers, Clint Murchison, Jr., said he would not "undertake the job again without the help of powers of condemnation."

CONDEMNATION POWER NEEDED

Murchison cited the difficulties in assembling large blocks of land as the major factor inhibiting downtown renewal, and he advances his reason for favoring cooperation between private enterprise and government, with its powers of eminent domain:

"The trouble with downtown Dallas," said Murchison, "is that so much of the property is tied up in trusts, in the estates of people who died. Property in trusts is controlled by lawyers, and lawyers are usually bad businessmen."

Incidentally, one legacy of Dallas's frontier heritage is evident in the problem Murchison raises. In the early days, the Texas pioneers were moved by a compulsion to amass landholdings. The more successful early settlers included portions of what is now downtown Dallas in their holdings. With the passing of years, these early property owners gave way to the persons who now, with their great monetary wealth, are rebuilding the central district.

Murchison stated that "the only way around this problem of putting together large enough sites for development is through condemnation. Urban renewal, even with all its dangers and disadvantages, probably will be necessary for the ultimate development of the Dallas central business district."

Efforts at land-assembling have also been influenced—sometimes spurred and perhaps sometimes inhibited—by tax assessing procedures. Former City Manager Crull stated that "The assessor has lowered taxes on downtown land and thus inspired some private urban renewal."

Dallas County Assessor Norman Register said he has adjusted property values for taxing purposes according to changing economic realities and not specifically to assist any development. Register says his office practices "continuous equalization," which brings every piece of property under reinspection and reassessment once every six years.

CENTER CITY ASSESSMENTS CUT IN HALF

Register said he has been fully conscious of the effect that suburban development, particularly shopping centers and motels, has had on reducing mid-town property values. The assessor said that since 1953 he has cut in half the total assessed valuations in the central business district. The most select mid-town property, which had been on the tax rolls at $20,000 a front foot ($200 a square foot) before feeling the full impact of suburban competition is now down to $10,000 a front foot ($100 a square foot).

Register also has reacted to shifting land values within the central district. The highest-valued land had been the southwest corner of Ervay and Elm Streets. Generally, land on the south side of Elm was given twice the value of the north side of Elm. Now, says Register, both sides of this top-ranked commercial street are practically the same.

To further refine his process, according to the assessor, he has used the "income factor" selectively in assessing central district property.

Register explained that he takes the income factor—the revenue produced by a commercial property—into account in assessing, but only when the owner lodges a protest that he is being called upon to pay too much in taxes.

The Dallas County Assessor is an appointed career official presumably free from political pressures. The net effect of Register's policies appears to have been to stimulate improvement, or at least assist the avoidance of deterioration, in central business district properties. The downtown merchant in competition with the out-of-sight suburban store owner has felt his tax burden gradually lighten even while he searched around for the cash with which to expand, improve, and upgrade.

Meanwhile, the Dallas central area continues to demonstrate a vitality which signals free-wheeling redevelopment.

In an exceedingly enlightened move, the Dallas City Council has encouraged unofficially the transformation of an awkwardly situated, blighted mid-town triangle (at Ervay, Pacific and Bryan Streets) into a compact mid-city park. Neighboring property owners were asked by a committee of businessmen to share the costs of acquiring, clearing and transforming this area into Thanksgiving Square. This, incidentally, was a procedure enthusiastically advanced by the 1950 ULI panel for turning the land triangles created by oddly-intersecting streets into central district beauty spots. This work has been moving slowly but with every indication of eventual success.

Many Dallas-ites were cheered in June, 1966, by word that an embarrassing mid-town "white elephant" at last would be corrected.

This is Cary Plaza, begun as a twin-towered hotel at Ross and Akard Streets. After the framework was completed, the developer ran out of money and the twin skeletons became the city's most elaborate eyesore. But on June 24, 1966, San Francisco hotelman Benjamin H. Swig announced he would complete the project with an investment of $15-million and turn it into "the finest convention facility in the country."

A GRAND DESIGN

More excitement was generated by New York architect I. M. Pei, who was hired to design the new Dallas city hall and who chose also to take a critical look at the entire central area within the express-way loop. Pei observed that there is both the space and a need within the central area for a new residential community. Pei said this would serve the desires of a portion of the population which wants in-town living but can't find it now. He said there should be garden apartments, town houses and some high-rise apartments, all "supported by amenities such as schools, recreation, open space and so on. A housewife should be able to walk around the corner to buy food. There must be community centers and playgrounds." The architect said this infusion of round-the-clock living into the central thousand acres of Dallas would eliminate the sense of barrenness which settles over the area after 5 p.m.

Dallas's aim, according to the architect, should be to make the center of the city "a center of culture, of life itself—a center in every sense of the word, and not just a place to do business. The center of Dallas is not performing that function."

Although Pei emphasized that he was merely making observations and not a proposal, his comments aroused much comment around the city, much of it approving.

There has been a ferment in Dallas concerning the central business area. There has been an outpouring of ideas and expression of aspirations from private developers and the rank-and-file citizens recruited for the Goals for Dallas drive.

The Dallas central district clearly has benefited from the profusion of wealth in the community and the willingness of entrepreneurs to invest, inspired by varying combinations of the profit motive and civic pride.

Pictured is one of the three buildings in Main Place which will provide Dallas with 2.4-million square feet of office space, a 300,000 square-foot department store, a 400-room hotel, 225,000 square feet of commercial and recreational space and a 3,000-car underground garage.

Dallas demonstrates that, even with its auspicious store of financial and human resources, a city nonetheless needs something more—a concept based on better planning, a grand design.

Few other cities its size can hope to match Dallas's accomplishments, particularly those brought about through home-grown enterprise and money. Still, because of the methods which Dallas is selecting to channel its affluence and ambitions into creating a city as nearly perfect as possible, Dallas is an example worth watching.

PEORIA, ILLINOIS

October 8-12, 1956. Peoria Metropolitan Area: Report to the Peoria Downtown Improvement Association, Sponsor.

Panel Members Participating

Boyd T. Barnard, Jackson-Cross Co., Philadelphia —Chairman

Gayle W. Arnold, Baltimore & Ohio Railroad, Baltimore

George W. Cox, Atchison, Topeka, & Santa Fe Railway System, Chicago

U. A. Denker, Wheeler Kelly & Hagny Investment Co., Wichita

James B. Douglas, Northgate Co., Seattle

Richard M. Hurd, Pringle-Hurd & Co., New York

Philip W. Kniskern, First Mortgage Co., Philadelphia

Laurence H. Lang, Cragin, Lang, Free & Co., Cleveland

Glenn McHugh, Equitable Life Assurance Society of the U.S., New York

Warren L. Morris, Ostendorf-Morris Co., Cleveland

Walter S. Schmidt, Frederick A. Schmidt, Inc., Cincinnati

Larry Smith, Larry Smith & Co., Seattle

Harley L. Swift, Harrisburg Railways Co., Harrisburg

C. C. Wiley, University of Illinois, Champaign

Richard S. Willis, New England Mutual Life Insurance Co., Boston

CHAPTER FIVE

PEORIA

REVITALIZING THE CENTRAL BUSINESS DISTRICT

Peoria, Ill., population (1950) 111,856, (1960) 103,162, (1965) 127,000.

1956—ULI was invited by business and industrial interests to look at the Peoria area as a whole, and in doing so to search out the reasons why the central city was deteriorating physically and in commercial vitality while the metropolitan region prospered.

The ULI Central City and Industrial Council panel found the answer contained in the statement of the problem. In a thriving regional economy buttressed by both agriculture and manufacture, Peorians were indeed prospering, and their tastes were becoming more sophisticated. As consumers, they were demanding more quality than could be found in a lackluster central business district.

ULI noted an awakening to problems and opportunities among the city's officials and private citizens in positions of leadership. The panel advised Peorians to discard their attitude that "blue-collar town" was synonymous with drabness. Suggestions on mobilizing the community leadership for central city improvement were offered—and heeded.

The unquestioned need for "saving" America's cities has inspired much cliche-bound thinking, including the notion that massive applications of public funds and vigorous shaking of the existing order of things are indispensable in all effective renewal efforts. Among the cities in this report there are some—Newark and Philadelphia, for example—in which nothing short of extraordinary measures would have made much difference.

However, to haul up another cliche, this is a big country. In its variety there can be found a city in which such prosaic events as routing an expressway close to the central business district and persuading the Sears department store management to stay downtown brought about a notable upsurge in urban vitality. This city is Peoria, Illinois.

Sitting in America's agricultural heartland, Peoria has grown to a considerable size (130,000 residents within the city limits, 325,-000 in the metropolitan area). This growth has been founded on a solid economic base, a happy blend of the riches produced by thriving farmlands and heavy industry. Peoria is far enough removed from the very large cities (the closest is Chicago, 150 miles to the northeast) to feel insulated from the worst urban afflictions. It has no major slum problem or racial conflict, no headlong abandonment of the central city by the middle class. Peoria once did experience an era in which its local government reached a low estate which is now remembered by Peorians for its ineptitude. But Peorians were too engrossed in what they regarded as more vital concerns to permit politics to become a major industry or a prime cause of public travail.

Bad government just before and after World War II was doing more harm than most Peorians realized—something they admitted later, after a shedding of complacent attitudes led to remarkable changes in this outwardly unflappable Midwestern city.

1956 ANNUAL LOSSES:
1,500 JOBS, $200,000 IN TAXES,
$25-MILLION RETAIL SALES

The Urban Land Institute made a Peoria panel study in 1956. The report was a blunt cataloguing of Peoria's unmet problems. These included the school problem, the leadership and planning problems, water supply and air pollution problems, just for starters. The sharpest criticism in the ULI report concerned the central business district problem. When Peoria merchants and business leaders learned the extent of their annual lost business, they reacted with a decisiveness the city probably had never seen before in civic affairs. ULI told Peoria it was losing $25-million a year in retail sales, and with it 1,500 jobs plus $200,000 annually in lost taxes. Confronted by such figures, Peoria's shocked leaders shed their complacent attitudes with finality.

Obviously, not all Peorians were content to see their city drift toward mediocrity. The contract with ULI for a panel study was evidence of some apprehension within the group known as the Peoria Downtown Improvement Association. A key figure in this turn of events was Harry D. Feltenstein, Jr., an official of the Central Illinois Light Company. Feltenstein later became a member and trustee of ULI.

Feltenstein saw first-hand the initial sproutings of the seeds of discontent—of the feeling that Peoria needed a new planting of civic effort and a new crop of ideas.

"What ended up as a major change for Peoria started with a small conversation," Feltenstein recalled in a recent interview. "An associate of mine at Central Illinois Light, George Hathway, who was a director of the Downtown Improvement Association, told me one day he was becoming increasingly concerned about the way things were going in the central business district.

"The way Hathway assessed the situation, competition from the successful suburban regional shopping center, Sheridan Village, was siphoning business away from downtown. The evidence of this was obvious—the increasing number of vacant stores in the center of town.

"Downtown Improvement Association members were aware of the shopping center's advantage in offering parking, plenty of it and free. Hathway asked me what I thought about having a downtown parking survey," Feltenstein continued. "I said I wouldn't give 15 cents for a parking survey. Downtown Peoria had a lot of problems besides parking, all of them interrelated. After thrashing this viewpoint over between us, we finally determined to attempt to get some expert help in surveying our overall downtown problem, in all its forms."

DORMANT CIVIC LEADERSHIP

The next move, Feltenstein recalled, was a job of salesmanship on the dormant civic leadership. "It is true that there were not enough people doing any coordinated thinking," he said. "Until people got together, typically, nothing happened."

"Hathway and I felt confident that there was enough leadership talent to cause a turnabout in•the city's direction and start it back uphill again. We knew there was a nucleus of leadership talent in Peoria, because it has the advantage of being a home office town. Caterpillar tractor has in the Peoria area the world's largest manufacturing plant for farm machinery. LeTourneau-Westinghouse, another big implement producer, has its headquarters in Peoria, as does Hiram Walker, probably the largest distillery anywhere. And of course there is quite a list of other important industries. The two railroads servicing Peoria, for example, helped underwrite the cost of the panel study."

After the determination to secure a comprehensive survey was implanted among the top echelon of leadership, a further decision was made to broaden the sponsorship. "One of the keys to the success we had later was the broad backing secured for the Peoria survey. The entire power structure contributed to the costs," Feltenstein said, "And we had the support of business, labor, the Negro community, Bradley University, and even political support. There was no opposition from city hall. Peoria had already moved along the road and achieved an effective city manager form of government."

Feltenstein said ULI—the Urban Land Institute was selected for the Peoria survey because the type of service ULI offered, a probing analysis of a city's problems by men who brought experience and objectivity to their task, appeared to fit Peoria's requirements at the time. The ULI panel was headed by Boyd T. Barnard of Philadelphia and included men from Chicago, Baltimore, Cleveland, New York City, Cincinnati, Seattle and other cities.

This panel turned its attention toward a city with a basically solid economy, built on diversified industry and drawing upon the affluence of the surrounding agricultural area, one of the most productive in the nation. In 1956, Peoria itself had a population of something over 100,000 with another 200,000 persons living outside the city boundaries but within what functioned as a homogenous metropolitan area. Peoria had previously rid itself of that insidious inhibitor of progress, local government which was self-serving or worse. In short, the city had no problems which required moving mountains before the base causes could be reached. It was merely asleep.

Perhaps Peoria had come to believe in the "image" which had been concocted for it in other parts of the country. *Time* magazine noted this bias in October, 1966, when it made this observation in an essay on provincialism:

"Sitting contentedly on the banks of the Illinois River in the very heartland of America, Peoria has for years been the butt of jokes, the gagman's tag for Nowheresville." *Time,* however, reported that "provincialism is dead," and noted that humor deprecating Peoria "is as stale as the idea of Peoria as a backwater of national life."

The criticism implied in the humor had more basis in fact a decade ago. The ULI panel avoided applying the handy but inadequate catchall labels for Peoria—among them "complacent" and "backwater"—in favor of a factual exposition based upon the experience of the panelists.

For example, Peorians tended to view the lack of vitality in the central business district, which contained about 1.5-million square feet of floor space, as a result of competition from Sheridan Village shopping center, which in 1956, had about 135,000 square feet of retail space plus the enticement of free parking for about 2,000 cars.

SELLING THEIR CITY SHORT

The ULI panel saw a problem with broader dimensions than the effects of competition between two retail centers, one downtown and the other suburban. Panelists sensed that Peoria was feeling the effects of what might be called the "blue-collar town" syndrome, which limited the horizons Peorians set for themselves and their city. Peoria needed to develop confidence that the overall quality of life there could improve and that the city could cope with problems brought by healthy expansion.

Before: Downtown Peoria, situated on the Illinois River, was losing an estimated $25 million retail trade annually before embarking on its vigorous urban renewal program. The photograph depicts Peoria before its multi-million dollar face-lifting and redevelopment

Panelists noted, in their report to the Peoria sponsors, that residents lamented somewhat defensively that the city "has not been a good place in which to do business." The Panel apparently was nettled by "comments that the Peoria population consists largely of wage-earners, on the assumption that style and quality merchandise would, therefore, not be favored." Peorians, apparently, were inclined in 1956 to sell themselves and their city short.

The ULI report said "it appears to the panel that the central business district community as a whole has not shown confidence in the changed purchasing power of Peoria shoppers during the last 20 years." Armed with this purchasing power, Peoria's workers were upgrading their demand for quality in a way unheeded by the merchants.

The panel report added that, "Certainly the industrial workers constitute the new American aristocracy, and with the disappearance of the so-called carriage trade, the high earning power of the American industrial and farm population provides a basis for the distribution of better quality merchandise than ever before." The panel went on to say that "In the case of Peoria it appears that there has been such an emphasis on the marketing of standard and

After: Peoria's new buildings—stores, banks, motels, restaurants, county courthouse—dot the river bank.

low-priced merchandise for a long period of years that the opportunity for better quality speciality stores in both apparel and home furnishing lines may not be evident to an individual entrepreneur."

This shortsightedness in Peoria was certainly evident to merchants in Chicago and St. Louis, who were the main beneficiaries of the estimated $25-million retail trade lost annually by downtown Peoria.

The panel observed that, in addition to the upgrading of merchandise quality, downtown Peoria needed about one million square feet of additional retail space, if it were to fulfill its role as the shopping hub for the metropolitan area.

"It therefore seems to be a matter for basic determination as to whether or not Peoria proposes offering a central business district which will adequately serve as a focal point for retail and commercial activity for the metropolitan area of which it is the dominant city." This was the key statement in the ULI report.

During a germination period of about five years, the idea of downtown Peoria's dominant role in its metropolitan area was nurtured and finally brought to fruition.

A MISSING SENSE OF URGENCY

Peorian Feltenstein observed that the city was beset by a number of interrelated problems, all of them in turn related to the absence of a sense of urgency about the need for corrective action. Perhaps it would be more accurate to state that a sense of urgency existed in latent fashion, needing only some triggering device to bring it bursting to the surface. The ULI panel proved to be such a device, and panelists were swamped with questions and requests for advice. The question and answer phase of the ULI session apparently served as a catharsis for Peorians and their pent-up concerns over their civic problems.

The list of problems included air pollution, an inadequate water supply, a physically-deteriorating school plant, a transit system troubled by dwindling patronage and archaic downtown traffic controls, and a taxation system which was not bringing in enough revenue to meet public needs and at the same time was overburdening mid-town property. In addition the absence of even rudimentary area-wide planning was apparent.

ULI's function in regard to the air and water problems was to point out the consequences of neglecting to take corrective steps, and to relate the technical approaches which have been successful elsewhere. A smoke abatement commission and a system of recharge pits using Illinois River water have brought the necessary relief.

SLOW ON SCHOOLS

ULI found the school plant in suburban communities "impressive," but noted with dismay that within Peoria itself only three schools had been built in the previous 19 years, and only nine in the previous 41 years. Nearly 1,000 children were attending on a shift basis. ULI advised that "new school facilities are required and the borrowing power is available."

Peoria voters had turned down several school bond issues prior to 1956 and rejected an attempt to increase the school tax rate. Feltenstein saw two factors at work. Much of the civic leadership had moved outside the boundaries of the city system. Secondly, according to Feltenstein, "the people had had poor government for many years, and this spread over into the school board. Voting against bond issues was the people's opportunity to rebel against what had been taking place." The School and Park Boards "were the first boards to get some good people on them" in Peoria's political renaissance, Feltenstein recalled. At the time of the turndowns at the polls, the School Board had regained respectability. But it felt the sting of the voters' pent-up resentment.

Government, as previously noted, was improving. The council-manager system was adopted in January, 1953, by a four-to-one margin of the voters. The executive vice president of the Peoria Association of Commerce, Herbert N. Johnson, told the panel session that "In four years we have experienced considerable improvement. Perhaps the major ones have been the reduction in prostitution and gambling. Also, there has been improvement in our elected city officials and in the manner in which they conduct the affairs of the city."

ULI's stand on schools contributed to the improving public attitude then developing. Feltenstein said, "ULI pointed out the need for new jobs and industries, and warned that new industry would not come in unless the educational system was improved." At any rate, the next school bond issue passed. In the last decade Peoria has had $34-million of new public and private school construction.

ULI found both the tax rate and bonded debt rate notably low. In Feltenstein's view this situation was evidence of a do-nothing government rather than the happy alternatives, government efficiency and a dearth of need for revenues.

At the panel hearing, Chairman Barnard put this question to Professor Thomas Coker of Bradley University: "Would we be right in assuming that, first, there is little uniformity of assessments in Peoria, and, second, the older downtown properties are assessed too high in relation to their true value and in relation to new construction outside the center of the city?" Coker, who had had 15 years experience with a public accounting firm that specializes in municipal tax problems, replied: "Yes, sir. I believe that statement is true in both cases." Coker added that inequitable taxing procedures were a statewide problem. "We have a situation here where one man has been the assessor for over 40 years, but that doesn't make our problem any worse." He said he had seen the same tax imbalance in other communities with newly-elected assessors.

A decade later, a downtown property owner and former merchant, Fred Bloom, ruefully recalled the status of assessments. "The assessments were political," he asserted. "Some property was taxed out of all proportion to what it was worth. This was the number one factor hurting downtown. The big stores could handle it," Bloom added, "but the tax situation tended to keep out the smaller specialty stores."

Bloom closed his store on one of the key downtown corners, Adams and Fultons Sts., in 1953, and a year later helped organize the Downtown Improvement Association.

CHAIN REACTION BEGINS: PEORIA DEVELOPMENT CORPORATION

The ULI panel recommended "a long-range program of careful study and action" on taxes and assessments. The panel urged securing "outside experts" to review assessments and set up uniform practices and standards. A reassessment study was underway in 1966, but by mid-1967 the new tax roll was still in the works. This reporter found indications that reassessment would trigger a new controversy. Certain property owners who claimed to have had advance knowledge of the new tax roll said property taxes would become "confiscatory."

ULI panelists and Peorians with whom they dealt came to grips with a series of ponderables, important factors which are, if properly handled, the raw materials for central city revitalization. Peoria has found, as have other cities, that mounting a program for civic betterment seems to generate unforeseen side benefits, which might appear to be the result of sheer luck unless closely analyzed. Action begets action. A chain reaction set in motion in the 1950's resulted in a remarkable downtown transformation in the 1960's. Peoria now boasts that half of its downtown area has been "renewed" in one form or another since 1950.

One of the elements in the renewal was the location of Interstate 74, the East-West expressway. The Peoria Realty Board was called in by the state highway department to estimate costs of alternate rights of way. F. M. Bourland, who is vice president of the First Federal Savings and Loan Association in Peoria, was a member of the board which found and recommended a feasible route for I-74 which touched the central business district. "The freeway and the Murray Baker Bridge over the river opened up the central core," Bourland said. This was a factor behind the next important event in the chain.

A major setback for downtown seemed imminent when the management of the Sears store revealed it would not renew its lease on the old, four-story building it occupied in the central area, which was leased through the Commercial National Bank of Peoria. Sears was intent on moving to a new suburban shopping center, near but not part of Sheridan Village.

"We agreed that the Sears downtown building was obsolete," said George Luthy, board chairman of the Commercial Bank. "But we, meaning myself and a few other people vitally interested in downtown, could not agree to let Sears get away without trying to do something about it." Luthy arranged an appointment with Sears executive Gordon Metcalf, who was then in charge of the region and is now board chairman. Metcalf's challenge to Luthy was: "Build us an 'A' store on a two-block site with at least 1,500 parking spaces adjoining, and we'll stay downtown."

Luthy and officials of seven other business firms with a stake in downtown formed the Peoria Development Corporation. For a target site they selected two rundown blocks along the Illinois River at the edge of downtown. Interestingly, the two major downtown department stores invested in the move to keep Sears downtown. A spokesman for Bergner's said the store's owners put $100,000 into the development corporation. An official of Carson Pirie Scott said that chain owned three lots in what became the Sears site, and swapped the land for stock in the Development Corporation.

"We started out with four investors who put up $50,000 each in pioneering money—money that they knew might be lost," Luthy recalled. Bourland, whose firm was one of the original investors, said that "all the initial investors went to their boards on the basis that we might never get our money back."

"We were willing to risk putting our money down the drain in an effort to stop Sears from going 10 miles out of town," Bourland continued. "Certainly, one of our motives was to help the city, and keep downtown healthy. But for us the profit motive was very real, too, although not so easy to see. From First Federal's viewpoint, we had to protect our own sizable investment in downtown.

"If Sears moved out," added Bourland, "we could see our own downtown interests going down the drain in 10 to 15 years. So, ultimately it wasn't a question of whether First Federal would make any money on a $150,000 investment, but whether the whole downtown area was going further downhill or would begin to come back."

New 1964-65 Construction in
Heart of Downtown PEORIA*
Without Using Federal Grants
*None more than one block from new Court House

Interst

New 4-story
PEORIA
SAVINGS &
LOAN Bldg.
(1964)

NEW 17-story
$5 Million
FIRST FEDERAL
SAVINGS BLDG.
(1965-66)

100 More Units
VOYAGER INN
$2 Million Project
(1965)

New
(1964)
3-story
DeKROYFT-
METZ
Bldg.

New 10
HOWARD
MOTOR L
RESTAL
105 Re
(196

Heart of
DOWNTOWN
PEORIA

$4.5 Million PEORIA
County Court House
Completed in July, 1964
— ONE SQUARE BLOCK —

Multi-Million Dollar
Caterpillar Tractor Co.
Headquarters Building (1965)
— ONE SQUARE BLOCK —

New 8-story
SECURITY
SAVINGS
& LOAN Bldg.
(1965)
New (1964)
KELLY SEED

$6 Million Project . . . New Homes for
SEARS, ROEBUCK & CO. and BISHOP CAFETERIA
Parking for 1200 Cars.
Completion in 1965
— TWO SQUARE BLOCKS PLUS 100 FEET —

Parking for 1500
Caterpillar Tractor Co.
Employees
— ONE SQUARE BLOCK —

ILLINOIS RIVER . . . Great Lakes-to-Gulf Waterway

The Peoria Development Corporation, formed by seven business firms with a stake in th
downtown area, selected two rundown blocks along the Illinois River at the edge of cent
city as a redevelopment target. The eleven projects detailed in the photograph above atte
to both commercial and community interest in urban renewal.

The Peoria Development Corporation assembled the two square blocks through purchase and lease. It secured a $4.7-million, 30 year mortgage to finance the building, and leased it to Sears for 30 years. *The Guarantor,* a publication of the Chicago Title and Trust Company, called the Peoria Development Corporation the only one of its kind in the United States. Banker Luthy, who originated the idea of the unique corporation, said it now "looks like one heck of a good investment."

SEARS DECIDES TO STAY DOWNTOWN

The Luthy-led group got its go-ahead from Sears in October, 1961. The new Sears store opened in August, 1965, with 170,000 square feet of floor space. Sears had only 50,000 square feet in its old store.

"When we got a major merchandiser like Sears to come in with a major new facility, that was the start of downtown improvement," Luthy said.

Although much negotiating skill and business acumen went into the keep-Sears-downtown project, an element of chance appears to have been a factor, as well. Sears had firm intentions of leaving downtown Peoria and relocating in a proposed shopping center just outside the city limits. However, this move was contingent on a rezoning of the suburban area, which encountered frustrating delay before the county commission. This delay gave the downtown Peoria group time to act, and to head off what would have been a major setback for the central city.

Other leading merchants hail the presence of Sears as a neighbor. John Roe, president of Carson's downtown store, said he regards Sears as a valued neighbor—"an aggressive merchant which attracts volume." Bergner's president and general manager, Thomas P. Liston, said his store's volume is 50 per cent higher than it was eight years ago.

As important as any dollars-and-cents yardstick was the removing of an aura of decadence from downtown. Potential investors began to take a new look at central Peoria, and some followed up with action.

"When we were about two-thirds of the way through in assembling the Sears land," Luthy said, "the two ranking officials of Caterpillar tractor came into my office unexpectedly one day." This major area employer had never had a facility inside Peoria proper. Caterpillar had completed plans for a new home office building in Moss-ville, near a Caterpillar research center about nine miles from the center of Peoria. "The president and chairman said they felt that Caterpillar ought to become part of Peoria, and they would change their home office plans under the right conditions." The result of this meeting was that four blocks of downtown land were assembled for Caterpillar, and its new home office building in downtown Peoria brings 2,000 employees into the city daily. Adjacent is a 1,600-car parking facility.

CATERPILLAR: NEW HOME OFFICE

The acceptability of the site to Caterpillar was contingent on another element in the chain reaction of downtown improvement, removal of the old county courthouse, an 1890s' eyesore.

"Caterpillar would not have taken the site if it had to look out onto the rundown courthouse in the square across the street," said Bourland. A new courthouse was built in the square's open space, and the old one razed.

Bourland said, "The community had turned down three bond issues for the courthouse. Finally, Peoria people got the legislature in Springfield to pass a law which eliminated the need for a refer-endum."

The law enables a community to form a Public Buildings Com-mission, which can float revenue bonds to erect a facility. The build-ing in turn is rented to a public agency.

At any rate, Courthouse Square is now an attractive focal point for downtown Peoria. First Federal Savings, Bourland's company, is one of the developers of a 15-story office building on the square, the first new general-purpose office building in Peoria since 1933. "Sears and Caterpillar's presence downtown is the principal reason for our building investment," Bourland said. "If they hadn't 'hap-pened' we wouldn't have 'happened' either."

All this revitalization was done by private enterprise, with the exception of the public buildings. The personal philosophies of a handful of Peoria leaders supplied the reason why there was no attempt to make use of eminent domain, federally-assisted urban re-newal, or any of the other public aids to revitalizing a central city.

Luthy summarized his viewpoint this way: "Personally I am a

firm believer that you get the best results through private enterprise, although I recognize that government help is necessary in some fields.

"I don't believe you could have gotten a public agency to move ahead as we did and get these things done. The land would still be unassembled, and you would still be having committee meetings," he said.

Bourland said private action was the only feasible means for land assemblage in both the Sears and Caterpillar projects, although in both cases the developer "paid through the nose for the land."

"The area that Sears went into was so rundown it might have been an urban renewal project, except that the time element made this impossible," Bourland said. "After Sears was talked into staying downtown, they wanted to move fast and get into operation. The whole thing would have taken three times as long under urban renewal.

"There was a slightly different situation in regard to Caterpillar, which feels rather sensitive about being such a big stick around here."

The land was assembled through a large number of real estate people, moving swiftly to secure options. "But the identities of the principals were not known to many of us, including myself. These were the best kept secrets of the century around here."

Luthy conceded that assembling the Sears land, in particular, without condemnation was extremely difficult. "We had every road block you could think of thrown in our way," he said. "We ended up paying much more than the appraised value of some land, and some of it we couldn't buy at all but had to lease for 99 years." The Luthy group never did succeed in acquiring an 18-foot strip on one side of the Sears tract although, as he said, "We were willing to pay a holdup price. As matters turned out, we didn't need this strip. It is now useless to the owners."

Private-enterpriser Luthy would like to see a modicum of governmental assistance made available to carry land-assemblage projects across the roughest part of the road, the last mile.

"Illinois ought to have a law saying that the last 20 per cent of the land in a tract could be picked up through an arbitration procedure, or something like that," Luthy said.

PROGRESS CENTER

Since its political clean-up Peoria has been a city in which a conservative, business-oriented approach has been the guiding factor in public affairs. In this city's experience, the prototype group which "gets things done" is not the public or quasi-public agency hacking it way through the labyrinth of some government program. Rather, the idea is a small group of "dedicated" (a word frequently heard) businessmen willing to invest their own time, and if necessary their companies' money, into a project in which civic improvement is the primary aim.

Luthy said, "A small group of the top people has to take the lead. They can't be looking for private gain. If a city hasn't enough top people willing to take on an undue burden and put money and untold hours into a project, it had better not start anything like we did here."

The Peoria Approach, as it might be called, has achieved impressive and obvious successes. Other formidable problems still await the application of a workable corrective formula.

A cordon of deteriorated housing in the core city offers an unsightly contrast to the nearby "Progress Center," as Peoria terms its revitalized central business district. Two limited-scale urban renewal projects were proposed. One was rejected by the voters. The other is proceeding. Ninety-five residences were cleared away between two hospitals, to make room for a medical facilities expansion.

But there obviously has not been sufficient progress made along the three guidelines for removing blight proposed by ULI in 1956: Encourage property owners to redevelop their property to its highest use. Strictly enforce building and sanitary codes. Redevelop where required, either under a federally-assisted program or through local effort.

The transit system is in serious trouble, and general manager Joseph P. Kelly said recently a cessation of service "is a possibility." A local syndicate bought the system for $325,000 after a five-month strike in 1964. Transit was propped up financially by a two-cent a mile city subsidy for a time, and later by a contract to handle school bus transportation. But Kelly said "the concept of protecting the core area of the city from decay requires some aid to transit"—more than it has received so far.

Metropolitan area planning, to which ULI gave top priority in its

1956 recommendations, has not gotten past the initial stages. There is a pro-forma tri-county planning group, covering Peoria County and neighboring Tazewell and Woodford counties. However, fairly recently, as noted by Bourland, "there has been a new atmosphere in this town, a whole new psychology."

1964 ANNEXATION: 20 SQUARE MILES

"Peoria has crossed the line. It used to be a small isolated central Illinois farm town. Now it is thinking of itself as an area metropolis."

The city was able, in November, 1964, to more than double its area by an annexation which brought 27,000 suburban residents into the city proper.

However, this annexation of 20 square miles of suburbia by 15-square-mile Peoria has brought on new difficulties for the central city. The equanimity which had built up around public affairs was torn by bitter rezoning battles and lawsuits over development in the annexed area.

At the start of the annexation campaign the Peoria City Council had pledged that the predominantly residential zoning of the county area would be preserved. This potential campaign issue was silenced, but soon after annexation the Council recanted and a rezoning controversy broiled up before the City Planning Commission. Two petitions were presented for rezoning separate 30-acre tracts in the newly-annexed area from low-density residential to commercial. Traders Development Corporation, a Peoria firm, proposed to develop a new regional shopping center of 314,000 square feet adjacent to Sheridan Village. Carson Pirie Scott and Company wanted commerical zoning about a mile away for a 330,000 square-foot shopping center.

After heated public hearings, at which the Peoria Development Corporation opposed the suburban re-zoning, the City Planning Commission rejected the Traders Development Corporation bid and approved the other. In June, 1965, the City Council approved both rezonings, reversing the Planning Commission on the Traders proposal.

The Sheridan Village operator and 25 downtown merchants then brought suit in circuit court to block the rezoning. The plaintiffs challenged the City's authority to carry out massive rezoning before city planners had a chance to extend Peoria's master plan to include the annexed area.

Another more conventional argument concerned probable damages to existing retail facilities in the central business district and Sheridan Village. It was stated that the two rezonings would add 644,000 square feet of commercial area in a city whose central business district contained only 670,000 square feet of major retail space. (The defendants called the figures grossly inaccurate, stating that at least two million square feet for all types of business were available downtown.)

However, the key issue was the relationship between planning and zoning.

ARE PLANNING AND ZONING INSEPARABLE?

"Planning and zoning are inseparable, and planning must precede zoning," said the plaintiffs' attorneys. They added that the major issue was "whether the requisite information required by the basic constitutional concepts of due process, equal protection and just compensation as required by the Illinois Zoning Enabling Act was furnished to or obtained by the Peoria City Council" prior to its adoption of the rezoning ordinances.

The defendants replied that "There is no requirement of law that a city have or follow a master plan or perform some fixed amount of planning to support zoning or rezoning." This side's attorneys added that to argue otherwise "is grossly misleading or is patent nonsense. . . . The two rezonings would have a great impact on the entire area. What of that? Good or bad? This is a matter of legislative determination under the settled law of Illinois."

This legal battle, waged over an issue crucial to the core city, cast as protagonists the most powerful business and political forces in Peoria. Former mayors were principal attorneys for each side, Robert Morgan for the rezoning forces, Eugene Leiter for the opponents. The Carson and Bergner stores, neighbors in the central business district, were maneuvering for favorable position in the suburbs. Bergner's had been a principal tenant in Sheridan Village. Carsons sought a comparable outlet in a new regional shopping center.

On May 16, 1966, the circuit court handed down a summary judgment dismissing the suit without a trial. The court held that the downtown properties were too far from the rezoned area to be concerned over damages, and that Sheridan Village faced merely increased business competition, which does not constitute damages. The court was silent on the key issue, whether master-planning is a prerequisite to rezoning.

However, this portentous issue still appears headed for a court determination in Illinois and perhaps, if the matter is carried to federal courts, for a landmark decision affecting many central business districts and potential suburban retail competitors. On March 9, 1967, the Appellate Court for the Third District of Illinois reversed the lower court and ordered the dispute sent back for trial.

The appeals court said that the lower court accepted "categorical assumptions" not supported by fact or law.

"One of the affiants admits that there will be an 'impact' from the rezoning 'on downtown'," the appellate decision said. "And, it was admitted that the findings and recommendations of the Planning and Zoning Commission made 'no findings with regard to possible adverse effect on the downtown merchants' properties'." Another finding was that there is no "rule of distance" to determine when one business venture is so far removed from another as to preclude damages.

Attorney Leiter, possibly over-interpreting the appeals court's opinion, stated later that "We had the good fortune of actually impressing the appellate court with the fact that CBD properties do have a legally protectible interest . . . against massive rezonings which, unresisted, would otherwise destroy CBD values."

But, at least, downtown business interests will have the opportunity to argue that crucial point before a trial judge and against the best arguments the other side can muster. The case could have ramifications reaching far beyond Peoria's 35 square miles of turbulent urbanization in the Illinois farmland.

This city has set some precedents in downtown renewal. It may set more, this time in the legal sphere, which will affect the health of core areas in growing, expanding metropolitan areas all over the nation.

MIDLAND, TEXAS

February 21-24, 1966. Midland, Texas: A Report to the Midland Chamber of Commerce.

Panel Members Participating

Hunter Moss, Hunter Moss & Co., Miami—Chairman

U. A. Denker, Wheeler Kelly & Hagny Investment Co., Wichita

Charles J. Detoy, Coldwell Banker and Co., Los Angeles

Charles Fleetwood, Prudential Insurance Co. of America (Southwestern Home Office), Houston

Gerald D. Hines, Gerald D. Hines Interests, Houston

William E. Listerman, Federated Department Stores, Inc., Cincinnati

Henry S. Miller, Jr., Henry S. Miller Co., Dallas

Paul B. Strasbaugh, Oklahoma City Chamber of Commerce, Oklahoma City

CHAPTER SIX

MIDLAND, TEXAS

THE TRAVAIL OF TWO CITIES: PART ONE

Midland, Tex., population (1950) 27,713, (1960) 62,625, (1965) 64,000.

1966—ULI Central City panels convened in two small cities having much in common although their geographical settings are dramatically different.

The oil capital on the Texas plains and the resort-and-industrial center in the Berkshire Mountains each has resources enough to be a diversified regional center. But each city has failed so far.

Midland's retail center had atrophied almost to nothingness. Pittsfield's center was downsliding in a slow decaying progress.

In each case, the proposed counter-action was a vigorous downtown renewal effort, initiated if necessary and sustained by a small group of persons willing to apply their leadership talent for the purpose.

Each city formed such a group; the objectives of each organization differed in specifics. "Conservative" Midland developed no enthusiasm at all for a downtown renewal project. Pittsfield's eagerness for a renewal effort spilled over into a proliferation of plans and political competition for control.

Urban Land Institute recommended an 18-square-block downtown federally-assisted renewal project for Midland, Texas. The ULI panel which studied Midland in February, 1966, pointed out the obvious—the main retail area was moribund, blighted, more befitting a ghost town than the prosperous, sophisticated regional oil capital that is Midland.

A year later, no renewal program was planned, contemplated, or likely in Midland in the near future. Mayor H. C. (Hank) Avery said, "If downtown isn't dead already, it is well on the way. And perhaps that is not a bad thing. We try to hang onto our institutions too long. When they stop functioning, they should be allowed to die."

Avery seemed a shade more pessimistic than some others in the "civic leader" category, but his stand was significant in that he spoke from a position of influence and leadership. An objective inspection of what passes for the "central business district" in Midland made Avery appear, if anything, a little too sanguine. The "downtown" built around Main Street is already dead as a center for shopping, recreation and entertainment. More than half the stores are vacant. Many others are marginal operations on a precarious month-to-month lease basis.

ABANDON MAIN STREET?

The ULI panel reported that "Main Street is not a vigorous area now, nor has it been one for some time. The panel concludes that it cannot realistically be expected to restore itself and, in fact, is not capable of being revitalized on any reasonable basis by anyone."

ULI advised the city to abandon Main Street as the nominal retail center and start afresh on building a central core. The key recommendation called for the renewal agency to acquire and demolish the county courthouse, an undersized box of neo-WPA architecture sitting where the retail hub of Midland should be located.

Midlanders tended to regard this suggestion as "preposterous," or else to consider this and the entire "downtown problem" not at all. Apathy to public problems and suggested solutions was itself recognized as a prevailing Midland problem, by ULI panelists and by ranking citizens such as Mayor Avery.

In this age of truly formidable urban crises throughout the United States, what becomes of downtown Midland is in one sense a miniscule matter. This small West Texas city (population about 70,000) sits in desert-gripped near-isolation midway in the arid, 600-mile stretch between Fort Worth and El Paso. (Midland's partner in isolation is Odessa, a sister-city with 90,000 population 22 miles to the west.)

However, the Midland "problem" has some attributes which make it worth more than passing notice.

The city's most striking feature is the juxtaposition of the downtrodden retail core and a remarkable cluster of tall office buildings, mostly oil company headquarters structures and a few banks. Midland ranks fifth in Texas in the amount of modern office space, outpaced only by Houston, Dallas, Fort Worth and San Antonio. Nearly 10,000 persons work in downtown Midland. How this city could avoid having a vibrant central business district presents an intriguing case study.

"As long as these buildings are in the downtown area, we are going to have a downtown shopping center," Ted Kruger, a jewelry store operator still holding onto a Main Street outlet, told the ULI panel. Kruger has hedged his commitment to downtown by opening a larger store in a shopping center. Other downtown merchants have not been as long-suffering as Kruger. The Kress company built a store on Main Street, and vacated it less than a year later. The most embarrassing monument to downtown futility is the Midland Mart Building, standing vacant on what should be the prime downtown corner, Main and Wall Streets. The Mart is a former hotel, given a garish facelifting in the early 1960's and hailed as the harbinger of downtown's rebirth. Within 18 months most of the specialty-shop tenants had given up. By the time the ULI panel convened in Midland, the Mart was a vacant, dusty eyesore, missing sections of its marbelized-glass facade.

Midland may be on the way toward demonstrating that a city in which most of the jobs are concentrated downtown can get by without any downtown retail district. This circumstance would mark Midland as a curiosity among cities.

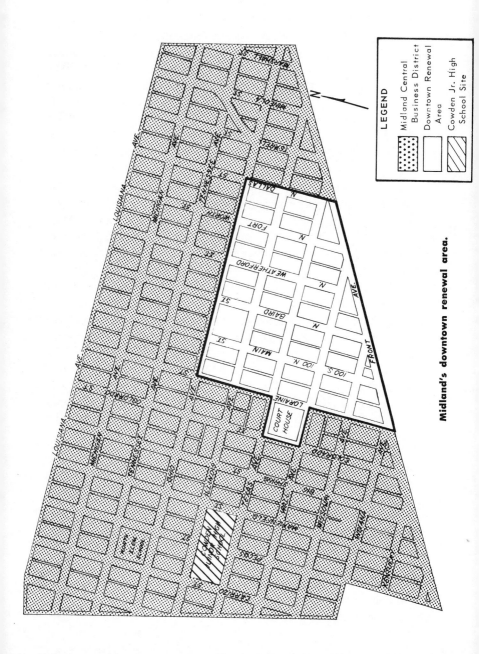

Midland's downtown renewal area.

LEGEND

Midland Central Business District

Downtown Renewal Area

Cowden Jr. High School Site

The most compelling reason for taking a close look at Midland arises from something more than the plight of its central business district. The abnormal situation there is symptomatic of larger problems besetting Midland and other cities. The people of Midland are aware of their city's deficiencies, and are capable, in terms of talent and financial resources, of correcting the city's ills. The imponderable is whether Midlanders will act to head off incipient crises before they become fully-developed and eventually too burdensome even for a city as richly endowed as Midland.

To put Midland in perspective, it is helpful to record a listing by ULI panel chairman Hunter Moss of the city's strengths and weaknesses:

STRONG COMMUNITY ASSETS

"We feel that Midland's strongest community assets are the high quality people; good supply and range of living accommodations; excellent air, highway and rail transportation; outstanding public school system; fine cultural activities such as the symphony, community theater, art colony; and the good climate.

"Its most serious drawbacks or weaknesses," Moss continued, "are the transient population; lack of institutions of higher learning; lack of diversification of industry; shortage of industrial labor supply, the blue collar workers; and the shortage of good quality industrial water supply."

Certainly one of Midland's assets is its general appearance. From the air the first impression of the city is startling. The monotony of the West Texas high plains is dramatically punctuated by the cluster of tall office buildings. On the ground, the upbeat first impression is bolstered by the parts of town which a Midland host makes sure a visitor sees first—the spacious residential neighborhoods, the bustling shopping centers. But inevitably, a tour of Midland touches on the problem areas, for which ULI's advice was sought.

Moss noted that "We feel that the general appearance of Midland would be most attractive to industrial or commercial prospects except for the blighted downtown retail area and blighted residential area on your east side."

The panel chairman's statement gave a more detailed breakdown of "the major problems and deficiencies in Midland's central business district." These are "the extreme deterioration of the retail district along Main Street; inadequate or potentially inadequate parking; lack of amusements and cultural activities."

In some of the cities whose problems have been studied by ULI, it is inescapably clear why these cities reached the state in which ULI found them. Often it is a case of the oldest sections of old cities, the core area, simply wearing out, in the absence of a vigilant maintenance-and-repair effort by government and private enterprise. Often a significant factor is the population turnover since World War II, marked by the influx of minimally-productive minorities, and the exodus of the middle class families—the reservoirs of taxpaying ability and civic leadership—to the comparatively problem-free suburban enclaves. The vitality of some cities has diminished along the same downward curve experienced by major home industries beset by obsolescence and competition from cheap labor markets.

None of these factors is the root of Midland's difficulties. A new city in the main, it nearly tripled in size between 1950 and 1960. Only a fraction of this growth carried the insubstantial characteristics of boom-time growth. There was a surge of speculative home-building aimed at a blue-collar market present for a short time when one phase of oil-drilling flourished with Midland as headquarters. When this activity tapered off, many workers and their families simply departed, abandoning their small equity in their heavily-mortgaged homes. Foreclosures placed about 2,000 homes in the hands of FHA and the Veterans Administration, and at the time of the ULI panel these two agencies still had 1,600 of these dwellings on their hands.

PETROLEUM ECONOMY

This boom-and-bust episode was a relatively small element in the substantial petroleum economy of the city. Midland is the administrative center of the staggeringly oil-rich Permian Basin. This area contains more than 90,000 producing wells, and about 20 per cent of the petroleum reserves in the United States. Midland and Odessa have a complementary relationship. Midlander Stanley Moore, president of Drilco Oil Tools, described the relationship aptly for the ULI panel when he said, "Odessa is where the work is done and Midland is where the decisions are made."

The Midland decision-makers are affluent citizens, indeed. The city claims the highest educational level among any urban populace in the United States, a level sustained by the advanced college degrees of the many geologists, engineers and managerial executives. Midland ranks near the top in spendable income, with 25 per cent of its families earning more than $10,000 a year. For these mobile, well-heeled people, downtown Dallas is where the serious shopping is done.

Permian Basin oil will be a source of wealth for generations to come. However, since Midland is a single-industry city, it is susceptible to the effects of periodic slumps experienced even by the super-stable oil industry. The effect of a backing-and-filling period in the industry is felt in public affairs principally.

Midland's experience with a 1963 bond election was cited for the ULI panel by Ray Herndon, general manager of KMID broadcasting company. The proposed $3.3-million issue would have provided a coliseum and auditorium plus courthouse and jail improvements. Unfortunately for Midland, the bond election coincided with a mild shakedown phase in the basic industry. The shock waves knocked down the bond issue.

"At the time there was an attitude that we didn't know where we might be headed," Herndon said. "One of the major oil companies had moved out five families, and some of the people thought we were going to pot. There was a public feeling that this is no time to spend money or make any obligations for anything. A week after the election the same company that moved out the five families moved in 10, but the damage was done."

The anecdote lends a sense of urgency to the statement by another man, an industrialist, whose business is an adjunct of the oil industry. He said he had been working with the Chamber of Commerce for 14 years on diversification of industry. "The thing we have felt for many years in Midland is we are too dependent on one industry," he told ULI. "Some people come in with the attitude 'You have the oil business, so what more do you need?' It is the greatest thing you could have, but depending on natural resources as it does, it leaves us feeling a little bit liable to being moved out from under it. Vulnerable would be a better word."

Midland realtor Jack Mogle told this reporter, "Oil is a wasting asset, and we have got to get away from total dependence on it, or we will waste away with it."

TRANSIENT POPULATION ATTITUDES

These statements are significant in the headquarters of the Permian Basin, which has total proven reserves of 7.5-billion barrels. It is a seemingly inexhaustable resource. But the fact that oil is a depleting asset, which might be supplanted by another dominant power source, joins with the uncertainties of a one-industry economy to create an underlying feeling of insecurity in Midland. This attitude shapes Midland's feelings about making long-term financial commitments for renewal.

This element in the collective mentality of Midland is only part of what Panel Chairman Moss meant when he listed the "transient population" as one of the city's "most serious weaknesses." Even when the oil business is at its booming best, which is most of the time, the major companies maintain a policy of shifting their employees periodically. The regional manager for Gulf Oil in Midland, Gene Hosford, said he had lived in that city four years, and this was the longest he had been in one place during his working life.

Hosford and a few other oil executives have become active in civic affairs, an interest which he says is encouraged by his employer. However, with disturbing frequency the "transient population" allies itself with what Mayor Avery calls "the agin'ers." They will vote for a school bond issue, because their families reap an immediate benefit from a first-rate school system. But they will not vote to tax themselves for long-term capital projects like a courthouse or civic center, when they might not even be around to see the dedication of the completed facility.

The Mayor told the ULI panel that "we have a certain group of the population here that looks upon its residence in Midland as they would a tour of duty in the Army. They do not really put their roots down."

Whether the temporary Midlanders could be persuaded to fund and support a renewal program is one of the crucial problems facing the city.

The editor of the *Midland Reporter-Telegram,* William Collyns, said the effect of the "turnover problem" on efforts to improve the city is "often overstated." He said that stay-put ranchers and landowners are, if anything, more opposed to change than the transients, but for a different reason. "They've got it made, and so they can't see why anything about Midland should be any different," he said.

Since they are the entrenched element of the city's elite, the ranchers and landowners are able to build up a base of influnce disproportionate to their numbers.

Oilman Hosford, whose outlook combines the outsider's viewpoint with that of the civic-minded resident, observed that "I don't like to walk downtown. It is so depressed that it depresses me. But when I do walk there, I think to myself that I'm not sure the people of Midland want anything different."

Another part of the population which should be enthusiastically in favor of a renewal program, the impoverished 5 to 10 per cent, is numerically and politically impotent. This group was unable to do any more than look on in dismay when the public transit system ceased operations about 10 years ago.

One Midlander was heard to remark that the transit system died because "only the Mexicans and Negroes rode it." Midland did indeed pioneer in the three-car family, now a commonplace thing. One of the vehicles is usually a company car which is driven downtown daily—straining even Midland's wide streets and spacious parking lots—and frequently is driven home for lunch, to the detriment of the downtown restaurant business. Those persons who normally would be the transit riders travel to work by taxicab, with the fare paid by the employer if they are housemaids, or else they depend upon the only jalopies evident on the city streets.

"We seem to have things in Midland which attract Ivy Leaguers but don't attract welders," said one business owner. "I could probably go out this morning and hire 15 college graduates before dark, but I couldn't find a welder at all. We have a reputation of being a place that has a high cost of living, which really it is not." However, the bus ride costing 20 or 25 cents is not one of the available economies.

"LOWEST CITY TAX RATE IN TEXAS"

The inner-directedness of most Midlanders, the reluctance to opt for taxes and public improvements, has had a salutary effect from one viewpoint. If the citizenry could be persuaded to undertake such costly efforts as downtown renewal, comprehensive planning, energetic industrial development and other such projects, it could do so without undue strain on public finances. All parties in the ULI-

Midland dialogue agreed that the city is capable of financing any project which reasonably might be recommended. as essential or desirable.

Mayor Avery told ULI, "We have the lowest city tax rate of any city our size or bigger in Texas."

Avery calculated that the ad valorem tax rate, after all adjustments are figured in, equals about one per cent of actual value of a piece of property.

Midland has a self-imposed bonding limit of 8 per cent of assessed value with a maximum authorized tax rate of two dollars for all purposes. (Assessed value was slightly more than $212,000,000, a figure based on 60 per cent of actual value.) Panel member U. A. Denker, investigating this phase of the study, reported that Midland was carrying a $5.75-million debt in general obligation bonds, had another $940,000 in authorized but unissued bonds. Denker said the city could issue an additional $10.3-million in general obligation bonds. "This is a healthy and somewhat unique financial position," he said.

The ULI report concluded "it would appear that at the date of this report Midland could legally finance almost any foreseeable projects that are within reason and which its citizens might approve."

Formulating and winning voter approval for public projects requires resourceful and dedicated leadership anywhere. Midland never has found a way to channel into public affairs the considerable leadership talent so obviously abundant in its business and industry. On this point, Mayor Avery is notably vocal and pessimistic.

"We've got an enormous number of talented people here who could do a terrific job," he said, "but they are beset by apathy and complacency." Avery made these remarks in an interview with this reporter, some six months after the ULI report was made.

"What we need are people with a selfish interest that happens to coincide with the town's best interest," Avery said. "No one gets moved just by civic pride. That's a fallacy. When I first became mayor I went looking for 11 people who would work with me because it was in their selfish interest to see the town grow and prosper because they would grow and prosper along with it. I haven't found them yet and I doubt if I ever will.

"People in this kind of affluent society just aren't motivated to give a good portion of their own time to the kind of work we need to do here. People already have things very good. They aren't motivated. I'll tell you what kind of town this is. We had a high school football coach here one time who said this was the only place he had ever been where the kids drove to practice in their own Cadillacs.

"I don't even know," Avery continued, "if I could get five people to go with me for a week on a trip to try to get some industry to come here. That's an indictment—I know it—and it's a tragic one.

"I'm afraid this town might have to see some bad days before it ever gets rejuvenated."

Avery said he will not quit trying to rouse the specially-motivated civic pride he regards as necessary. His principal effort, to formulate a program patterned after the Goals for Dallas idea of Mayor Erik Jonsson in that city, was examined earlier in this report. To emulate Dallas's bustling, upbeat approach to its problems is one Avery goal. Perhaps a more urgent aim of the Mayor's is to guide Midland away from the declining spiral which some of his state's cities are experiencing.

"I can show you the map of Texas," he said, "and point out cities which are breathing their last gasping breath because they have been beset by complacency and apathy on the part of civic leaders. Any community that does not have some real hard-core dedicated people, motivated by selfish interests, will never go anyplace but down."

"AGGRESSIVELY CONSERVATIVE" LEADERSHIP

One other factor in Midland's background which should be taken into account, for a better understanding of the impact made by the ULI recommendations, is the city's "conservatism." It is a word commonly heard when Midlanders describe their city and its people. What the label actually connotes is hard to determine precisely.

"We oppose government assistance," said newspaper editor Collyns. He said he believed that private enterprise can and should handle affairs like housing improvement.

The president of the city's leading bank, C. J. Kelly, described his bank as "aggressively conservative." He added, on the subject of renewal, other than through private enterprise, that "If at all possible we don't want to take federal assistance. We don't go for that."

Oilman Hosford commented that "The natives here are more conservative than the oil people. Government assistance per se is not bad, but when it gets out from local control, that's bad. Most oil men talk anti-federal, but what they really feel depends on the particular program." Hosford added that, in his view, "being conservative means using what you've got."

Attorney Thornton Hardie, Jr., state Democratic committeeman, said that the politics of the local segments of both major parties is conservative. "All of us who are trying to do something for Midland are of the same mind," he said.

Another Midland business leader told the panel that "This area in general, I would say, would. be a little more suspicious and disdainful of government programs than perhaps the average in the United States. That's partly because of the heritage, and maybe partly because of the sophistication and educational level of the people here."

The ULI panel, although certainly not unaware of prevalent attitudes in Midland, approached the city's physical problems subjectively; that is, panelists drew upon their experiences in many parts of the nation and made "universal" recommendations, applicable to any city, anywhere, with comparable physical problems.

Midland, to be sure, is not unique in all respects, any more than Pittsfield or Peoria. Office workers by nature seem loath to walk more than two blocks to shop downtown. In Midland, if Main Street were a functioning retail area, the trek between office and store would involve an inordinately long stroll past the county courthouse square.

"We looked at the courthouse, we studied it, and certainly coveted that large piece of lawn," Panel Chairman Moss told Midlanders. The panel's key recommendation in downtown renewal was acquisition of the courthouse square by the renewal agency and conversion of the site into the new downtown retail hub. "We felt very strongly we had to say things the way they came out, and that is one of the keys to the future revival of downtown Midland," Moss said later.

The panel suggested creating a government complex, with new courthouse, post office and federal buildings, civic center plus parking facilities, on the languishing east side of central Midland.

Midland's high-rise office buildings break the monotony of the West Texas plains. ULI recommended that the county courthouse, lower right foreground, be demolished and that the land be redeveloped as Midland's retail hub.

QUESTIONS OF RENEWAL "PHILOSOPHY"

This recommendation inevitably led to a discussion of the philosophy of renewal. "If the city of Midland and the county choose to do so, they can accomplish the renewal job without federal assistance," Moss said. "Terminology is a funny thing. Renewal is acceptable. When you get to urban renewal, it starts to get a little bit hazy. What we are talking about in our report is 'renewal,' and I think you'll find that the term 'urban renewal' wasn't even used."

Editor Collyns, who maintained that the conservative editorial policy of *The Reporter-Telegram* is a major factor in shaping Midland attitudes, was still pondering the problem half a year later. He conceded that the city needs some sort of major downtown overhauling. The crucial, still unanswered question, he said, is whether "our wealthy conservatives are willing to tax themselves to finance the inevitable programs locally."

In a renewed and revived CBD, Midland's shortcomings in parking and traffic circulation would require correction. ULI recommended creation of a special parking and traffic district for the central area; elimination of curb parking on major streets; better design and landscaping for parking lots than Midland has been accustomed to; improvement in traffic circulation—particularly one-way streets to the west and north of the central core, and a connection with Interstate 20 from the South.

ULI noted a deficiency in comprehensive planning for the city's growth, by whatever means or route it takes place. Panelist Charles J. Detoy of Los Angeles called Midland's 12-year-old master plan out of date.

"All of us on the panel feel that Midland has reached a juncture, a rather historic 'continental divide,' where the city has the opportunity to cross over into a different 'watershed'," Detoy said. "You, as an entire community, must think through very carefully what you want Midland to become and how this can best be attained.

"One of the most fitting and most persuasive instruments you can use to impress this philosophy (i.e., what you want Midland to represent) on the community and to help the community to grow to fit that philosophy is a general plan. You need a new plan now," Detoy continued, "even if one was prepared five years ago."

Specifically, the recommendation was that the city enlarge its planning department, which consisted of one planner and a drafts-man, and in addition contract with a "community planning con-sultant of proven ability and national standing in his profession." ULI urged creation of "a top level citizens committee" to support the planning effort, the group being made up of representatives of "all major areas of influence in this community." Detoy pressed the point that "it is essential that the entire com-munity become involved, since depth of understanding is of the greatest value to final implementation of the plan." He gave Mid-landers one final thought to ponder: "Outside assistance in this effort can come from the federal government to help with profes-sional fees."

A check six months after the ULI recommendation showed that Midland had taken a first small step toward better planning. The city council and county commission each budgeted $12,500 for additional planning services. However, there was no evidence that the next step, expending the funds, was imminent. Midland planning director George Wolf said he had no idea when master plan devel-opment might begin.

AREA-WIDE ECONOMIC DEVELOPMENT

In other key recommendations, ULI suggested cooperation by Midland and Odessa for area-wide benefit. "Weld the leadership of Midland and Odessa into a cooperative area-wide economic develop-ment effort," the panel report said. Specific suggestions were estab-lishment of a Community Development Corporation with a capital fund, and a $50,000 annual increase in the Midland Chamber of Commerce's industrial development budget.

The panel said that an important attraction for industry which might be considering Midland-Odessa as a site would be the estab-lishment of a four-year college. The area is the most populous in the state without such an institution. Later, tentative agreement was reached between the two cities on a college site near the airport midway between them, which serves both Midland and Odessa. A committee was beginning to work on acceptance of the college plan at the legislature in Austin.

There were, indeed, deep stirrings of social and civic conscious-ness in Midland during the second half of 1966. It was as if the townspeople were becoming aware that their aloofness from the problems in their midst could not be sustained indefinitely. The ULI panel report dealt a jolt to complacency. Midland might not be inspired to rush into planning and funding a downtown renewal program. But, after the town heard as experienced and thoughtful a group as the ULI panel catalogue its shortcomings, matters could never again be the same as they were before February, 1966. The panel carried Midlanders to the point of self-examination, and from that point the beginning of the process was almost automatic.

The Midland Chamber of Commerce, which sponsored the ULI study, followed up by assigning the executive committee to determine what sort of implementation should be made of the panel recommendations. Chamber leaders met with the three local government bodies, the city council, county commission and school board, and from these sessions evolved the "goals" concept. The influence of Mayor Avery, who had attended the Dallas "goals" sessions as an observer, predominated at this phase.

The first position paper to come out of the new civic action movement contained some significant statements:

"Since the Urban Land Institute study, it has become apparent to the City Council that there is a lack of objectives and plans for the city, with any established priorities for undertaking these objectives."

Under the heading of "Objectives for Midland" were these noteworthy observations:

"Each of us has his own aspirations, and consciously or not we set personal objectives. However, each person in a community cannot go entirely his own way, pursuing his own objectives, oblivious of the aims of his neighbor. There should be some shared aims, objectives which affect all or at least most of the people in a community. Therefore, objectives for the community are needed to provide the opportunities and the atmosphere which will permit and inspire every citizen to lead a satisfying and meaningful life."

Further on, the position paper said, "The easy course for a community, just as for an individual, is to meet problems as they arise, to set no objectives, to live from day to day. But a community which has no objectives is destined for a lot of trouble. . . . The question facing us is: Do we wish to work together to set common objectives for Midland and thereby create an even better community, or do we want to continue to meet problems as they arise from day to day?"

The ULI panel might easily have posed precisely the same question. Wisely, the outsiders stopped one step short. The fact that Midlanders themselves were induced to make the self-examination lays a sounder basis for constructive action.

However, it appeared to this reporter that a long period of reappraisal lay ahead for Midland before any plan of action will show results. This city is no more suspended in time than any other place, and the dimensions of its early-1966 condition are already changing.

Midland's future "action" and "goals" will have to be shaped to fit some unpredictable future condition, and they will reflect the attitudes of whoever emerges as the civic leaders in a constantly changing power structure.

CREATING A PUBLIC HOUSING AUTHORITY

As has been indicated in this report, Midland does not turn a monolithic facade of indifference toward its present situation. One example of an ambivalent attitude on government-citizen relationships is a proposal to create a Public Housing Authority.

During the past three years the city government, through enforcement of a housing code, brought about demolition of 466 substandard and unrepairable residential buildings. City Manager James Brown conceded that at best this program could achieve only a partial solution to the problem of substandard housing for subachieving families. Midland has no relocation procedure; all the demolished dwellings were vacant. Some families would like to move from slum to adequate housing, but can't afford it. There is no official machinery for helping that situation, either.

Real estate man Mogle was named head of a Chamber of Commerce committee on housing, with the mission of finding some means of interaction between two phenomena—the several hundred families living in hovels, and the hundreds of vacant homes repossessed by FHA and VA. The Mogle committee's first report said, "Consider the two together—families crowded into shacks, often on dirt lanes, while a few blocks away good houses are empty. You have a situation which should disturb every citizen."

The Mogle committee studied the problem and alternatives, and recommended that a Public Housing Authority be created to acquire some of the vacant houses and make them available to Midland's poor. "I'm no socialist," chairman Mogle told the reporter, "but I am not afraid of every form of government assistance. After all, we are the government. We have got to assist ourselves with the means at hand.

"Another thing we have got to remember," Mogle continued, "is that there would be no 'encroachment' in our affairs if we had taken care of our problems ourselves."

Mogle's plan won the unanimous endorsement of the Chamber of Commerce's board of directors. A varied arsenal of arguments was used. There was the old standby, that Midland pays out considerable federal taxes, and gets nothing back from the portion which goes into "giveaway" programs.

Then, there was the companion argument for economic practicability. It was estimated that the Housing Authority would need $500,000 to get started, and annual expenditures of $100,000 thereafter. If Midland tried to fund a city housing agency unassisted, "it would divert funds which are urgently needed for streets and sewers."

"Citizens in the poverty sector of our city are aware that assistance is available," the committee report said. "If we refuse to permit their receiving it without meeting their needs with local funds, we may reap a harvest of bitterness and perhaps violence."

Another warning sounded by the committee to the Chamber board: "Unscrupulous promoters" might come into Midland to build subsidized housing under other federal programs, by "taking advantage" of non-profit sponsoring organizations. "It is easier than you think," the board was told. "The need is here for a subsidized housing program. If we eliminate this need in our own way, no outsiders can come in with any of their housing deals."

That was sufficient argument to swing the full prestige of the Midland Chamber of Commerce over to the side of a locally-conceived public housing program with federal assistance. Midland leaders chose what they considered the lesser of two evils to combat a problem which they were compelled reluctantly to admit existed.

Of course, there was still no guarantee that the Chamber's housing authority proposal would culminate in actual creation of the agency. A possible political battle in city hall lay ahead. But, for Midland, the progression of events leading up to this point was significant. A precedent of sorts was set.

In Midland, undeveloped land, often a scarce resource in urbanized areas, does exist in scattered parcels throughout downtown.

Perhaps there are arguments which will, in time, be used to build the case for a downtown renewal program. Traditional stances, old prejudices, and habitual viewpoints are subject to challenge. Change does not mean surrender of principle, but rather adjustment to harsh reality. Realizing this, Midland can mature as a city of the 1970's.

PITTSFIELD, MASS.

September 1966. Pittsfield, Massachusetts: A Report to the Sponsors on Redevelopment of the City's Central Business District.

Panel Members Participating

F. Lawrence Dow, Dow & Condon, Inc., Hartford, Conn.—Chairman

Boyd T. Barnard, Jackson-Cross Co., Philadelphia

Ronald L. Campbell, David D. Bohannon Organization, San Mateo

John W. Combs, John W. Combs Ltd., Willowdale, Ontario, Canada

Randall H. Cooper, Chicago Central Area Committee, Chicago

Hunter A. Hogan, Goodman-Segar-Hogan, Inc., Norfolk, Virginia

Warren L. Morris, Ostendorf-Morris Co., Cleveland

Fred F. Stockwell, R. M. Bradley & Co., Inc., Boston

CHAPTER SEVEN

PITTSFIELD

THE TRAVAIL OF TWO CITIES: PART TWO

Pittsfield, Mass., population (1950) 53,348, (1960) 57,879, (1965) 57,000.

In contrast with the Texas plains, the Berkshire Mountains in western Massachusetts are renowned for many attractions. Visitors come by the thousands to see one of the most glorious displays of colorful autumnal foliage to be found anywhere. At different seasons they come for the Tanglewood music festival or for the skiing. While the visitors are circulating around this lavishly-endowed part of the United States, they usually discover its principal city, Pittsfield.

Among the 58,000 residents of Pittsfield there seems to be a preoccupation with preserving (or creating) an "image" bespeaking "quality" in their community. It is part of the local mystique, along with a pretention to New England quaintness. Harboring these views, the City of Pittsfield itself might be expected to qualify for a place among the attractions of its region. But it does not, although more exciting times may lie ahead.

Mid-town Pittsfield has a somnolent business district which several Urban Land Institute panelists criticized for its shabbiness and untidiness. When the ULI Central City Council panel convened in September, 1966, it found downtown barren of after-dark entertainment attractions, first-rate dining places, and hotel accommodations. The Pittsfield panel made its headquarters not in that city at all, but at the Holiday Inn of Lenox, the next town down the road. Pittsfield had a hotel once, the Wendell, located on what *The Berkshire Eagle* newspaper described as "the city's most important corner." The Wendell moldered with the years and in 1965 was torn down. Pittsfield's "most important corner," at West and North Streets, was acquired by the city's most important home-based business enterprise, The Berkshire Life Insurance Company. However, plans for redevelopment were floundering at the time of the ULI panel.

1966: PERIOD OF SELF-EXAMINATION AMIDST PROSPERITY

It was a period of self-examination for Pittsfield, a time for inventorying civic assets and recognizing the community's points of strength, in order to correct the weaknesses. To an outsider it appeared that one of Pittsfield's more generative assets was a citizenry with a genuine affection for their town and region. Even the lackluster central area possessed a focus for civic identity, an oval town "square" called Park Square. Its potential attractiveness was diminished by the polyglot activities fronting on Park Square, including a gracefully crumbling public library, a 135-year-old city hall whose lines have a stark colonial New England attractiveness, a peanut vendor's stand, and a hiatus where the old Wendell Hotel once stood. Since the main retail street, North, connected at its south end with Park Square, Pittsfield obviously had a ready-made setting for a downtown rejuvenation effort.

A spinoff of Pittsfield's pervading civic pride was a group of business leaders who were awakening to the opportunities for improving both the community in general and their own companies' fortunes through central city revitalization. (ULI's most immediately-felt and perhaps most significant service to this study city, as in many

The Massachusetts Turnpike and the Interstate Highway System provide Central Berkshire with overnight delivery of manufactured goods and raw materials throughout Megalopolis and over an area extending west to Cleveland and north to Quebec.

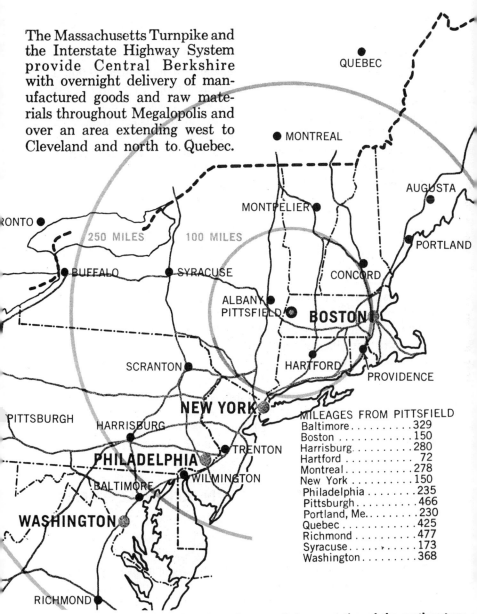

MILEAGES FROM PITTSFIELD

Baltimore	329
Boston	150
Harrisburg	280
Hartford	72
Montreal	278
New York	150
Philadelphia	235
Pittsburgh	466
Portland, Me.	230
Quebec	425
Richmond	477
Syracuse	173
Washington	368

Central Berkshire County lies on the fringe, but out of the congestion of the northeastern megalopolis. Within this 150-mile strip extending along the coast from southern New Hampshire to the Virginia Capes live and work 40-million people in the contiguous urban areas of five of the nation's thirteen largest cities.

others, was its advice on mobilizing the civic leadership for concerted effort.)

One more of Pittsfield's prime assets is its basic prosperity. United States Census Bureau figures show incomes of more than $9,000 a year for 35 per cent of families in Pittsfield proper, and also in the Standard Metropolitan Statistical Area with 75,000 population.

What the Census Bureau listed as the total Pittsfield trade area contained about 160,000 persons, with about 30 per cent of families receiving more than $9,000 income a year and with an average family income of roughly $8,000. In Pittsfield proper, nearly as many families (16.7 per cent) have incomes of more than $12,000 as have incomes under $4,000. The underlying reason for the relatively high and broad plateau of economic strength in Pittsfield is healthy and diversified industry. Berkshire County has 24,000 manufacturing jobs, the bulk (9,880) in the General Electric plant and the rest in the 45 other plants which can be classified as sizable (employing more than 50 persons). Pittsfield by definition is a blue-collar town, but in a milieu which encourages a search for "quality" in style of living.

The 300-acres which Pittsfield considered to be its central business district qualifies as the only regional shopping center in the entire trading area. The "advance kit" prepared for the ULI panel refers in one place to "downtown Pittsfield" as "one of the Northeast's more attractive small-city business districts," but in another section concedes that the area has "fallen short of realizing its full commercial potential." The ULI panel later found the first part of the local self-evaluation overstated, the latter observation correct as far as it went.

1967: JUBILEE DOWNTOWN REDEVELOPMENT

Early in 1967, seven months after the ULI study, a New York entrepreneur, J. Allen Ornstein, surveyed the Pittsfield market, remarked that at least $100-million in consumer dollars was leaving the area every year, and offered a downtown redevelopment proposal on a scale which made Pittsfielders boggle. The 600,000-square foot Ornstein development would occupy the prime 7.5-acre slice of the 61-acre Jubilee urban renewal area, located entirely inside the central business district with a 200-foot-wide mall connector to North Street.

Creation of Jubilee had been one of the Pittsfield leadership's landmark attempts to recoup on opportunities lost. Another urban renewal area, the 25-acre Columbus project, was conceived in 1963 to clear out an island of moderate mid-town residential blight and to complement Jubilee. Columbus is near Jubilee's north boundary, separated from the main renewal area by the Penn Central railroad tracks. This smaller renewal project would provide rights-of-way for major new traffic arteries serving Jubilee and the CBD.

Pittsfield turned to urban renewal in 1962 as the means to reconstruct its downtown area. Progress in executing the concept was inchmeal for nearly five years. However, the native caution which contributed to the city's dormancy was put to a more constructive purpose in the latter half of 1966. Finally conceding openly they were not proceeding in the most expeditious manner, and unsure how to stimulate downtown renewal, Pittsfield leaders called upon ULI to review their plans. Sponsors of the study were the Association of Business and Commerce of Central Berkshire County, a sort of supra-chamber of commerce; the city government of Pittsfield; and the Pittsfield Housing Authority, which is the local public agency for urban renewal. An ABC spokesman said the idea for a ULI central city study originated with a Berkshire Life Insurance executive, John E. Sylvester, Jr.

The timing of ULI's investigation and panel study in Pittsfield gave this reporter the opportunity to observe first-hand the workings of the Central City Council, and also to gain first-hand knowledge of the study city at the sides of panel members.

To this observer it appeared that an underlying reason behind Pittsfield's invitation to ULI was the hope that the panel's recommendations would break an impasse over urban renewal by mediating the controversy over Jubilee's re-use. The Pittsfield Housing Authority and Berkshire Life had been unable to achieve much coordination in their desires for downtown improvement, and to complicate the situation Mayor Remo Del Gallo had mounted a drive to oust PHA from renewal control. Each of the several sides in this tangle of course hoped for ULI endorsement—one gathered this was the case even if this meant the visitors would forego genuinely critical evaluation of the existing rival plans.

What Pittsfield got from ULI was a searching analysis of renewal plans leading up to a series of objective and sometimes unpopular recommendations. The panel's production of constructive criticism had something for nearly everybody. Renewal planners were told, in effect, they were being beguiled by visions of a glamorous but grandiose air-conditioned mall in Jubilee. Berkshire Life was advised to drop plans for a department store in its development of the Wendell Hotel site as an appendage to Jubilee. The city as a whole was chided for its readiness to write off the long-established main retail strip, North Street, as a prospect for dramatic upgrading. In other aspects, Pittsfield's leaders were told they underestimated the potential demand for new facilities, principally in plans for a new mid-town hotel and for modern office space.

HIDDEN DEFECT: NO COMPREHENSIVE PLANNING

ULI's review of the Public Housing Authority's record in urban renewal led to the judgment that this agency was understaffed and incapable of carrying out both the public housing and renewal functions. Creation of a separate renewal agency was recommended.

In blunt terms, Pittsfield was advised to re-group the public and private bodies interested in revivifying downtown, and to turn these combined forces first toward a clean-up of North Street, with the goal of making it attractive to shoppers in the entire region. Then, it was suggested, the prospective proprietors of a major new department store might be attracted to a North Street location. The panel said proposed renewal plans "would tend to pull uses away from North Street, which should be strengthened." ULI advised comprehensive planning for a balanced, multi-purpose central area. Jubilee's uses should complement the existing CBD, which then could be anchored on the opposite (east) side by a government, civic and cultural complex.

ULI's recommendations came after four days of intensive investigation of conditions in Pittsfield, interspersed with candid, sometimes heated discussions among ULI panelists in late-evening work sessions. The end product was the uncompromising dissection of a renewal plan which had a fine surface glossiness but serious defects underneath. The panel's performance was consistent with the make-up of its membership—men experienced in redevelopment in many parts of the country; men to whom none of Pittsfield's brand of problems and mistakes was anything new.

The panel included vigorous younger men, typified by the chairman, ULI Central City Council Chairman F. Lawrence Dow of Hartford, plus a leavening of wise older heads. Boyd T. Barnard, a former ULI president and president of the American Institute of Real Estate Counselors, had guided the panel whose work set new directions for downtown in his home city, Philadelphia, 15 years before. Warren L. Morris, another former ULI president, had built the largest real estate firm in Cleveland.

Less experienced in panel activity, but contributing fresh viewpoints, were Ronald L. Campbell, a city planner and vice-president of the David D. Bohannon organization in San Mateo, California; John W. Combs, president of a consultant firm in Ontario, Canada; Hunter A. Hogan, a shopping center specialist in Norfolk, Virginia; Fred F. Stockwell, mortgage banker and real estate firm executive from Boston. Another phase of experience was brought to the panel by Randall H. Cooper, executive director of the Chicago Central Area Committee.

Before the panel got its first look at the long expanse of North Street, set against a background of the lovely Berkshire Hills, the panelists were given one of the most voluminous advance information kits prepared by any panel sponsor in any city.

PREDOMINANT LAND USE: RESIDENTIAL

The compilation of data included the information that the predominant land use in the business district was residential (102 acres). All of the housing units were old, and most were substandard. CBD housing was concentrated in the urban renewal areas. The area contained 70 businesses, a few rooming houses, and 118 family residences.

Pre-renewal Jubilee was by no means an unrelieved expanse of squalid slum by usual standards. However, none of these structures were a notable adornment to the center of a city which is striving for an "image of quality." Plans called for demolition of all structures except two commercial properties and one dwelling. Jubilee is urban renewal of the genre which looks for what city planners call "the highest and best use" of a sector, with slum clearance as an ancillary goal. Clearance began in January, 1966.

Jubilee's first proposed reuse included about a million square feet for commerce, a quarter of a million square feet for residences, a small park, parking and considerable use for rights-of-way essential to better downtown traffic circulation.

Progress on Jubilee had languished until Berkshire Life Insurance Company acquired the three-acre Wendell parcel contiguous to the renewal area, with frontage on South and West Streets at the key downtown intersection. The insurance company decided to demolish the hotel, and hired a consultant to produce a redevelopment plan which would be both profitable to the company and beneficial to the community. The consultant, Spencer M. Hurtt Associates, Inc., said a three-acre development would not be as desirable as a larger one, and so Berkshire Life's planning area was expanded to include five adjacent acres in the Jubilee tract. Even on the enlarged site, plans included only modest-sized hotel, office and merchandising space.

Meanwhile, the Adams Supermarket organization became interested in five acres of Jubilee just north of the Berkshire Life complex. Adams' plans were anchored by a supermarket and filled out with a moderate-sized department store, office tower and parking space.

Some Pittsfield leaders awoke to the possibility that the profusion of renewal planning would result in three uncoordinated, inadequate downtown retail centers—deteriorating North Street, Berkshire Life's development, and the Adams supermarket cluster. It became apparent that the two local business firms expressing the strongest interest in renewal should integrate their planning with an eye toward complementing the existing central business district.

Still, panel chairman Dow was unimpressed, and at an early stage of the fact-finding he commented, "The Housing Authority got itself one consultant and said 'Make a plan.' PHA bought it, and said this must be urban renewal. Then Berkshire Life brought in another consultant and he took the PHA plan apart." Further action was needed to bring order from the disarray.

PITTSFIELD HOUSING AUTHORITY: JUBILEE NORTH PLAN

The Pittsfield Housing Authority had stepped in to exercise its function as the renewal agency and brought in still another architectural and design consultant, Hoberman and Wasserman of New York, to achieve some unity in the overall planning. The result was the Jubilee North Plan. Its concession to the continuing importance of North Street was a narrow pedestrian mall linking North with a larger enclosed mall, which would be the hub of an elaborate regional retail center.

PHA consultant Joseph Wasserman keyed his redevelopment plan for downtown to a two-level, 85,000-square foot department store, with 37,000 square feet of satellite specialty stores. The principal store in this plan was a scale-down from the total 140,000-square foot department store space allocation in the earlier Adams and Berkshire Life plans for Jubilee. Wasserman raised the earlier office space allotment a scant 2,000 square feet, up to 50,000. He included a 160-room motel, a theater and super market, all with controlled parking. A public parking garage with three levels, 900 spaces, was envisioned by Wasserman.

The 25-acre Columbus urban renewal area, based on a simpler concept than Jubilee, was spared the change and uncertainty of the other. Columbus was laid out to provide better street access to the central business district and Jubilee. The plan was filled out by a miscellany of commercial usage and a 100-unit housing project for the elderly.

All this planning and re-planning was carried on under the aegis of the Pittsfield Housing Authority, which in 1962 was named local public agency for renewal by the mayor and city council. When Pittsfield elected a new mayor, Del Gallo, early in 1966, a latent disagreement over urban renewal jurisdiction became a public issue.

The region's influential newspaper, *The Berkshire Eagle,* had long been stumping editorially for a separate urban renewal authority. The paper's position reflected the attitudes of Pittsfield's power structure. Berkshire Life was reportedly concerned about the PHA's seeming equivocation on guaranteeing access to the Pittsfield by-pass of U.S. Highway 7. There was a widespread concern that PHA was spreading itself too thin, in attempting to handle both public housing and urban renewal.

In his inaugural address Mayor Del Gallo announced he would create a Pittsfield Urban Redevelopment Authority and give it the mission of carrying out the city's urban renewal plans. To justify his position, Del Gallo said he believed the Jubilee was in danger of failing, and he laid the blame on PHA leadership. The five men Del Gallo nominated for his new URA were quickly confirmed by the City Council.

PITTSFIELD URBAN REDEVELOPMENT AUTHORITY

Later, after the council voted 7 to 2 to transfer Jubilee jurisdiction from the PHA to URA, it was discovered that under state law the change in renewal control could not be forced if PHA resisted, and resist it did. A controversy broiled through the spring and early summer of 1966, quieting down after a "compromise" which was no real solution. URA members could attend PHA meetings and cast unofficial "votes" on matters concerning Jubilee and Columbus, but the votes would carry no legal weight. URA would have control of any future urban renewal projects—a hollow consolation, since, if Jubilee and Columbus soured, the prospects for future renewal projects in Pittsfield would be dim.

The ULI panel, after a painstaking review of this situation, offered a clear-cut recommendation for splitting the housing and renewal functions.

ULI found that the Pittsfield Housing Authority was following "standard procedures" for acquiring and disposing of renewal property, but beyond this pro forma compliance the PHA was performing inadequately, causing "confusion and misunderstanding."

The panel concluded that the PHA was "understaffed" for handling both public housing and urban renewal. Panel chairman Dow told the public meeting at the end of the panel study that "With the present set-up you can't possibly do the job." He added that "You must realize that something is radically wrong with the situation, and you must take steps about the lack of progress in urban renewal."

Panelist Barnard added that "The present organizational structure seems illogical compared to areas where urban renewal has moved much faster and farther than it has here. It is that simple, and it has nothing to do with personalities or professional talents."

The closest ULI came to offering specific guidelines for revamping urban renewal administration was this advice from Dow: "You cannot have dual responsibility in two fields as important as housing and urban renewal. You need professionals in both fields. You have (professionals) in housing, where you have a fine director and good staff men. You need professionals in urban renewal."

From that cautiously-worded admonition, it was just one easy step for Pittsfield observers of the panel's work to draw a blunter conclusion. *The Berkshire Eagle* reported that "the panel backed to the hilt Mayor Remo Del Gallo's call for separating renewal from the PHA." That paragraph from the newspaper's report was interpretive, but in the main accurate.

ULI's panelists were told at one point in the Pittsfield study that the sponsors' charge to them "could be summarized in one overall question: 'How can we (Pittsfield) develop our central business district to its fullest possible potential (including commercial, housing, civic and cultural uses), with a quality approach, and make it economically feasible and attractive to investors?' " This statement was accurate as far as it went, but it skimmed over some of the subtleties of the situation.

When panelists got into the legwork phase of their study, their inquiries quickly turned up evidence that ULI was, in effect, being called in to arbitrate a disputed situation. One point of contention was the location of the new department store in Jubilee. Berkshire Life wanted the store on the south side of West Street, as close as possible to its three-acre tract adjoining Jubilee. But PHA consultant Wasserman's re-design for Jubilee North placed the department store north of West Street. ULI panelists got an indication of the intensity of the disagreement at a meeting in the PHA offices, attended by Housing Authority executive director Arthur C. McGill and architect-consultant Wasserman.

The insurance company was remaining aloof from the more overt forms of controversial expression.

The ULI men quickly learned that the delicate tasks of purchasing Jubilee urban renewal properties, assisting area businesses to relocate, and clearing the land were not proceeding with any marked degree of success.

"TIME IS RUNNING OUT"

The ULI report to Pittsfield warned that "Time is running out." The report went on to say that "The days and the weeks and the months go by, and even the years. It has been four years since Pittsfield's urban renewal program was initiated. It has been eight months since the contract for the Jubilee Project was signed. What has been accomplished?

Jubilee North, Pittsfield's major urban renewal effort, will utilize the land in the lower left-hand corner of the photograph. The street at right is North Street, which slices through the heart of Pittsfield's central business district.

"Approximately 50 per cent of the property has been acquired. Most of the properties acquired are still being operated under use-and-occupancy agreements and are paying rent. However," the ULI report continued, "very little thought has been given to relocation." The panel noted that between January and September, 1966, only two Jubilee area businesses moved out of the district.

ULI's Dow observed that "there was no sense of urgency to vacate transmitted by the PHA to occupants of the renewal area."

The vacillation in Jubilee clearance, besides creating hardship for businessmen in the area, was found to be harming the renewal effort in another way—by discouraging prospective re-developers. The panel said it "heard of prospective developers who have no idea of land costs; who are far from settling in a satisfactory manner the purchase of their own property; and some who cannot afford to wait for the time when a site might be prepared for them." Pittsfield was advised: it is preferable to have cleared land ready for sale to a developer, than it is to condemn property, take it off the tax rolls, and permit former owners to remain as tenants, paying nominal rents.

ULI learned that many businessmen in Jubilee wanted to return to the area after redevelopment, but "they have very little information as to how this can be done; what sites might be available; whether they are suitable; what they will cost," and so on. In this clouded situation, most of the Jubilee area businessmen adopted a tactic of hanging on as long as possible in their old locations, especially since they were under no pressure to move out. However, the ULI panel noted, the apparent status quo was neither desirable nor capable of being sustained indefinitely.

Panelists found little merit in an attitude expressed by renewal officials—that "time is on our side." The panel report stated, "No one running a business would want to land in limbo for as long as some of the proprietors of businesses in the Jubilee area have. If no action is taken, time will continue to go by, just as it has, but it will definitely not 'be on your side.' "

Investigations by ULI members turned up unrest and disillusionment among renewal area businessmen. The operator of a tire-recapping business said PHA had promised to give him a sketch of the site on which he could re-locate in Jubilee, "but they have never come in with it." What he did receive from PHA, the businessman said, "Was an offer of $25,000 for my business, which my own

In the Columbus Project, conceived in 1963, land in the upper left corner will be cleared ▸ retard mid-town residential blight and to compliment Jubilee. Columbus is near Jubilee's orth boundary, separated from the main renewal area by the Penn Central railroad tracks.

appraisers value at $43,000." He lamented that "Unless we get fair prices for our properties, we may not be able to go back into business at all."

Another Jubilee area businessman with a typical complaint, an auto parts dealer, said, "The urban renewal agency just is not paying enough attention to us little guys."

No matter how, or by whom, downtown Pittsfield was to be revitalized, some unequivocal guidelines seemed pertinent to the ULI panel. The panel urged that the city concentrate on upgrading its principal commercial asset, North Street, by beautifying it, by recruiting a new department store operator for the street (instead of for the Jubilee area), and by organizing a new "minute-man" group of downtown business leaders to press for continued improvement of North Street.

Several panelists thought the city's leaders had done an inadequate job of "selling" a downtown Pittsfield location to the large merchandising organizations. "I am constantly amazed," said Panelist Stockwell, "at the lack of contact made by this community with the store chains around the country." Dow remarked that many Pittsfielders had become accustomed to going to Springfield, 57 miles away, to do their major shopping at stores of the caliber of Forbes-Wallace, and that Pittsfield merchants had grown accustomed to this drain-off of business.

Panelist Barnard said this kind of apathy could be attacked most effectively by "a small group of the city's top-flight citizens, ideally about a half dozen, perhaps led by a still-vigorous retired executive who could make it a full-time job."

The final ULI report stated that "either some existing organization or preferably a new one should be created for the sole purpose of carrying on a selling and public relations program . . . a professional type of promotion" aimed at luring new businesses to the central business district. The report did underscore the belief that such a program "is of prime necessity if Pittsfield is going to share in the country's increasing economic growth."

CONFLICTING OPINIONS

"Direct and vigorous action on the part of business and political leaders is necessary," panelist Campbell reiterated. He said that "Step number one should be the adoption of a strong zoning ordinance that will rigidly confine retail commercial uses to the snugged-up CBD; that will prohibit the stringing-out of CBD uses along the major arteries fanning out from the CBD."

The Jubilee North Plan embracing a new department store as the keystone of a thriving new urban hub was called impractical, because "no major store operator will want to take a back street location," as panelist Stockwell put it. He added that "Our feeling is that another department store is needed, but that it more logically should be located on North Street, to help the present retail stores on both sides of the street hold or improve their volumes." Several panelists cited their experience with the habits of shoppers and their liking for the opportunity to do comparison shopping. Women, they said, like to shop at more than one store, and they like to be able to walk between stores—but not very far.

It is interesting to note that consultant Wasserman was critical of the ULI findings, while Berkshire Life president Furey characterized himself as "delighted" with the report.

Furey said after the study report he would be pleased to have the ULI-backed motel, high-rise office building, and specialty shops in the Berkshire Life portion of Jubilee. He would let the department store go. But Wasserman contended his plan would have generated business for North Street rather than draining it off. What ULI saw as a "back street location," Wasserman viewed as the future retail core for Pittsfield.

Wasserman concluded that the ULI recommendation would lead to "fragmented" development of Jubilee, and would "set the renewal program back many months."

This was a simple case of conflicting opinions—Wasserman's, and the opposing view representing the accumulated experience of the ULI panel. It was impossible to say with certainty where the wisdom lay in this disagreement.

Some tactical steps were suggested by ULI for concentrating the commercial core in a compact area. On the east side, the CBD should be bounded by a complex of civic buildings, an enlarged city hall relocated in the former post office, plus a federal building and library. The old city hall could be remodeled for private office use. Panelist Combs observed that "The benefits to the CBD will be substantial, in that the employees (of nearby government agencies) will become customers of the retail and service stores of the center core."

Jubilee would be the confining element of the CBD on the west. The hotel, specialty shops, perhaps a theater, facilities such as the proposed new Western Massachusetts Electric Company headquarters building would provide a sound nucleus for a redevelopment area compatible with a revitalized North Street. Parking would be another important land use.

Panelist Barnard made a strong case for a downtown theatre, clubs and restaurants to bring some "activity after-dark" to an urban core which is notably barren of amenities. He also suggested apartments downtown for upper-income families—"the segment of the population which is now being neglected most, except in the large metropolitan areas."

The consistent theme of the entire ULI approach to the case of Pittsfield can be summarized in the advice to conserve and improve existing downtown assets. North Street was the principal neglected asset.

Panelist Campbell said "You can make the central business district in fact a major regional shopping center for a large area. But it must be clean and orderly. For a starter, take the architectural excresences off the buildings. Take down the ugly signs. Make the facades on North Street uniform and attractive."

Panelist Hogan gave the bluntest advice. "You have just plain let downtown wear out," he said. "The sidewalks look miserable, because they are patched with black tar and in some places grass is growing through the concrete.

"You can't put any more trash in the containers downtown because they haven't been emptied. Pittsfield looks like an old worn out city. When you leave here," Hogan told the audience of civic leaders, "walk down your streets and see what kind of city you have. Downtown Pittsfield is dying because you are not doing anything about it."

The panel did not, in the final analysis, put Pittsfield down as a desperate case of civic neglect. ULI found that the city had a desire to re-assert itself as a quality center for a large region possessing considerable endowments in natural beauty and economic strength. The city had a reservoir of leadership talent.

What Pittsfield needed was a catalyst, a force which would jar its complacency and divert it from some dead-end paths in renewal. At the close of the session the panel felt that it had performed its function with integrity, candor and—it was hoped—a fair degree of success.

1967 RESULT: STRONG CITIZEN PARTICIPATION "ACTION COMMITTEE"

Eight months after the panel session, a re-check of Pittsfield turned up evidence of widespread ferment. Although not all the activity was along the guidelines recommended by ULI, the catalytic value of the panel study was evident on all sides. "The really remarkable immediate result of the ULI panel," said Albert R. Neill, ABC executive director, "is that we have at long last achieved strong citizen participation in the central-city improvement program."

The ULI report had recommended "an aggressive citizens program to promote Pittsfield's CBD." The result was "The Action Committee for Downtown Development," a 13-member group headed by Gardner L. Brown, a banker and president of the Association of Business and Commerce. In organizational structure, the Action Committee was an offspring of a 100-member Downtown Pittsfield Development Panel named by Mayor Del Gallo and the ABC. Broad community support was enlisted for the work of the compact "action" nucleus. Subordinated to the "Action Committee" were 15 "Action Teams for Downtown Development," each assigned a sharply-defined mission. These missions included CBD beautification, business relocation, multiple housing development, parking, traffic and pedestrian flow.

How effectively this intricate structure could respond to the challenge presented by Pittsfield's downtown problems is a matter which must be judged by the results. Some of the early results have been impressive. Not the least of these is one claimed by Action Committee Chairman Brown—"We have achieved a constructive attitude and unanimity of thinking that things can be accomplished."

Pittsfield's "Action" program has moved most rapidly in executing a ULI suggestion for the future of the old city hall on Park Place. Panelist Combs had said there was a way to achieve the seemingly incompatible goals of preserving the historic city hall building on Park Place and securing more roomy quarters for city government, both at minimum public expense. Combs suggested leasing city hall to a developer who would preserve the colonial exterior while remodeling the inside of the building for private office use. The existing federal post office building, soon to be vacated by the move of that agency to a new federal building, would make an excellent city hall,

Pittsfield from the air—the town square in the lower left portion of the picture—is distinguishable by the "cross" inside an oval, created by intersecting walkways. At the top of the town square is the construction area for Berkshire Life's new home-office building.

Combs pointed out, if a swap between the local and federal government could be arranged.

This recommendation was carried out to the letter. The city traded a mid-town parking lot for the post office, and the terms of a 30-year lease of the old city hall to a developer would net the city an estimated $250,000.

"Action Teams" and the parent committee for downtown development were instrumental in these developments. Other "teams" were moving more slowly, including the one assigned the downtown cleanup suggested so pungently by ULI's Hogan. However, the caliber of membership on the guiding group, the 13-man "Action Committee," suggests that Pittsfield may be mobilized for a successful campaign against the prinicpal deficiencies which are susceptible to this type of activity.

The presence of Robert L. Gibson, general manager for General Electric in Pittsfield, indicates a more active concern with civic affairs by that company. Mayor Del Gallo and City Council President Joseph Scelsi brought governmental involvement to the group. Another Action Committee member was Pittsfield radio station president, Richard Jackson, who also serves as chairman of the semi-powerless Urban Redevelopment Authority.

The vice chairman of the Pittsfield Housing Authority is a committee member, but not the chairman, Ralph J. Froio. *The Berkshire Eagle,* commenting on the implications of Action Committee membership, termed this committee's role in urban renewal problems as "imprecise," and added that "One thing appears certain—the Action Committee will have little chance of implementing the ULI recommendations for major changes in the Housing Authority plans for Jubilee."

Mayor Del Gallo, for one, was not willing to accept that estimation. On April 18, 1967, after assuring himself that the Action Committee and its satellite groups had been organized sufficiently, Del Gallo wrote a letter to Gardner Brown which caused some consternation among the group's top echelon. The mayor suggested pointedly that if the committee really wanted action in redeveloping downtown, it should support Del Gallo's renewed efforts to wrest urban renewal control from the PHA.

"I just do not have much confidence in PHA members," Del Gallo explained to this reporter. "They mean well, but they are not the pros in the business who should be in charge of urban renewal. Shortly, the city is going to be asked to use some of its bonding capacity for the Jubilee project. If I don't have confidence in the people I am dealing with, it will be hard to go along with their plans."

Action Committee Chairman Brown, to whom the Mayor's letter was directed, assigned an "action team" to study the matter, but privately Brown seemed more intent on smoothing over the dispute rather than becoming a partisan.

"The ULI recommendation for separating public housing and urban renewal functions was constructive as a theory," Brown told this reporter, "but in practice sometimes you have to make do with what you have. In this case, many of the difficulties with PHA have been overcome, and the original criticism is not as valid as it was a few months ago."

Several sources in Pittsfield said that the formerly strained relationship between PHA and Berkshire over renewal plans had improved.

PHA director McGill, contending all along there was nothing wrong with his organization except understaffing, said he had secured three new aides since the ULI session and Jubilee was moving apace. McGill added that, by the end of May, 1967, acquisition in Jubilee was 80 per cent complete and demolition had reached the 55 per cent mark. Several small redevelopers had been found for the back-street sections of Jubilee, among them Western Massachusetts Electric Company, the Salvation Army, an auto dealer, and a tire merchant.

This much progress in renewal was enough to keep PHA's critics off balance. Ultimate full-scale success for PHA as the renewal agency depended upon the disposition and development of the Jubilee portions nearest North Street. McNeill and PHA announced March 10, 1967, that they had found a developer who would take on the job of turning the prime 7.5 acres of Jubilee into a new core for downtown Pittsfield. The developer was J. Allen Ornstein, a New York attorney with extensive real estate interests on Long Island and suburban New Jersey. Ornstein said that everyone had so far underestimated downtown Pittsfield's potential as the retail and commerce center for a large, fallow region. He talked of a department store development far surpassing Jubilee North's dimensions, and calling for a 1,500-car municipal garage to handle the traffic his development would generate.

"LIFESAVER FOR DOWNTOWN?"

The next significant event in the see-saw course of downtown renewal in Pittsfield was Mayor Del Gallo's latest expression of no-confidence in PHA. "Before I would commit $3.5 to $4-million in public funds to a parking garage in Jubilee I would need to know a lot of things," Del Gallo said. "I'd have to know what this would do to the city's borrowing power, credit rating, and tax structure," he said, "and I would need to work with a renewal agency in which I had confidence."

PHA's obvious counter-move to the Mayor's criticism was to make public more detail on the Ornstein plan, and when it came it bedazzled most of the city's public and civic figures. The New York developer told Pittsfield it was ready for—and he would provide—a 600,000-square foot shopping plaza anchored by a "major" department store with as much as 200,000 square feet. Two other department stores, one with about 100,000 square feet and another possibly 75,000 square feet were included among the stores envisioned in a three-level development structured on the land sloping westward from North Street. Ornstein included an office building of undetermined size. The sketches presented to Pittsfield public and civic figures showed the major store at the western end of a broad plaza fronting grandly on North Street. Ornstein talked of a 250-foot width for the pedestrian plaza.

City Councilmen, who would have to vote on the parking bond issue and redrawing some of Jubilee's boundaries to accommodate the Ornstein plan, praised the concept in such terms as "tremendous, exciting, a lifesaver for downtown." *The Berkshire Eagle* reported only one official as non-committal—Mayor Del Gallo.

Ornstein received an informal designation as the major Jubilee developer from PHA.

Later, in his New York office, Ornstein elaborated on his ideas. The Jubilee North Plan had included merely an 80-foot pedestrian connector to North Street and roughly one-third as much usable space as the new proposal. Ornstein called the Jubilee North Plan "terrible," and belittled its mall onto North Street as "an alleyway which would fail to attract shoppers and would discourage any prospective major department store operator." Ornstein, however, hired PHA consultant Hoberman and Wasserman as his architects, and declared that "Out of their Jubilee North Plan came the concept I have."

Ornstein said he studied the Pittsfield regional market and concluded "There is probably no place else in the country like it, for opportunity in the retail field.

"This region has a shopper population of between 250,000 and 300,000 people, all within less than an hour's drive of downtown Pittsfield. This includes the permanent residents and a part-time population which comes in for schools and camps, plus a sizable year-round tourist group. And what have they got around here for major, diversified shopping? Not a thing. Nothing," Ornstein said. "Our figures show that these people spend only $55-million a year in the Berkshire County area, but another $100-million, perhaps more, is drained off from this area. This retail trade goes to Hartford, Springfield and Albany."

Jubilee North, in Ornstein's view, would have been just another minor shopping center. "It would not have brought anybody new into downtown Pittsfield to do major shopping. Instead, it would have created just another slice in an already well cut-up pie," meaning the volume of "necessity" shopping.

Ornstein said he had met the Berkshire Life officials "And there is no conflict over phasing our office building construction. I hope they go ahead first."

The insurance company had retrenched its plans for the Wendell Hotel site. Berkshire Life planned a 150-room motor hotel, a 40,000-square foot office building, and 30,000 square feet for specialty shops. A bond between Berkshire Life and Ornstein was the demand by each for a publicly-financed parking garage. The insurance company estimated that it needed a facility for 300 to 400 cars. Ornstein called municipal parking an absolute prerequisite for his plan.

"As soon as the city assures us it will provide the parking, I will be ready to go with my store leases," he said. "My personal time-table calls for the start of construction on the plaza by April, 1968. If it is not possible to begin on that date, I'll say I can't do it. But somebody else will be able to build this regional center. The potential is there in Pittsfield."

ULI panel chairman Dow reviewed Ornstein's plan and criticized it principally for being "overambitious."

"Pittsfield needs another major department store to provide, along with England Brothers on North Street, the basis for comparative shopping," Dow said during an interview in his Hartford office.

"But 50 stores? I do not see how, by anybody's estimate, Pittsfield could hope to absorb this much new retail space."

Although the ULI panel had rejected the notion of what it called a "back street location" for the new major store, Dow saw merit in Ornstein's idea for, in effect, turning North Street "around the corner" into a broad, attractive pedestrian mall. "It should work, if Ornstein can get that first olive out of the bottle and bring in the major department store," Dow said. "His wide plaza would co-ordinate the entire downtown retail area between the new store and England's.

"I believe the panel accomplished a lot in Pittsfield," Dow said. "It got the city to take another look at itself, and inspired the city's leaders to get organized for some constructive downtown improvement."

By mid-1967 Pittsfield was deeply into the frequently frustrating and excruciating process of planning and creating. Doing nothing is infinitely less painful and risky, but only for the moment. Assuming that Pittsfield, like most cities, will make some mistakes and achieve less than the ideal in downtown redevelopment, the city may still reflect in later decades that idle submission to slow decay would have been the most painful choice of all.

DENVER, COLORADO

April 27-30, 1955. Downtown Denver:
A Report to Downtown Denver, Inc.,
the Sponsor

Panel Members Participating

Boyd T. Barnard, Jackson-Cross Co., Philadelphia
—Chairman

U. A. Denker, Wheeler Kelly & Hagny Investment
Co., Wichita

Joseph W. Lund, R. M. Bradley & Co., Inc., Boston

Frederic B. Martin, Carl G. Stifel Realty Co., St.
Louis

Warren L. Morris, Ostendorf-Morris Co., Cleveland
—President, ULI*

Lloyd B. Reid, Traffic and Transportation Engineer,
Detroit

Richard J. Seltzer, R. J. Seltzer, Philadelphia

Larry Smith, Larry Smith & Co., Seattle

Harley L. Swift, Harrisburg Railways Co., Harrisburg

Howard J. Tobin, Northwestern Mutual Life Insurance Co., Milwaukee

CHAPTER EIGHT

DENVER

MILE-HIGH CITY—AN EXERCISE IN DIVERSITY

Denver, Colo., population (1950) 415,786, (1960) 493,887, (1965) 520,000.

1955—ULI Central City Council panel study.

1964—Denver revisited; ULI takes another look.

The postwar development opportunities in Denver were sensed and acted upon first by outsiders. Their activities accelerated a central city construction episode which would have been inevitable, to some degree.

One end of an elongated central business district benefited almost exclusively from downtown redevelopment through the early 1960's. What had once been the prime retail section of downtown became shabby and unproductive. ULI pointed out that a high order of ingenuity was needed to plan and guide development of complementary re-uses for the blighted section of mid-city, and again cited the merits of organizing a "mover" group of the city's most influential citizens.

Although Denver's enlistment of the "power structure" did not achieve ideal continuity, it did produce a master development plan and finally the ambitious Skyline urban renewal project. Skyline survived a classic political fight, and gives every indication of contributing diversity to downtown Denver, the lack of which had been its major shortcoming.

The most important piece of commercial real estate in the vast west-central section of the United States, by almost any acceptable measurement, is the 338-acre Denver central business district. To find the Denver retail core's equal in business volume and vigor, one must look eastward to Kansas City or as far west as San Francisco.

Serving as it does an isolated metropolitan region with more than a million population, and situated as it is at the center of an increasingly popular convention and vacation area, downtown Denver has prospered. Circumstances make some degree of affluence inevitable.

The city's history has conditioned its residents to accept good fortune with equanimity. Discovery of gold near Denver in 1858 created the circumstances which resulted in the small frontier town's first boom period. Eventually the gold in Cherry Creek petered out. Deep-rooted in the cumulative Denver personality is the urge to prepare for the day when the pan turns up only sand.

Modern Denver is attempting to renew the worn-out parts of the central city before the effects of blight can spread. Some initial successes have been achieved, but there is evidence that Denver has failed to avail itself fully of one device with proven effectiveness. This is an organization of the most influential community leaders, determined to exert as much time and effort as may be required to guide a renewal plan though all the stages from conception to completion.

Denver has made some starts in the direction of a power structure exercising its power, but these efforts have been diffused and sporadic, and hence inconclusive.

1955: DOWNTOWN DENVER, INCORPORATED

As far back as 1955 a group of concerned businessmen formed Downtown Denver, Incorporated (DDI), an informal organization with 75 members who felt they had sufficient reason to militate for

This 28-floor tower office building, containing 635,000 square feet including parking was built in 1957. The estimated $10-million development includes the tower, a four-floor renovated structure integrated with the base and a new six-level, 400-car garage with a motor bank at street level.

Central Business District uplift in ways not compatible with traditional Chamber of Commerce programs.

DDI's concern developed from the list of urban ills which has become a familiar litany in practically all major cities. There was obsolescence and blight in the core area; traffic glut on the accesses to the central city and on streets within the CBD; aggressive competition from suburban shopping centers. The most unnerving problem of all, to the thoughtful civic leaders, was the absence of a plan of counter-action expertly-enough conceived to win widespread acceptance, and cogent enough to retain popular support during the inevitable controversies springing from downtown renewal.

The Downtown Denver group's first major response to the challenge it had accepted was to sponsor an Urban Land Institute Central City Council panel study in 1955. Later developments indicated that this was a productive beginning. ULI's recommendations helped generate new retail store and hotel development downtown by private interests, and planted the concept of unified planning for the renewal of the CBD's blighted end with the development of a culture-and-convention center. The Skyline urban renewal project evolved from the early ULI recommendation. It was a tortuous evolution, complicated by political haymaking. This phase of downtown renewal finally came to an end in May, 1967, when Skyline won overwhelming approval in a popular referendum, a bizarre election held on what the opposition figure called the "moral issue in urban renewal's basic philosophy." Denver's voters decided that renewal was morally acceptable, and no real harm came of the episode except for a loss of time. However, the entire flap, stirred up after the public financing of Skyline had been settled, might have been avoided by a determined exercise of civic leadership.

In 1955 ULI had suggested guidelines for setting up a permanent, more effective successor to Downtown Denver, Inc.

The panel placed an emphasis, almost insistence, on the formation of a "mover" organization—"a small, militant, and effective hard-core nucleus which meets weekly, or as often as need be, and has no axe to grind other than the welfare of the entire central city, and whose members can and will subordinate their individual interests to that end." The panel added, with underscoring, another criterion—"non-political."

These recommendations were followed in part, leading first to creation of a broader-based group, the Downtown Denver Improvement Association, and later to an offshoot with impressive power-structure credentials, the Downtown Denver Master Plan Committee.

The Downtown Denver Improvement Association, with members from 176 firms, was non-political in membership and financing, but violated the guideline on compactness. By 1961 the need for a smaller group was apparent.

1961: THE MASTER PLAN COMMITTEE

The Master Plan Committee sought political credentials, and its official creation in 1961 was by an ordinance of the Denver City Council.

In the formation of the Master Plan Committee ULI's cautions against political involvement were disregarded in several ways. The mayor nominated committee members, and initial one-year financing was derived from private subscription ($80,000) and a city council appropriation of another $80,000. The second year, with private contributions carrying a less-than-equal share of the load, the total master plan budget was increased to $250,000. There was no provision for the continuity stressed so earnestly by the ULI panel.

Nonetheless, the Master Plan Committee and other civic groups have assisted in guiding downtown Denver through a notable growth spurt.

Meanwhile, the Master Plan staff was busy producing a massive, detailed, and for the most part astute "Development Guide for Downtown Denver," issued in 1964.

All the bustle in organizing of associations and committees gave the impression of a genuinely aroused and resolute attitude in the highest civic and political councils of the city.

Ten years after the panel study, a ULI team took a new look at Denver and reported in a Technical Bulletin that downtown revitalization "went beyond surface treatments and isolated projects." [1] The report said the effort "involved the whole range of community leadership in achieving a program that attracted new investment."

This 1965 report went on to say that "The downtown Denver resurgence was based on a practical, realistic approach that made maximum use of local and national talent to determine feasibility before embarking on projects. One of the most important lessons to be learned from the Denver story is the necessity of involving the

---

[1] *Downtown Denver—A Guide to Central City Development* (Technical Bulletin 54). Edited by Mechlin D. Moore. Washington: *Urban Land Institute,* 1965. 64 pages. $5.00.

power structure of the community in the planning process from the beginning."

These observations described an ideal situation, but in fact Denver fell short of the ideal in one important respect, the depth of the power structure's involvement.

It would be unfair to disparage the abilities and dedication to civic improvement of the individuals prominent in Denver's public affairs. Members of the 1955 ULI panel, the observers who visited Denver 10 years later, and this reporter all developed a high regard for the talents of the bankers, real estate operatives, merchants and others active in civic affairs.

CUSTODIANS OF POWER

The restrictions on full utilization of the leaders' talents have come from outside the men themselves, and from outside their civic organizations. In a real but obscured sense, the men who play out the role of the power structure are the custodians but not controllers of power in Denver public life. The wealth of the city is not readily brought to bear on the side of progress during a public crisis. Instead, the wealth is imbedded in trusts and estates, by nature impersonal, conservative, isolated from the community mainstream.

An insight into the nature of Denver's leadership came from Perry Anderson, executive director of the Downtown Denver Improvement Association. "This city's leadership is the managerial type," he told this reporter. "It's purpose is to conserve the entrenched wealth entrusted to them, not to take risks or blaze any trails."

Some other cities, including St. Louis, Detroit and Philadelphia, had highly effective "mover" organizations because their members were men who could command that the prestige and some of the wealth of their private businesses be enlisted on the spot for public improvement efforts. Denver's functioning power structure had lacked that sort of heft.

The vacuum left by the shortcomings of local enterprise in Denver was filled in a spectacular manner by outside entrepreneurs soon after World War II.

The 1955 ULI panel report made one reference to Denver's "blue line," a mysterious-sounding designation until one learns the history of Denver's confrontation with its water problem. The city had drawn most of its water supply from the relatively scant snowfall on the eastern slope of the Rockies. Denver's expedient reaction to the perennial water crisis was to restrict its own growth by decree. Beyond the arbitrary blue line on a city map, no one could expect or demand city water. The solution was simple in theory, but costly. A 23-mile water tunnel through the Rockies tapped the abundant snow supply on the western slope, and a huge reservoir was constructed. The blue line was erased, at a cost of $70-million in property liens to finance the new water system.

A much more easily-waived limitation had prevented Denver's man-made downtown Skyline from competing with the vista of the nearby Rockies. Hudson Moore, Jr., a realty company president who has served on all the major downtown improvement groups, recalled that "Until several years after World War II we had a 12-story height limitation on buildings. Then it dawned on people that you could have height in buildings without blocking the natural view simply by providing open space between the structures." Denver architecture entered the modern era when the height restriction was lifted.

OUTSIDE INVESTORS: A BUILDING BOOM

Roger D. Knight, board chairman of the Denver U. S. National Bank, said that "The revitalization of downtown Denver has lived up to any standard that could be set," but he added, with candor, that "without the pioneer developments by investors from other parts of the country who recognized the potential of Denver, the story might have been different."

New York developer William Zeckendorf got in early on Denver's resurgence during the frenetic 1950's. He developed the $16-million, 22-floor Mile High Center office building with 574,000 gross square feet of floor space. The builder's *quid pro quo* for exceeding the still sentimentally potent 12-story barrier was to build a plaza, the first open, landscaped, ground-floor treatment for an office development in the city. This was in 1954, and five years later the Denver U. S. National Bank bought the property. Banker Knight said "Zeckendorf was the spark for a great period of growth in downtown Denver."

Other investors, some home-grown, followed with six more downtown skyscrapers, the tallest being the 30-story Security Life Building. The Murchison interests of Texas joined the boom with the $10-million, 28-floor First National Bank Building, completed in 1957.

The square foot totals for downtown buildings in Denver rose from 1.8-million in 1950, to 2.7-million square feet in 1960, and to 3.65-million by 1964. The ratio of downtown space to population remained steady during the 14-year period, about 3.18 square feet per capita.

Throughout this period, Denver grappled with the effects of an unusually high vacancy rate in its downtown office buildings. In 1955, during the earliest stirrings of the downtown building boom, the ULI panel found a 15 per cent office vacancy rate. With two new major office buildings then under construction, the ULI panel cautioned that "From all appearances there is now enough space available for the next few years."

However, much of the available space was in obsolete, unattractive structures, and the incentive to investors who sensed the demand for new, top-quality offices took the brakes off any caution based on a statistical recitation of vacancy rates. And so the new towers were built.

1966: HIGH VACANCY RATE

By 1964, reported Gerald T. Hart, a realtor and member of the Master Plan Committee, "It appears that there is a tremendous excess of space in Denver." Vacancies in the older downtown buildings were 19.3 per cent. In the modern buildings the rate was 13 per cent—or, if Lincoln Tower several blocks off the main financial street were included, the vacancy rate was 22 per cent. Hart saw one advantage to the high vacancy rates downtown. From one viewpoint there was vacant space in profusion, but in the eyes of a company considering a move to Denver this meant immediately available prime space. A major oil company shifted its division headquarters from Casper, Wyoming, and occupied 50,000 square feet in downtown Denver in one sweep.

Hart said that an economically-sound office space vacancy rate would be 8 per cent. The office tower boom ground to a halt.

In late 1966, Denver still was far over the ideal 8 per cent level. Realty company president Moore estimated the office building vacancy rate at 18 per cent in new buildings and 27 per cent in pre-1945 structures. The shakedown period in downtown office building occupancy was not yet completed.

Zeckendorf's interests in the Denver business district ranged beyond the comparatively prosaic effort of tapping a market for modern office space.

This entrepreneur acquired the site of the former county courthouse, located at the eastern end of 16th Street, the main retail street. Zeckendorf built one of the largest department stores in the nation, with underground parking for 1,200 cars. This was in 1957. Apparently the department store structure was built on speculation. However, by the time it was completed, the pressure was not on developer Zeckendorf but on two of the city's oldest retail establishments, Daniels-and-Fisher and the May Company. What they had in common before Zeckendorf was obsolete stores at the deteriorating western part of the main retail strip. What the two retailers shared after Zeckendorf was a merged identity as May-D&F and joint tenancy of the most attractive commercial building in town.

However, the balance of the business district was seriously upset, and remains so to this day.

Since the May-D&F store, located more than seven blocks away from the old D&F store with its landmark tower, is obviously there to stay, the solution to upgrading and delimiting the entire core area requires a high order of ingenuity.

In its November, 1964, reexamination of Denver, the ULI observed that "The movement of the May-D&F store to the present location has accentuated the retail problem by creating a major retail street that is too long for convenient comparative shopping." The ULI Central City Council recommended "a quality discount store" for the west end of the CBD, and added, "The feeling is that even though a discount operation is a change in the retail pattern, it would tend to strengthen the retail core by making a more complete center of downtown."

There does indeed appear to be a potential of walk-in customers on the west side of the CBD. Nearby is the sprawling federal office complex. This is also the neighborhood of the renovated city auditorium and the convention center under construction.

One man who has given downtown Denver a hard look, from a vantage point based on business experience plus the insights of an

Urban Land Institute president, is Hunter Moss of Miami. Moss was chairman of the ULI's Central City Council when it re-visited Denver late in 1964. Reflecting on the distention of the CBD, Moss said late in 1966 that "Denver had a frankenstein created in its midst when the main shopping street was stretched to its present length.

"OVER-EXTENDED BUSINESS DISTRICT"

"There is no ideal answer to this type of problem," Moss added. The discount store proposal would help rejuvenate a rundown area, although it would not correct the situation of an over-extended business district.

"The panel thought long and hard about the problem, and no one was able to offer what might be regarded as a neat, surefire answer. Of course, unless the Skyline urban renewal area can get off the ground, the problem of the spread-out business district will be immeasurably more critical."

The old May Co. store on 16th and Champa Streets has been cleared for a parking lot. D&F's archaic old building still sits empty, its anachronistic tower an impossible-to-ignore remainder of the Skyline urban renewal area in which it is located. Realtor Moore recalled that at the time of the merger and relocation "There was public endorsement for anyone willing to invest that much money in the downtown district."

The May-D&F store cost over $8-million. Zeckendorf had some courthouse-square land left over, and perhaps another $26-million available for investment in Denver. In 1960-61 these assets went into the 884-room Hilton Hotel and office annex. This largest Denver hotel was built near the city's only other first-rate hotels, the Brown Palace and the Cosmopolitan, on the eastern, that is, the "up" end of the see-sawing business district.

Denver's initial thrust in downtown rehabilitation produced remarkable results. However, by the mid-1960's there were signs that the first effort had lost its momentum. Formidable problems which had never been mastered, plus a new crop of incipient crises, called for a strong second effort by Denver leaders.

These were the dimensions of the problem in the mid-1960's:

The Denver economy was experiencing an unusual period of softening. Denver's geographical isolation had been paralleled by another form of insulation—this from the extreme peaks and valleys of the national economy. While Denver had no seam-bursting booms, it also experienced no severe recessions, even when most of the rest of the nation was stung by them. Geography had much to do with it. Denver has been the major distribution center for a multi-state area. The metropolitan region enjoyed a healthy leavening of major industry, principally rubber products and luggage. Another stabilizing factor has been the huge governmental work force, state and federal. Moreover, the convention business has shown signs of becoming a stable major industry, propelled upward by the public's enthusiastic acceptance of jet aircraft travel. Denver is still the colorful far-off mile-high city by the Rockies, and getting there is no exhausting challenge at 600-plus miles an hour.

And yet, in the face of all these pluses, Denver was feeling the strain of a braking effect on its pell-mell growth of the 1950's and early 1960's. A major employer, the Martin Company, began reducing its work force in 1962, and since then has eliminated more than 10,000 jobs. A recent study prepared by consultants for the Denver Urban Renewal Authority stated that "This sizable reduction (by Martin) has adversely affected numeorous parts of the Denver economy." Overall, employment has managed to hold steady since 1962, propped by gains in wholesale and retail trades, the insurance business, finance and real estate, and government employment. The slump has been felt in mining, construction, manufacturing and related activities.

DENVER URBAN RENEWAL AUTHORITY: A TURNING POINT

Since 1962, which was apparently a turning point for the city, the population has increased little, if at all. A market analysis prepared by the Real Estate Research Corporation for the Urban Renewal Authority predicted "significant improvements" by 1967 in the area's economy, but foresaw that Denver's next wave of growth will occur "in newly annexed outlying areas." This is not a startling prediction, since population within the central urban area decreased nine per cent even during the halcyon 1950-60 decade and nothing has happened to change the trend.

The notably effective Downtown Denver Master Plan Committee,

Denver's Courthouse Square Project, an urban renewal complex of 1,725,000 gross square feet, houses the May-D&F Store, foreground; and the Hilton Hotel, background. The development represents an approximate $32-million investment in downtown renewal.

which carried the development guide through its initial achievements, has become in a sense a casualty of its own success. Founded and funded for a two-year life, the committee gave its staff a year and a half extension, finally closing its offices on December 31, 1964. The key organization of movers, therefore, was in a dismantling process during a period when several signs pointed toward a time for girding for renewed effort. The Committee itself remained intact, and in fact holds occasional meetings on the call of its chairman, but for staff work it relies upon the already heavily-committed members of the city planning department.

This circumstance calls to mind an admonition by the 1955 ULI panel in Denver, when it laid down the guidelines for an effective downtown association. The panel observed that "An official city commission or authority inevitably takes on political flavor. It has been proved in other cities that the public interest must be paramount to secure the active participation of top people from every field of economic endeavor."

By September, 1966, the Master Plan Committee had a scant $1,000 left in its operating fund. Staffless, it was by then merely one of several civic organizations interested in downtown betterment. One former master plan staffer complained that "The private money available for this kind of activity is being thinned out."

The principal beneficiary of an intensified effort by civic leaders would be the Skyline urban renewal area, the 37-square block, 158-acre sector anchoring the west end of Denver's elongated retail and financial districts, which run parallel for about nine blocks along 16th and 17th streets.

The Skyline project suffered one setback when voters turned down an $8-million urban renewal allocation in a 1964 bond election. For two years Skyline remained a political battleground.

As it stands, the area designated for renewal contains Denver's sizable skid row, lying athwart the city's two most important downtown streets. Within Skyline's confines is concentrated the worst blight in downtown Denver. Because Denver's largest retail store and hotel are located nine blocks away, at the east end of the central business district, and have tipped the spread-out business district's balance precariously away from Skyline, what happens next in the proposed renewal area is of overriding importance.

This aerial view shows the large volume of land given over to parking space in downtown Denver.

SKYLINE URBAN RENEWAL—
37 SQUARE BLOCKS

The downtown master plan strongly recommended moving ahead with Skyline urban renewal, and the Master Plan Committee's endorsement was abetted by that of the Downtown Improvement Association. Watson A. Bowes, a realtor and prominent figure in Denver civic life, commented that the 500-member improvement association swung public opinion around in favor of Skyline renewal, despite the 1964 setback at the polls.

Bowes, who is a vice chairman of the Master Plan Committee, said that "Ten years ago no one could have sold federally-assisted urban renewal to the Downtown Improvement Association." In the meantime the efforts of the 25-member Master Plan Committee gradually won over the larger group. Bowes says that ultimately urban renewal gained the backing of 95 per cent of the improvement association's members.

Downtown Denver's causes for concern are not all contained within the Skyline urban renewal area. Transit ridership into the central business district has been in a steady decline. Denver Tramway Corporation's total ridership, which was 37.8-million paid fares in 1961, was down to 24.7-million fares in 1965. The decline had the double-edged effect of limiting the transit company's resources for service improvement, and burdening the business district's feeder arteries and streets with ever-increasing auto traffic. A tax-saving lease arrangement with city government, or possibly outright sale, was in the works.

Not all the structural deterioration and obsolescence has been limited to the renewal area. Sixty-seven per cent of the structures in the central business district were built before 1920. Forty-seven per cent of the usable floor space was rated in no better than "poor" or "fair" condition by the master plan staff. In the buildings rated "poor," the vacancy ratio was one square foot out of every eight. The necessity for broad-scale rehabilitation was manifest.

Denver's good record in planning and executing solutions to its past difficulties rules out a flatly pessimistic forecast about the outcome of present probelms. The city has a record of success, sometimes inspiring, in the face of adversity.

The blighted area of the CBD may, indeed, be on the threshold of a remarkable renaissance. Skyline urban renewal would be the foremost factor in revitalization, but there are others of importance. One is Larimer Square, an attempt by private developers to establish a tourist attraction on what was once Denver's main downtown street, but which for years has been a notorious bums' beach, where the blight left its mark on more than the buildings.

METRO STATE COLLEGE

Spreading southward of the convention complex and the Skyline area is the prospective site for a new four-year higher-education facility, Metropolitan State College. A mayor's committee charged with site selection has recommended the 176-acre tract bounded by Speer Boulevard, Colfax, Sixth and Wazee Streets, an area now used for low-grade residential and low-yield industrial purposes. Metro State's impact on the neighboring renewal area would be major, if planning for redevelopment capitalizes on the customary demand near colleges for specialty shops, recreation facilities, and medium-rent apartments.

ULI's Hunter Moss said after the reinspection of Denver in 1964 that "There is too little evidence of residential development in the downtown area to date. This is a disappointment to men who were in Denver 10 years ago. The market exists."

An attempt to tap the upper strata of that market has been launched by the developers of Brooks Tower. Already underway, this will be a 42-story thrust into Denver's skyline, located inside the Skyline renewal area but nonetheless a private development.

The ULI panel had offered advice on the difficulties of land acquisition solely through private enterprise. The panel was asked whether it would be practical for private business interests to form an unofficial redevelopment authority. This approach was considered feasible by ULI "on a limited scale."

The Brooks Tower developer and public agencies later learned by experience in the Skyline area that the panel had offered a valuable insight on renewal 10 years before:

"Based on our experience, the panel must state that any large-scale, bold project, such as seems to be desired by the citizens of Denver, must at some time resort to the powers of eminent domain to acquire properties from individuals who, through greed or stupidity, are willing to prevent desirable improvements."

Armond Asborno, an officer of the Central Bank and Trust Company, which provided the basis for the Brooks Tower development organization, described the project: 42 stories; the ground floor for retail shops; second level, office space; third level for some recreational use; two levels of parking with 400 spaces; and 537 apartment units, with rents ranging from about $130 a month to $485. This will be Denver's first downtown apartment structure.

BROOKS TOWER APARTMENTS

The Brooks Tower syndicate's acquisition of two and a fraction square blocks in the renewal area was cited by urban renewal opponents as proof that private enterprise can handle the renewal job, but this contention was rejected by the developers themselves.

Land purchased by this developer, but not required for the Tower itself, is being put to first-class use. One section was sold as a site for a new $7.5-million Federal Reserve bank building. Another section is earmarked for a new hotel. After a look at the surface results, it might have appeared that private capial was available and private land-assemblage practical.

Not so, said Asborno emphatically. "What we proved to ourselves is that it is impossible to assemble large tracts of downtown land on an economical basis without help from an urban renewal agency; that is, without resort to the power of eminent domain." Asborno spoke from the experience, often bitter, of dealing with 68 property owners. One holdout never did come to terms. He wanted $2-million for land worth $300,000. He didn't get it, and so four lots remain an island of resistance to change in a turbulent neighborhood.

Operating as quietly as possible, the Brooks Tower organization at first acquired some land for as little as $8 a square foot, but later had to pay as much as $48 a square foot. One of the most knowledgeable real estate men in Denver disclosed that the cost of the cleared land acquired for Brooks Tower and the Federal Reserve Bank ran about $30 a square foot, in an area where scattered sales unrelated to large-scale assemblage were running $8 to $10 a foot. The redevelopment tract had been appraised at $1.2-million before asemblage. The most reliable estimates available indicated that the same land could have been acquired for $1.8-million through condemnation. The redevelopers ended up paying $3-million. Developer spokesman Asborno says he would never again undertake land assemblage on the same scale without the assistance of an agency with power of eminent domain.

Banker Bruce M. Rockwell said flatly "There will be no more private land assemblage in Denver at economical prices." Rockwell, senior vice president of the Colorado National Bank, is former chairman of the Denver Urban Renewal Authority and a director of the Master Plan Committee.

The late Elwood M. Brooks, banker and civic leader who pioneered the Tower development which will bear his name, had said, "A well conceived urban renewal program to revitalize the heart of the city is absolutely essential. Only in this way can the difficulties of land assembly be overcome, so that private enterprise can function effectively in redeveloping the center of metropolitan life and preserving the tax base upon which the entire community depends."

Securing the financing for Brooks Tower was a difficulty second only to land assemblage, Asborno recalled. He and his associates worked for four years to raise the equity capital, and succeeded only after it appeared reasonably certain that the surrounding land would be rejuvenated by the Skyline urban renewal project.

Councilman Gibson led the fight against Skyline urban renewal in the classic style—decrying the resale of condemned land to private developers as "immoral" and urging a waiting period as long as 10 years for "the private investment potential which does exist in this area to exert itself." Testifying in March, 1966, before the House Committee on Banking and Currency in Washington, Gibson called Skyline "a fraud upon the people of Denver." Meanwhile the Councilman busied himself with collecting voters' signatures on a petition to force referendum which, he hoped, would kill the project.

The "fraud" allegation concerned the local contribution to Skyline renewal financing. In a 1964 bond election, $8-million for urban renewal in Skyline and five other Denver projects was one of 10 items on the ballot. Six passed, and four failed, including urban renewal.

A member of the Downtown Improvement Association, realtor Royal Judd, headed the "Taxpayers' Protective Council," which opposed the urban renewal bond issue item. Judd said later, "My opposition was not based on the feeling that urban renewal is wrong per se. Skyline has possibilities if it is properly planned. This idea of flying by the seat of your pants leaves me cold. Their plans were

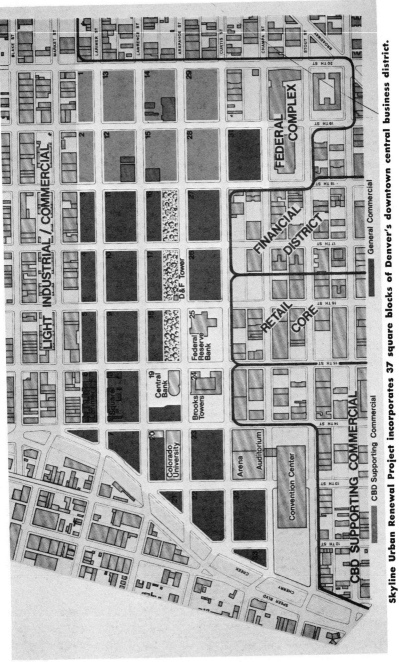

Skyline Urban Renewal Project incorporates 37 square blocks of Denver's downtown central business district.

SKYLINE PROJECT AREA
LAND USE MAP

too nebulous. If they (the renewal planners) produce first-rate plans and can tell me where they're going, I'm 100 per cent for them. My interest is purely monetary."

POLITICAL UPS AND DOWNS

Mayor Tom Currigan told the same Congressional hearing to which Gibson made his charge that "I did not regard the rejection of the bond issue as a vote against the principles of urban renewal." (The vote was 29,344 for, 34,300 against). Currigan added that he did view the result as indication that the majority of voters did not want bond funds used for the city's share of the cost, but favored some other method.

Except for Gibson's continuing efforts, the issue of local financing would have become moot when Congress later voted to accept Denver's previously authorized $11-million expenditure for its convention center as the city's matching funds for the project. The Skyline area was enlarged from 29 to 37 blocks to include the nearby convention hall area. Gibson contended that extending the boundaries to take in "the convention center and other areas that are not blighted is a fraud upon the people of Denver." The Mayor and City Council majority then argued that no further public vote was necessary to proceed with Skyline, because no local bond money was required for the city's share of project expense.

A rider to the Federal Housing Act of 1965 ostensibly gave Denver's pro-urban renewal forces the means to sidestep more political struggles on the Skyline project. Denver leaders credit Congressman Byron Rogers with engineering the legislative coup that permitted the city to apply its convention hall outlay to its urban renewal obligation. The intent was "to do something for Denver" to help it recover from the economic ill-effects of the disastrous Platte River flood that year. Even though the funds hassle appeared to have a happy outcome, from the Denver Urban Renewal Authority's viewpoint, a DURA spokesman said he wished it had proceeded differently in the whole affair. The decision to include Skyline and other projects in the bond issue had been made because of eagerness to "establish a priority" for urban renewal among the city's capital improvement projects. Rockwell, the banker and former DURA chairman, said that all the group proved to itself was that "We could not sell a program to a confused and apathetic public." Rockwell was one of the civic leaders who insisted that, after a thorough briefing on Skyline, Denver citizens could not logically disapprove either the broad principle of urban renewal or the detailed Skyline plan.

Rockwell said during a series of debates with Gibson that Skyline required broad-scale clearance and renewal, and not the lesser ministrations of rehabilitation and code enforcement.

"The area has entirely too many uses incompatible with the central business district," said Rockwell. "For instance, skid row has got to be rooted out. The Urban Renewal Agency could compromise itself right out of the project by being too minimal. There has to be something close to total clearance in the Skyline area to permit redevelopment on a magnitude that can be truly beneficial to the area."

Such frankness, far from disarming the anti-Skyline forces, gave Gibson a rallying point for his referendum movement, which had lagged in the summer of 1966.

In the early months of 1967 there was confusion on both sides of the Skyline controversy over how many signatures Gibson needed and how many valid ones Gibson had secured on his petition. As the day approached for preparing the ballot for the spring elections, in which the offices of mayor and councilmen would be contested, the City Council abruptly agreed to put the Skyline issue up to a popular vote. Mayor Currigan and six incumbent councilmen were seeking reelection, and they did not want to face the embarrassing charge that they denied the voters a chance to be heard on a vital civic issue like Skyline.

The Skyline referendeum technically was merely a straw vote with no binding legal significance. All the public financing had been arranged. Nothing in state or local law required another public endorsement. However, both sides in the controversy agreed that in practical effect the future of publicly-assisted urban renewal in Denver rode on the outcome.

"While the May 16 vote is specifically for Skyline," Mayor Currigan said, "a negative vote could only be interpreted as against the concept of urban renewal." He added "there would be no hope whatsoever" of proceeding with other urban renewal projects in the city if Skyline fell to public disapproval. Elected officials would not dare buck the mandate.

Gibson made the drawing of battle lines complete by announcing he would run for mayor on a staunch anti-urban renewal platform. Currigan was just as unequivocally pro-Skyline. A third major candidate, Don Nicholson, attempted to straddle the Skyline issue but showed a slight leaning in favor of the renewal project. (Denver city elections are non-partisan. In party affiliation, Currigan is a Democrat, Nicholson a Republican. Gibson styled himself as "independent.")

"CITIZENS FOR SKYLINE, INC."

"Citizens for Skyline, Inc." was formed to handle the "pro" side in the referendum campaign. Its support was channeled through the Downtown Denver Improvement Association. Chairmanship of the citizens' group went to a clergyman, the Rev. Arthur L. Miller, in a move to counter Gibson's raising of a "moral" issue.

The main event in this political battle was still Currigan versus Gibson. The mayor had the establishment behind him.

"A negative vote would undoubtedly remove us from contention in our request for model city approval," Currigan said at one point.

The climax of Gibson's campaign was a rally featuring Harvard professor Martin Anderson, author of *"The Federal Bulldozer."* An unseasonable snow storm hit Denver the evening of the rally and fewer than 100 persons turned out. Despite the portents, including polls indicating strong Skyline support, urban renewal adherents awaited the election returns with some apprehension.

They might as well have relaxed. The vote on May 16, 1967, was 73,908 in favor of Skyline, 29,803 opposed. Mayor Currigan won reelection with 55.7 per cent of the vote. Gibson ran third with 10.3 per cent.

J. Robert Cameron, executive director of DURA, said the day after the election that detailed plans for Skyline would be ready for the required City Council review and presumably its approval when that body began its new term on July 1, 1967. Allowing time for public hearings and final agreements between DURA and the Department of Housing and Urban Development, Cameron estimated that execution of the Skyline plan would start in January, 1968.

"In the meantime," said Cameron, "we've got to think in terms of setting up a redevelopment corporation to get this thing going. We will study what places like Philadelphia have done to interest the biggest developers and the best builders."

Members of Citizens Committee for Skyline agreed to keep the organization in existence. "But we need something a little more high powered," Cameron said. "We need to get more of the power structure involved."

As DURA member Rockwell had said so candidly during the early stages of the confrontation with Gibson, massive clearance will be carried out in Skyline. Nearly half the structures are more than 75 years old and a DURA survey rated only 10 per cent to be in "good" or better condition. Few of the old buildings had enough historical or esthetic value to merit retention.

In DURA plans, the D&F tower would be preserved but the rest of the dusty old store would be razed and the site converted to public park use. Authority officials had given assurances to operators of garment factories and other light industries within Skyline that they would have the opportunity to relocate. The land use and market-ability study prepared for DURA by Real Estate Research Corporation allocated 650,000 square feet to light industrial and commercial activities. The consultant warned that "it might not be economic" for low-overhead activities like a garment industry to return to renewed Skyline.

The emphasis during the early stages of thinking on Skyline re-use was on making the area complementary to the adjacent central business district and to the pacesetter within the renewal area, Brooks Tower. Parking would be structured around terminals serving the proposed freeway which will skirt the renewal area. An estimated 500 to 700 apartment units in addition to Brooks Tower's 537 units would be absorbed by 1971. A new major department store would be feasible between 1973 and 1975. Because of the high office-space vacancy rate in downtown Denver, allocation for this use in Skyline was a nominal 250,000 square feet. There was recognition of the future desirability of a new hotel near the convention center.

What these sketchy early estimates of Skyline utilization seemed to indicate was an opportunity for a redeveloper with a creative approach.

Clearly, an expertly planned and executed Skyline redevelopment would be as potent a stimulus for downtown Denver as Zeckendorf's efforts were in an earlier decade.

The influence of the 1955 ULI panel could be traced throughout the pattern of core city revitalization. Zeckendorf's overturning of the long-time CBD alignment with the new store was a *fait accompli.* The panel counseled against rushing into insufficiently considered schemes which would cause further over-extension of the mid-town commercial area.

The ULI panel gave its stamp of approval to another major downtown hotel, to remodeling the municipal auditorium, to creating an expressway belt around the central business district, and to establishment of a one-way grid system for downtown streets—all proposals which have been completed or are underway. The panel warned that downtown Denver required a healthy transit system and that the city might have to make some sacrifices to assist this vital utility.

The panel also implanted the idea for a large-scale rehabilitation of the lower (western) edge of the CBD, an idea which became the Skyline concept.

Perhaps the panel's principal contribution to Denver was the one cited by Anderson, the DDIA director. "For the first time an outside group looked us over and pointed out the necessity for mobilizing the top-ranked civic leaders to get this city moving."

Keeping the central city moving along wisely conceived directions is a challenge of indefinite duration for Denver leadership. By the time a Skyline redeveloper can begin construction on the variety of new central city uses, the Master Plan Committee's development guide for downtown Denver would be at least five years old and in need of updating even without the necessity of achieving compatibility between master plan theories and the Skyline actuality.

The core city will have an enhanced role as the metropolitan business and retail center, and as the culture focus for the entire region. The CBD's composition will be diversified by medium-to-high-rent apartments. By 1974 the CBD will be housing an estimated 5,000 residents, a throng of conventioners, and 75,000 persons who will work in the core city. For the remaining million-plus persons in the metropolitan area, the Denver CBD will be compelled to offer the lure of first-rate comparison shopping.

PARKING AND TRANSPORTATION

Denver's planners and thinkers admit to a necessity for some enlightened decision-making about parking and transportation for the central district.

Skyline will transform Denver's core into the metropolitan business and retail center as well as the culture focus for the entire region.

Denver's experience with costly solutions to the parking problem has caused it to move cautiously. In 1958 a $4-million revenue bond issue was approved by voters who thought they were assuring adequate CBD parking for the predictable future. The money went for three garages and three surface lots, about 1,700 spaces in all.

After the bond-financed facilities opened around 1960 downtown parking was too abundant, about 27,000 spaces in all. Caught in a buyer's market for parking space, the Denver city agency found that revenues would not cover the bond payments. Parking meter receipts were diverted to parking bond debt service. After the city had lost about $1.5-million on its parking operation, it sought to bail out of a money-losing proposition by leasing the facilities for enough money to cover the bonds. The first private operator defaulted. A second operator, a national firm, was faring better in late 1966. But the city was holding in escrow $9,000 a month in parking meter revenues as a backstop if it proves utterly impossible for the city parking facilities to pay off the bonds.

The master development plan predicted a need for an 83 per cent increase in core area parking space by 1980. The cleared-out land in the Skyline urban renewal area provides an obvious location for much of the new parking space needed. However, Denver planners may have to scale down their early plans.

The master plan had recommended a five-level, 1,300-space garage in Skyline. The Denver Planning Office's study of the proposal showed that gross annual income would be about $312,000, and annual expenses $483,600. The Planning Office, in a report to the Urban Renewal Authority, made a rather ambiguous recommendation for subsidizing "necessary" parking with city general revenues. A further attempt at parking subsidy could be expected to generate political opposition.

The 1964 ULI review of Denver saw "tremendous design problems" in the city's then extant parking plans. In August, 1966, ULI Central City Council Chairman Moss said that no city is realistic when it defines its parking problem in the context of the necessary facilities' ability to pay for themselves. Speaking about parking and a not-too-distantly related concern, transit, Moss said, "I can't get excited about the profit motive when it comes to these two topics. Parking and transit are such integral parts of a city's life blood that any objections based on dollar considerations are unfortunate. What

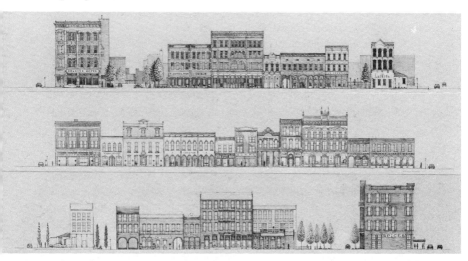

Larimer Square is an attempt by private developers to establish a tourist attraction on what was once Denver's main downtown street.

has to be considered is the lower right hand corner of the balance sheet. Every city has a colossal investment in downtown and a tremendous dependence on the taxes derived from downtown. Whatever is required in the way of parking and transit must be provided." Moss concluded, "I feel very strongly about subsidized parking."

Denver has not yet channeled any sort of subsidy into the privately owned transit system, but the time may not be far distant. The Denver Tramway Corporation has requested several forms of tax relief—from city and county gross receipts taxes and state fuel taxes.

The system's difficulties were not unique—fewer riders, higher costs. Between 1961 and 1965, revenues dropped about $500,000 while operating expenses rose about $120,000. Denver Tramway's main boost has been that it hasn't stopped operating in the black, and continued to pay its 8-to-9 per cent return in dividends. The corporation's charter requires that at least 50 per cent of net income be paid as dividends to first preferred stockholders. The company's board in 1965 dipped heavily into net income to maintain the dividend rate.

From the transit rider's viewpoint, service is not getting any better. Those thousands of downtown workers and shoppers who deserted the bus for automobile transit are not the objects of any campaign to lure them back into the mass-use vehicle. Tramway company spokesmen sound resigned to the predominance of the automobile, and to the decentralizing effects of the suburban shopping center.

Others outside the transit business would like to see a revival. Knowledgeable realtor Watson Bowes said "If we're going to have a core area designed around the automobile, the CBD is about as vigorous now as it will ever get. We need six or eight other 'central' business districts dispersed around the area just to accommodate the automobile traffic. "I believe transit should play a bigger role in the core area, and I feel that an adequate system will need some form of subsidy," Bowes continued.

Spread-out Denver, with its relatively low population density (6,600 persons a square mile) presents obstacles to profitable transit operation. The Development Guide noted that "In light of low density development at the fringes of the Denver Area, high automobile ownership and increasing family incomes, local transit will do well to hold onto the patronage it now has." The same Guide put an "infeasible" label on rapid rail transit. ULI's Moss took issue. "The panel considers it a mistake to write off rail rapid transit without further study," Moss wrote in 1964. "Subsidy will be required, whether it be for the highway and parking terminal system or for rail transit. Therefore, additional study should be given in order that the city may know the comparative costs."

The Downtown Improvement Association did take some notice of the room for transit improvement in its "program for action." This group "urged" Denver Tramway to run express buses on the freeways and called for a continuing study of rapid rail transit. However in late 1966 there was little evidence of any concerted movement to assign a top priority to significant transit improvements.

INCREASED DOWNTOWN EMPLOYMENT

One ULI panelist noted with some dismay Denver's unflustered anticipation of a 54 per cent increase in CBD employment during a period when transit patronage would continue to drop. This panelist was Donald C. Hyde, general manager of the Cleveland Transit System.

Hyde observed that "The inner core cannot accommodate the increased traffic to be generated by its recommendations and plans." Parking garage planning, according to Hyde, minimized both costs and parking fees. He warned of an annual subsidy of $3 to $4-million a year for the parking terminals, or else of rates triple or quadruple those recommended by the Development Guide. Hyde said conditions might compel downtown employers to move to outlying office buildings, leaving the optimistic downtown growth estimates in shambles and the whole CBD program in a state of collapse. Hyde's analysis of the Development Guide's parking and transportation plans led to one conclusion: Denver must revise the plans "to provide a better balance between transit and the private vehicle."

Compared with the peacefulness of the Rocky Mountain foothills a few miles away, downtown Denver at rush hour may seem like a hectic place indeed. But by objective measurement movement within the Denver CBD goes on with a comparative serenity unknown for many decades in some other cities of no greater size. The elongation of the business district, the reason for many of the downtown difficulties, helps dissipate congestion by dispersing traffic.

This factor is assisted by the results of enlightened planning—one-way street pairings, open curb lanes for buses, ample parking on the CBD periphery. All these antidotes to traffic strangulation were suggested by the 1955 ULI panel.

Downtown Denver will require new peaks in planning enlightenment if it is to succeed in coping with the rejuvenated lower end of downtown while attracting a new CBD work force anything close to current predictions in size. Movement within the core could become a valid cause for concern. There is disagreement on this point.

"Movement within downtown does not and will not present any problem," said Denver Tramway spokesman Baker. But planning consultant John Demsey said Denver would be prudent to start work on preparations for the style of downtown which residents will demand in a few years. Demsey, who had directed the Development Guide staff, toyed with some far-out ideas about what will be required for intra-CBD pedestrian movement—including "a second-level walkway, some development of the moving sidewalk concept, running about 1,400 feet along the main commercial street." He decided not to turn his idea into a serious proposal.

The broader issue will be whether the Master Plan Committee will gear itself for a new effort characterized by the vigor which produced the development guide in the early 1960's. Demsey said, "Denver would lose heavily by having its power structure dissolve."

The decade between 1955 and 1965 provided ample demonstration that Denver possesses capable leadership and that its downtown difficulties are not beyond correction. What seems called for in the next decade is a higher order of resourcefulness in integrating the Skyline area and the vigorous existing central business district into a far larger and better balanced core for a notably attractive city.

The 24-floor Western Federal Savings Building, built in 1962, towers over Denver. The ffice complex contains 201,000 gross square feet and was built on a 13,000 square-foot te at an estimated cost of $6.5-million.

ST. LOUIS, MISSOURI

October 11-15, 1954. Downtown St. Louis.

Panel Members Participating

Boyd T. Barnard, Jackson-Cross Co., Philadelphia —Chairman

C. J. Faherty, Prudential Insurance Co. of America, Newark

Newton C. Farr, Farr, Chinnock & Sampson, Chicago

Ernest M. Fisher, Institute for Urban Land Use & Housing Studies, Columbia Univ., New York

Joseph W. Lund, R. M. Bradley & Co., Boston

Paul L. McCord, Paul L. McCord Co., Indianapolis

Glenn McHugh, Equitable Life Assurance Society of the U.S., New York City

L. D. McKendry, Chicago Title & Trust Co., Chicago

Henry S. Miller Sr., Henry S. Miller Co., Dallas

Warren L. Morris, Ostendorf-Morris Co., Cleveland

John McC. Mowbray, Roland Park Realty Co., Baltimore

Lloyd B. Reid, Traffic and Transportation Engineer, Detroit

Walter S. Schmidt, Frederick A. Schmidt, Inc., Cincinnati

Larry Smith, Larry Smith Co., Seattle

Harley L. Swift, Harrisburg Railways Co., Harrisburg

Foster Winter, J. L. Hudson Co., Detroit

CHAPTER NINE

ST. LOUIS

IN ONE DECADE, UNSURPASSED CENTRAL CITY REVITALIZATION

St. Louis, Mo., population (1950) 856,796, (1960) 750,026, (1965) 710,000.

1954—The city was losing population, commerce and vitality during the years before the ULI panel. Its downtown retail area was suffering from suburban competition, and downtown shabbiness was growing more pronounced yearly. Although the CBD was diminishing in importance in its region, its streets were becoming traffic-clogged at a rate which compounded its problems.

The panel urged that the 16-year expressway program be compressed into five years; that transit and parking facilities be modernized; and that the local governments work toward metropolitan-level administrations of regional services.

St. Louis's record in central city revitalization during the next decade was surpassed by few, other cities. A unique organization called Civic Progress, Incorporated, and a notably effective state redevelopment law brought about a remarkable downtown transformation. It has been climaxed by construction of the Gateway Arch.

The opening line in Urban Land Institute's panel report to the sponsors of this study stated, "St. Louis must be a more convenient city in which to live and work." This simple statement could have come as no shock, or even as a mild surprise, to the civic leaders and public officials who had invited ULI to study their city and offer guidance. St. Louis in 1954 was decrepit, a city old enough to have required a massive revitalization several decades before any official assistance programs were set up and it became commonplace for political leaders—and voters—to think in terms of huge outlays for renewal.

St. Louis was a 160-year-old city, and a decaying one, when the onslaught of the Depression of the 1930's made maintaining the status quo goal enough for any city. The economy was barely set aright when World War II brought its demands on the public purpose and purse. Comparatively new cities which went through these periods suffering merely a denial of natural growth had problems enough coping with postwar expansion. But old St. Louis was crammed into 61 square miles, practically all of its land occupied, much of it by obsolescent structures. A decade and a half of unavoidable stagnation, coming at a period when time simply caught up with the buildings constructed during St. Louis's turn-of-the-century heyday, created a uniquely discouraging situation.

1946: CENTRAL CITY BLIGHT

One national magazine, *The Saturday Evening Post,* described St. Louis at the end of World War II in these terms:

"Many commercial enterprises had moved out of the city. No new office building had been built in 25 years. Schools and hospitals were mostly old and overcrowded. Downtown traffic was an impossible daily snarl (while pedestrian traffic was showing a 40 per cent drop since 1929). Slum areas infringed on the railroad station and business district. An estimated 39 per cent of all blocks in the city were blighted or ripe for wrecking.

"In the six years prior to 1952, the voters had turned down no less than five proposed bond issues for much needed public improvements," the *Post* continued. "Political and civic leadership had declined toward the vanishing point. Conservatism and complacency had engulfed a once-bustling business community."

Another publication, *Fortune* magazine, added a few gloomy figures to round out the picture. St. Louis was a city on the downgrade. In 1870 it was the third largest city in the United States. By the 1950 census, it ranked eighth, with a population of 856,800. Although industrial payrolls stood at an all-time high for St. Louis during the early stages of the post WW II boom, and the city had the lowest per capita public debt of any major city, its government was impoverished. The municipal budget for fiscal 1953 was a modest (for a city this size) $45-million. Even so, St. Louis city hall faced a $4-million budget deficit that year.

By the date of the ULI study in October, 1954, imminent disaster had been averted, through passage of an earnings tax in a popular referendum. The fact of the increased revenue, and public inclination toward improvement which the election outcome had illustrated, provided an upbeat background for the ULI panel.

At that time, any searching report on St. Louis necessarily would have given prominence to an observation that the city must, somehow, be made into a more convenient place to live and work. No matter which words were chosen to convey the thought, its essential meaning was plain. In view of the human predilection for comfort and pleasant surroundings, thousands of persons whose economic circumstances permitted them the option of leaving the city would do so. Their places would be filled by others whose economic status left them no choice but to dwell in the decaying buidings. The warning to act speedily or face an accelerated flight of the middle class residents was the unspoken "or else" suffixed to the deceptively simple statement which began the ULI report.

The ULI panel, of course, followed with more specific recommendations. Principal among these: Raze and rebuild "great segments of the close-in city." Plan and work toward "rendering regional services through a central source." Speed up the 16-year expressway plan, aiming for a five-year completion date. Vastly increase downtown parking, particularly on the rim of the core area.

ULI participated in, or at least was witness to, the beginnings

Pre-renewal St. Louis was crammed into 61 square miles, practically all of it occupied, much of it by obsolescent structures and transportation facilities.

of one of the most remarkable eras of rejuvenation experienced by any major American city. The statistics are impressive; the new visage of St. Louis even more so.

In the decade following the ULI panel, St. Louis demolished 2.5 square miles of residential slum and commercial blight. According to the urban renewal agency in that city (full title: Land Clearance for Redevelopment and Housing Authorities of St. Louis) the decade saw a $72.5-million commitment of private redevelopment funds and $126-million overall, in just one area, Mill Creek Valley. This investment is resulting in about 2,000 new dwelling units and more than 80 new commercial and industrial developments.

GATEWAY ARCH: NEW SPIRIT OF ST. LOUIS

Chamber of Commerce figures show that for 1954, the year of the ULI panel, the investment for industrial and commercial expansion in the St. Louis Metropolitan Area totalled $173.7-million. By 1966, the annual figure was up to $591.3-million.

The Chamber of Commerce trumpeted that, at the close of 1966, $2.3-billion was being spent on or was committed for industrial and commercial expansion in the metropolitan area, with an additional amount estimated at $400-million to $1-billion going for residential construction, schools and churches. The redevelopment of "great segments of the close-in city" suggested by the ULI panel is taking place with a vigor impossible to foresee in 1954.

No amount of statistical recitation can convey the new spirit of St. Louis as well as a first-hand look. Gateway Arch, a 630-foot-tall stainless steel parabola, is an audacious expression of St. Louis's ambitions as a city. The Arch stands in a national park stretching about a half mile along the Mississippi riverfront. For more than 20 years the area had been a parking lot, before that the site of a rundown warehouse district. Thirty million dollars are going into the park, three-quarters of it federal money.

No city requires a large, expensive monument in order to function as a city. Once the site for it is cleared, a monument does nothing further in a practical way to assist slum clearance, and it has no direct bearing at all on such common municipal ills as an ailing transit system or an archaic, multi-segmented metropolitan government system. St. Louis still has formidable problems in all three categories, slums, transit and governmental efficiency. But it seems clear that the existence of Gateway Arch will have an influence on St. Louis's attitude toward and attack upon its problems. Any city which can afford to invest $6-million in such a splendid geegaw can hardly claim indigence when confronted by basic concerns needing correction.

The Arch seems to fill St. Louis's need for an identity which takes into account the city's past, when it was literally the gateway for western expansion, and its future as a metropolis which is both highly industrialized and desirable as a place to live.

In addition, the Gateway Arch designed by the late Eero Saarinen is simply a beautiful and inspiring creation.

The blight which lay within the shadow of the arch was naturally regarded as incompatible, and something had to be done. Eighty-eight acres were cleared to make way for Busch Memorial Stadium, a laudable sports colosseum designed by Edward Durrell Stone and a St. Louis firm. Around the stadium are four garages with space for 7,400 cars. The rest of this redevelopment project is taken up by two office buildings, a motel and restaurant. In all, it represents an $85-million investment, all private money.

MANSION HOUSE CENTER DEVELOPMENT

Just upstream from the stadium complex, near the north base of the Arch, more of the city's downtown obsolesence has been cleared away. In its place is Mansion House Center, three 28-story apartment towers joined at the base by three-story commercial buildings. This is a $52-million investment, put together by Paul W. Lashley, a lawyer and former St. Louis Plan Commission member, and Lewis E. Kitchen, a developer headquartered in Kansas City.

Mansion House is located in an area which, to the ULI panel in 1954, seemed destined for office building use. The panel reported that high land values near the national park, between Washington Avenue and Chestnut Street, eliminated a number of reuses including motels and residential development.

"The negative factor of high land value plus the fact that it would be impossible to establish a sufficiently large residential environment acts against the development of luxury apartments there," the panel said. In 1954, this was true. But St. Louis had become a different investment market once it had proved, to itself and the rest of the country, that it could halt its downslide.

Business Week offered an interesting sidelight on the Mansion House developers' efforts to win approval and financing. Lashley, who was described as "not of the Establishment but now being accepted," said he received "a lot of support from the right business leaders" at home. But apparently this was not easy, at first. "St. Louis is still a city which does not really appreciate its own worth," Lashley told *Business Week.* "At first, I often found it easier to sell outsiders than some of our own citizens. Fortunately, this attitude is changing."

When Lashley and Kitchen went looking for capital, they found the stadium developers had dried up available St. Louis financing sources, according to the *Business Week* account. Mansion House, and in effect the future of downtown St. Louis, had to be "sold" to outsiders, and this was done. The General Electric pension fund acquired the land under a leaseback arrangement. Alcoa Aluminum provided preliminary financing. Mellon National Bank and Trust Co. and John Hancock Mutual Life Insurance Company handled the permanent financing through FHA-backed loans.

A St. Louis realtor and ULI trustee, Clarence M. Turley, said he "questioned the implication" of the *Business Week* account and called it "unfair to local interests."

Turley recalled that two rival plans for redeveloping this area had been submitted, one exclusively by St. Louis interests, the other the Lashley-Kitchen Mansion House proposal. The City Plan Commission and Board of Aldermen decision in favor of Mansion House, according to Turley, "Was largely influenced by Kitchen's apparent success in the downtown development of Quality Hill in Kansas City.

"Although Lashley was identified with the (Mansion House) project as vice president and counsel, Kitchen was put forward as the real developer," Turley continued. "As it turned out, Lashley became the active party in connection with the program. While Kitchen is now chairman of the board, Lashley became president and general counsel, and we hear very little of Mr. Kitchen's actual connection with the project."

Turley said that St. Louis financing was not necessarily unavailable.

"In spite of what Lashley had to say about local money, Kitchen brought in Alcoa at a time when its activities were expanding," Turley said. "And in addition to the initial money it put up, Alcoa was touted as the financial and development entity behind the project. As things developed in the Alcoa picture nationally, they bowed out of this project."

There was local financial involvement in Mansion House from the beginning, Turley explained. "The original money for land acquisition was supplied principally by three downtown St. Louis banks," he said. "And when the present so-called.limited partnership arrangement was worked out, the Mercantile Trust Company turned out to be the largest owner of limited partnership interest in the project."

The overriding fact in all this is that there was no scarcity of investment funds in what became a successful venture.

Kitchen told this reporter that ULI's 1954 recommendation for office buildings in what became the Mansion House area was probably the correct one at the time. "But times change," said Kitchen, "and so do conditions, the most significant shift in this case being widespread revitalization of the area around Gateway Arch and plaza.

"We have learned that pinpoint renewal just will not work," Kitchen said. "But when the overall environment is improved, as it was here, then all sorts of possibilities are opened."

Mansion House's 1,250 apartments were 40 per cent occupied at the time of the Kitchen interview, in April, 1967. "All things considered, we have a successful project," Kitchen said. The market for downtown middle-class apartments is "limited," according to the developer. "But in a city this size, when only two or three per cent of the population constitute a market, that still means 10,000 to 15,000 people. We have about 1,900 persons in Mansion House already. We have no complaints with the way this has turned out."

URBAN REDEVELOPMENT CORPORATION LAW OF 1949

The design for St. Louis's reemergence was beginning to take shape at the time of the ULI panel. Two elements in the St. Louis story predominate—a law and a civic organization. Without the Urban Redevelopment Corporation Law of 1949, and without Civic Progress Inc., renewal could not have proceeded so rapidly or so well.

The redevelopment law was designed to encourage private investment in central city renewal, principally through a 25-year partial abatement on ad valorem taxes. The Missouri Legislature made the act applicable only to cities with more than 350,000 population; it is a St. Louis and Kansas City law.

Former Mayor (1943-49) Aloys Kaufmann said the language of the redevelopment law was "practically written" in the offices of New York insurance companies.

Kaufman had come to regard the then-new federal urban renewal program as potentially the most effective weapon against St. Louis's enormous blight problem, and he wanted to move quickly. Kaufman's foray into New York financial circles produced only disappointment. "They performed a service for us, however," the former mayor said. "They told us in detail why St. Louis was a bad risk." The redevelopment act was drafted in direct rebuttal to the objections raised in New York.

Redevelopment corporations are permitted an 8 per cent annual return on their investments. The tax break is considerable. For the first ten years the corporation pays no taxes on improvements, and the land is taxed only on the pre-redevelopment assessment. Then, for the next fifteen years taxes are based on half the total updated land plus improvements. By one expert calculation, the city reaches the break-even point in ad valorem taxes from a redevelopment project at about the 13th year. Once clearance has begun, the city reaps a saving in services it would have provided, principally police and fire protection, if the area had been left in its blighted state.

A redevelopment corporation may function only in an area declared blighted by the City Board of Aldermen. State law endows the redevelopment corporation with the power of eminent domain.

Restrictions on redevelopment corporations are loose. The law stipulates that such corporations must be organized "to serve a public purpose" and that what it builds must "promote the public health, safety and welfare."

A former federal deputy commissioner for urban renewal, Charles L. Farris, was director of the Clearance for Redevelopment Authority when it began administering the act. Farris told the ULI panel that a redeveloper must participate in competitive bidding (though the "best" plan and not necessarily the highest dollar bid may be accepted). The winning bidder must begin construction "without unnecessary delay."

"But other than that," Farris told the ULI panel, "there are no restrictions on the redeveloper, except the proviso he has in his contract to extend priority to low-middle-income displaced families, and the usual terminology that you find in government contracts." In practice, redevelopments under the Missouri corporation law often have taken place in blighted, non-residential parts of St. Louis. The sports stadium and Mansion House projects both had the assistance of the redevelopment corporation law, but had no worries about rehousing lower income displaced families.

1951: TAX ABATEMENT FOR PLAZA SQUARE: $1-MILLION TAX GAIN

The first renewal project in St. Louis, Plaza Square, did involve some displacement of persons. This pilot project cleared a 14-acre slum tract which included "skid row" and lay embarrassingly close to city hall and the main commerical district. The skid row inhabitants did not fit any category in the law which gave any sort of priority for relocation in the old neighborhood after redevelopment. The Plaza area was rebuilt to contain an office building, six middle-class apartment towers (with rents currently ranging from $95 to $195 a month), and a two-acre park along a major traffic artery.

As the pilot project, Plaza Square had implications and an importance farther-reaching than the boundaries of its area. "If Plaza Square had failed, I honestly believe it would have been the end of urban renewal in St. Louis," former Mayor Kaufmann said. However, this project bore out the ULI panel's endorsement: "This proposed multi-family residential reconstruction will be successful," the panel report said, although it pointed out that commercial re-use under the 1954 housing act would have been less costly to federal and city agencies involved.

The history of Plaza Square in effect educated St. Louis on the workings of renewal and the redevelopment act, illustrating that temporary setbacks do not rule out a successful venture overall.

The pioneer Urban Redevelopment Corporation was formed in 1951 for the Plaza Square project. The *St. Louis Post-Dispatch* got the funding drive started with subscription of $250,000. Despite the tax advantages for such corporations, it was a tedious process funding the initial redevelopment corporation. About 70 individuals and businesses became partners in Plaza Square. The public funds investment was not approved until late 1953. A $1.5-million bond issue item was turned down in March of that year and finally passed on resubmission to the voters in November, 1953. At the time of the ULI panel, Farris was predicting that demolition would begin in January, 1955.

More difficulties were to come. Occupancy in what turned out to be a $21-million dollar project lagged, and, as reported by *Business Week,* Plaza Square was "in technical default to FHA since the first payment was due." Plaza Square's shakedown period was continuing as recently as September, 1965, when a nonprofit group took over one of the apartment towers as a residence for elderly persons.

By early 1967, Plaza Square was 95 per cent occupied, its FHA loan was current, and all delinquencies were paid up.

In summary, Plaza Square must be regarded as a successful venture. It removed the worst mid-town eyesore. St. Louis residents and outsiders had a demonstration that the various laws covering redevelopment carried safeguards against financial disaster. St. Louis also had the satisfaction of seeing an urban renewal project carried through to completion, the only one wrapped up as of March, 1967.

Finally, there was a case history of how the tax abatement works in practice, and evidence that the theoretical arithmetic actually does rebound to the city treasury's advantage over the long haul.

Figures compiled by the Land Clearance for Redevelopment Authority show:

Before redevelopment, annual ad valorem tax receipts of $61,000 from the Plaza area. For the first 10 years after redevelopment, tax receipts of $35,878 a year, and for 1971 through 1986 (the period of 50 per cent payment) $146,232 a year. During the 25 year term of tax abatement, the gain in ad valorem revenues to the city would be roughly $1-million.

This kind of ledger-book evidence silenced the commonly heard complaints against tax abatements by owners of property not covered by the exemption. Clarence M. Turley, the realtor who is a member of Civic Progress, Inc. and an Urban Land Institute trustee, recently recalled that "Complaints against the tax benefits were heard in the beginning, but not lately. People came to realize how little taxes the city was getting from the old buildings. Besides the increased property taxes from the redeveloped areas, the city has benefitted by the sales taxes and the impetus to the construction industry brought about by redevelopment."

Some understandable resentment did arise when the current mayor, A. J. Cervantes, suggested that perhaps the way to stimulate scattered redevelopment in the midst of the central business district would be to apply an official "blighted" designation to the entire district. With that done, the redevelopment law's tax advantages and eminent domain powers could be used to promote redevelopment of midtown's many vacant lots and obsolete old buildings. The newer, more productive existing structures would, of course, be unaffected directly. But the indirect effect of the tax abatement would have been considerable.

Downtown property owners were pleased to see some of the scruffiest areas converted to bright, new uses such as a sports stadium. However, the prospect of seeing a new competitive structure arise next door, its developers bolstered by the advantage of tax abatement, was more than most property owners would abide.

The Cervantes plan was quickly scaled down to cover three separate square blocks downtown. However, progress on these pocket-sized redevelopments was delayed while city and state attorneys pondered the ambiguities of the redevelopment law concerning the minimum size for a "blighted" area. There was a possibility of litigation to settle the question of tax-advantaged redevelopment of relatively small central city parcels. Apparently such a court test would be a "friendly" suit, but all-out legal assaults on the redevelopment law have been many—and have established the basic constitutionality of its key provisions.

The United States Supreme Court has upheld the validity of the tax abatement feature, finding in effect that the law did not impinge on the rights of owners whose property was not covered by the tax abatement.

CIVIC CENTER REDEVELOPMENT CORPORATION AND BUSCH MEMORIAL STADIUM

Refinements in application of the redevelopment act were worked out in recent St. Louis projects. The Civic Center Redevelopment Corporation, organized for the $89-million sports stadium and other buildings in the complex, worked in close partnership with the Land Clearance for Redevelopment Authority. Former Authority Director Farris told of some of the details of the cooperation. The land acquired and cleared by the authority was held in public ownership as long as possible so there would be no taxes due on it. Meanwhile, the initial $22-million capitalization for the project raised locally was held on deposit and accrued interest. Satisfied with both the overall economic feasibility and the acumen of the St. Louis developers, The Equitable Life Assurance Society made a $33.5-million, 30-year, 6 per cent mortgage loan on the stadium. This home arena of the baseball and football Cardinals is a deficit operation itself, but revenues from the parking garages and ground rentals on adjacent project sites, such as the one for the new Pet Milk Company headquarters office building, are holding the entire project over the break-even point.

The success of the Busch Memorial Stadium complex required a high degree of business acumen abetted by the tax abatement under Missouri's redevelopment corporation law. The list of officers and directors of the Civic Center Redevelopment Corporation was practically synonymous with a roster of the city's business elite. For example, the president is James P. Hickock, board chairman of the First National Bank of St. Louis; chairman of the executive committee is Preston Estep, board chairman of the Bank of St. Louis.

With all the high-powered help it received, the stadium complex project was still spread over the better part of a decade, from the idea to the actual use. Chairman Farris of the Land Clearance for Redevelopment Authority conceived the proposal in 1958 for this reuse of a sorely blighted downtown area. The first baseball game was played in new Busch Stadium in May, 1966. It was difficult to find anyone in St. Louis who did not contend, enthusiastically, that the result was worth the effort.

Many cities have had the experience of one downtown renewal project begetting another. The Stadium Project and Mansion House eventually will be joined, on the upriver side, by another major high-rise structure and possibly satellite buildings. Two bidders are competing for the right to redevelop the riverfront area between Eads and Veterans bridges. One proposal calls for a 46-story tower building.

Gateway Arch seems to fill St. Louis's need for an identity which takes into account the city's past and its future. It was literally the gateway for western expansion. Its future is as a metropolis which is both highly industrialized and a desirable place to live.

MILL CREEK VALLEY: 460 ACRES OF BLIGHT

St. Louis's largest urban renewal project, Mill Creek Valley, required ingenious application of state and federal renewal aids because of the area's sheer vastness and dilapidation.

Four hundred and sixty acres of extreme blight constituted this not-so-green "valley" on the western periphery of the central core. The pre-renewal inventory of Mill Creek Valley made by the St. Louis renewal agency presented a grim recitation: 99 per cent of the 2,100 structures needed major repairs; 80 per cent of dwelling units had no bath or toilet, and more than two-thirds lacked even running water.

The city had plans for redevelopment. At the late-1964 stage of this planning, the area was parceled out among a variety of uses: residential, commercial, industrial, expressway rights-of-way, and a 22-acre expansion area for St. Louis University. ULI panelists studied the proposal and observed in their report that "We approve the general plan for this area as it has been presented to us." ULI particularly applauded using the portion served by railroad tracks and close to the expressways for industrial uses. "St. Louis is seriously short of land available for industrial uses," the panel said "and feels very strongly that this is an ideal location for the placement of light industry." ULI trustee Turley observed seven years later that "The Mill Creek Valley project has been laid out substantially as approved by the panel." The only major deviation was the shifting of one area from heavy to light industrial use to make best use of the final railroad track and expressway delineation.

When Mill Creek Valley is completed by 1970, it will contain a private investment of more than $200-million. The public portion of the financing involved some write-down of cleared land costs, and a complex interworking of two redevelopment corporations, one St. Louis-based and the other a New York combine.

The St. Louis Redevelopment Corporation ended up with about 65 per cent of the total Valley area, including all the industrial and commercial acreage plus about half the residential. However, according to Turley, an official of the redevelopment corporation, the St. Louis group, all realtors, has provided between 80 and 85 per cent of the total private investment in Mill Creek Valley.

Mill Creek Valley—460 acres of blight before renewal—will, when completed, reflect a private investment of more than $200-million.

"This required lots of capital," Turley said. "State law says 6 per cent is the most we can pay for mortgage money, and the anti-speculation feature of federal law prevents any resale until construction is completed."

Turley, who is treasurer and executive committee chairman of the St. Louis Redevelopment Corporation, was the object of considerable public criticism after the vast Mill Creek Valley tract was cleared and for a time sat vacant. "Hiroshima Flats" was a name popularly given to the area.

"Time has proven that we were right," Turley said. "This was such a lousy slum (sic) that it would have been disastrous to try to demolish part of it and rebuild some new housing in the midst of the old. If we tried to get respectable people to live in there, surrounded by the slums and the crime that was prevalent, there would have been extreme difficulty."

Now, the term "Hiroshima Flats" is part of St. Louis's dimly-remembered past. Mill Creek Valley is widely applauded.

Mill Creek Valley adds up to a tremendous net plus for the local economy as a result of helpful public renewal laws, a general business climate encouraging investment, and skill in putting together investment packages.

1953: CIVIC PROGRESS, INC.

Members of the ULI 1964 panel such as Glenn McHugh, a New York investment consultant, recently expressed no surprise at St. Louis's rejuvenation. ULI's report contained the observation that "It is the judgment of this panel that this city can have an extraordinary future if its citizens band together in a strong and energetic movement to reach a group of specifically designated objectives. There is evidence that many of your community leaders have become infused with zeal in this cause." The reference was to Civic Progress Inc., one of the sponsors of the panel study.

This organization began inauspiciously, organized by city counselor James E. Crowe at the behest of the 1949-53 mayor, Joseph M. Darst. *The St. Louis Post-Dispatch* reported that Darst felt "Something new was needed because he could not seem to get anything done in St. Louis." Mayor Darst, unfortunately, did not work a great transformation in his city during his term, although he did initiate public housing.

The Post-Dispatch at the time was attempting to arouse civic and political leaders with a series of reports titled "Progress or Decay? St. Louis Must Choose." It is significant that the politicians were first to become aroused, if only enough to recruit a blue-ribbon civic committee ostensibly to help achieve progress instead of surrendering to decay. *Business Week* records a "deep-rooted apathy" in St. Louis at that time, and added that "In the city's decline, the old Establishment had taken to suburban living, turning its back on city problems."

Fortune magazine said "The traditional contentment of St. Louis had turned to stagnation; the stagnation had become decay."

The unproductive early days of Civic Progress, Inc. demonstrated that such organizations do not thrive when there is no empathy with local political leaders.

This situation changed with the 1953 election, which put an educator, Raymond R. Tucker, into city hall. Tucker, who was chairman of the Department of Mechanical Engineering at Washington University, was not exactly a neophyte in government. He had been an executive assistant to a pre-war mayor, was a former Director of Public Safety and Civil Defense Director. Recollections are now a little hazy around St. Louis as to precisely what prompted business executive Sidney Salomon, formerly treasurer of the Democratic National Committee, to recruit Tucker. But obviously the move was not that standard ploy in the game of politics, the search by a worried organization for a "respectable" but naive and malleable outsider as a candidate.

Tucker did not fit that mold, and twenty-three of the twenty-eight city Democratic ward leaders supported not the college professor but an "organization man," Mark Eagleton. There followed the most significant campaign in St. Louis history, with the "citizens committee" backed by business leaders brought at last into active open combat with the dominant political organization. Tucker received the Democratic nomination for mayor by a mere 1,500-vote margin but won easily in the general election. He took office in April, 1953. When Tucker surveyed the state of municipal affairs, he concluded, like Mayor Darst before him, that resources greater than those then available to city hall were needed. The difference in Tucker's case was that he was able to elicit the full confidence of the business community. The first meaningful meeting of Civic Progress, Inc. was held in Tucker's office on September 10, 1953, five months after the new mayor took office.

Civic Progress, Inc. is a loosely-knit coalition of the business community's elite. Its general makeup has changed little since the beginning, and in 1967 the membership included the presidents or board chairmen of six banks; the presidents of Anheuser-Busch and Falstaff brewing companies, Pet (Milk) Inc., Monsanto (Chemical) Co.; the board chairmen of Union Electric Co., Emerson Electric Co., Ralston Purina; the president of St. Louis University and the Chancellor of Washington University.

This organization's rules of procedure have proven extremely effective:

The members themselves perform the work of the organization. There is no delegating to subordinates. The nature of the St. Louis "establishment," with its predominance of personal and family control of business and industry, permitted the top men to devote the necessary time for civic work.

Civic Progress does not initiate projects. It offers (or withholds) support from activities suggested by others.

The 1967 Chairman of the Board of Civic Progress, David R. Calhoun, said "We are careful not to initiate civic projects. We don't have a planned objective, a program to put across. There has never been a desire in the organization to dominate. Possibly we are not as imaginative as we should be, but then that was not what Civic Progress was created for."

Calhoun, who is board chairman and president of St. Louis Union Trust Co., gave this explanation to illustrate an unwritten policy for Civic Progress members—that they do not want the organization to become established as, or be regarded as, the "power structure" of the community. However, that is what it is.

Certainly all the elements of what is usually regarded as a community's power structure are present in Civic Progress. However, the organization has chosen to speak softly and carry no stick at all. Instead the members apply their talents towards fund-raising and public educational campaigns for worthwhile but easily misrepresented causes, such as tax increases and bond issue proposals.

To the outside observer, these tactics seem peculiarly suited for St. Louis. Civic Progress as an entity receives almost no publicity. In the political guerrilla warfare which usualy crops up during controversial referenda, Civic Progress presents a diffused image, a hard-to-define target for the highly organized opposition groups such as political machines and labor organizations.

The organization has no staff, except for the part-time services of a public relations firm executive, Harry B. Wilson.

Wilson said the cost of maintaining a staff had no bearing on the decision to proceed without one. "The Civic Progress people decided very early that the top men, the members themselves, would do the work," Wilson said. "So if there was no staff to take over the responsibilities, the members themselves would have to take on these responsibilities."

Wilson cited other reasons. "A staff tends to find ways to keep busy to justify its continued existence. The Civic Progress members did not want to be pulled into all sorts of projects dreamed up by a staff trying to keep busy."

Campaigning to pass bond issues has been a prime accomplishment of the organization, but it does not become involved in political races between candidates. "This is not a particularly powerful group of men in political affairs," Wilson said. "Politics has never been much of an avocation with many of them. Probably they could not swing much political weight, in the sense of influencing votes for candidates, if they tried. These mens' homes and businesses are scattered all over the metroplitan area; there's not enough of them in any one community or district.

"And don't forget that this is a heavily unionized city," Wilson said. The unions are politically active, he added, and "I think most Civic Progress members would have trouble influencing their own employees' vote if they wanted to, which they don't."

Despite its limitations, most of them self-imposed, Civic Progress has been a remarkably successful mover and shaker. The organization has been called "the driving force behind every major civic improvement since its organization" by former mayor Tucker.

1954: ½% EARNINGS TAX PASSED

Civic Progress's first contribution toward the success of Mayor Tucker's 12-year tenure was one of its most significant. This was assistance in passing the half per cent earnings tax which staved off bankruptcy for the City of St. Louis. A temporary tax granted by the Missouri Legislature was expiring. First, Tucker and former Mayor Kaufmann stumped the state together and won support for a new bill making the tax permanent. But it had to pass a city referendum.

The late Powell McHaney, who was president of General American Life Insurance and first president of Civic Progress, took charge of the campaign. About $50,000 was raised for advertising and other expenses, and donated aid including billboard space and free radio-TV time was worth an estimated $50,000.

The pro-politicians were in an ambivalent position. They knew the earnings tax revenue was needed, but they worried about a voter rebellion against it. Civic Progress, in addition to spending money, sent some members on personal stumping tours into the neighorhoods.

The tax carried by an astonishing 6 to 1 margin.

The following year, 1955, Civic Progress waged a similar campaign for Tucker's $110-million public improvements bond issue. The once moribund city, its electorate noted for reluctance to incur public debt, approved the huge issue by an 8 to 1 margin. The same year a $39-million St. Louis County bond issue was put across.

Another notable success for Civic Progress was its role in passing a 1962 bond issue to finance the first area-wide service for the St. Louis area's jumble of political jurisdictions. This was the $95-million Metropolitan Sewer District.

Civic Progress members have been active in downtown renewal efforts. For illustration, all but two of the 13 members of the board of directors of the Civic Center Redevelopment Corporation are also Civic Progress members. One exception is board deputy of an industry whose president and chief executive officer is in Civic Progress, and the other is a labor organization official.

Currently, with Tucker out of public life and back at Washington University, and the big revenue and bond battles won, there is some question whether Civic Progress will maintain its former effectiveness. The concensus seems to be that it will, but with its operations recast to fit changing conditions.

SOCIO-ECONOMIC PROBLEMS NOW PREDOMINATE

St. Louis's present-day problems concern minority groups and poverty, the extension of metropolitan governmental services and the plight of its floundering transit system. A continuing problem is slum eradication and better housing. *The St. Louis Globe-Democrat* noted in an editorial April 15, 1967, that "About 25 per cent of the residential sections of St. Louis are rated as slums. This is a shockingly high figure, and much work must be done to correct the situation. How do we go about it? . . . We need law enforcement, minimum standards of decency on the part of both landlords and tenants, and more initiative on the part of investors."

Civic Progress's part-time aide, Harry Wilson, spoke frankly and realistically of Civic Progress's current role. "The time has passed when the most pressing problems were the kind that businessmen are equipped to deal with," he said, "matters like passing bond issues and building things. But now we are in a period when the city's problems are socio-economic, and this kind of group has no special competence in this field."

However, Civic Progress is making the attempt. Its work in cooperation with the anti-poverty program has been important, although peripheral. Civic Progress assisted in starting the organization "Work Opportunities Unlimited," a retraining and job-placement agency for persons at the lower end of the economy. Civic Progress pays half the salary of the director, pushing the figure high enough to attract a top-grade administrator, and it provides office space for this agency.

In the direct attack on blight, St. Louis has been attempting to persuade the Legislature to pass enabling laws for an Industrial Expansion Authority, which could offer special inducements to new industry and provide the sites, cleared slum areas.

If the 1954 ULI panel could be brought back into session, its greatest disappointment in viewing St. Louis 13 years later would probably concern the transit system. The panel used the word "splendid" to describe the system and recommended certain tax exemptions as an aid to transit's competition with private automobile travel into downtown. By 1967, the transit system was operated by the quasi-public Bi-State Development Agency, and was in desperate financial shape. *The Globe-Democrat* reported that the system had a net operating loss of $1.25-million a year. The newspaper commented that, in regarding the transit problem, "We must confess that we do not have the answer any more than the transit officials or the public officials involved."

The aspect which would probably bring the 1954 panel the greatest sense of accomplishment, if it could take another look at St. Louis,

would be the expressway system. ULI looked at the 1954 expressway plans, and advised a rapid speed-up in what was then considered
a 16-year program.

The acceleration did take place, and downtown St. Louis is ser-
viced, or soon will be, by four major super-highways and an expressway loop around mid-city—all either built, under construction,
or approved.

The super-roads are part of the St. Louis rebirth in terms of
concrete and steel. The city began moving slowly, but soon achieved
a pace and record of success which place it back among the "first
rank" of American cities, a position which the city had lost in the
mid-1950's.

The efforts toward physical revitalization and human rehabilitation, the socio-economic challenge concerning Civic Progress and
others, appear to be more closely entwined than do similar efforts
in other cities. St. Louis has the opportunity now to become a
pace-setter among big cities in the more sophisticated total renewal
effort of the years ahead.

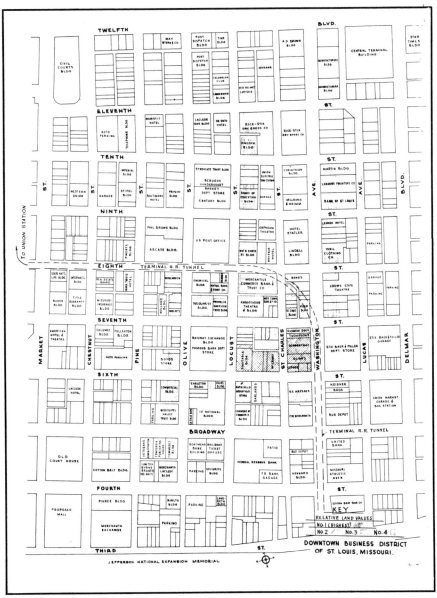

St. Louis's Downtown Business District.

DETROIT, MICHIGAN

February 14-18, 1955. Downtown Detroit: A Report to The Detroit News, Sponsor.

Panel Members Participating

Clarence M. Turley, Clarence M. Turley, Inc., St. Louis—Chairman

David D. Bohannon, David D. Bohannon Organization, San Mateo, California

Randall H. Cooper, President, State Street Council, Chicago

Newton C. Farr, Farr, Chinnock & Sampson, Realtors, Chicago

Cyrus A. Hackstaff, Frederick R. Ross Investment Co., Denver

Philip W. Kniskern, First Mortgage Corporation, Philadelphia

Warren L. Morris, Ostendorf-Morris Co., Cleveland —President, ULI

B. R. Sayer, The Austin Co., Cleveland

Walter S. Schmidt, Frederick A. Schmidt, Inc., Cincinnati—Chairman, Industrial Council, ULI

Larry Smith, Larry Smith & Co., Seattle & New York

Roswell F. Thoma, Niagara Frontier Transit System, Buffalo

Richard S. Willis, New England Mutual Life Insurance Co., Boston

CHAPTER TEN

DETROIT

REMOLDING THE STYLE AND SUBSTANCE OF LIVING IN THE CORE OF MOTOR CITY

Detroit, Mich., population (1950) 1,849,568, (1960) 1,670,144, (1965) 1,660,000.

1955—This city had hoped to move rapidly, as soon as post-World War II conditions permitted, in ridding itself of one of the nation's classic mid-town residential slums, a degraded spread of inferior construction which had become worse through neglect. In-decision—or more accurately a welter of conflicting decisions—impeded planning for this urgent renewal effort.

The ULI panel which answered Detroit's call for objective advice was one of the most far-sighted in the long history of the Central City Council. The panel's advice helped guide Detroit away from the then prevalent notion that the only persons willing to inhabit the central city were those who had neither the choice nor the means to do otherwise. Detroit was advised that the heart of the city should be made available to, and attractive for, the more productive portion of the population.

The success of Detroit's central city renewal effort has placed it in the front rank of American cities which have made city life once again a varied, interesting, comfortable experience. And, Detroit has demonstrated that accommodation of the automobile and of urban esthetics are not necessarily incompatible goals.

During the 1960's the inadequacies of urban life in the intensely urbanized United States became the source material for public debate, legislation, protest, riot, emotional lamentations, and also for meaningful planning and reconstruction. In many cities which have made significant progress in renewal, there has been much concern with the search for civic identity; an "image," in the jargon of the times.

Dallas residents underwent an examination of civic conscience in search of "goals." St. Louis rediscovered its history as a "gateway" to American expansion and hoped the remembrance of glories past could enhance the uncertain future. Philadelphia stripped away the decadence surrounding its "cradle of liberty" made an unabashed commitment to a modern application of the old, simple virtues like patriotism and civic pride.

In short, the renewal of the great cities was found to involve more than the replacement of one era's bricks and mortar with another's glass and steel. The quality of human existence possible within a city became the ultimate criterion for its successes in renewal.

One city which has made a conscious effort to weave esthetic considerations into the fabric of its renewal effort is Detroit. One recent public utterance of the City Plan Commission includes these observations:

"In the contemporary American city, the places where people spend most of their lives are those places where our society has all too often created confusion and visual blight. . . . It is inconsistent to attempt to teach civic pride and a full appreciation of the creative arts to children, while denying them beautiful surroundings.

"Children today do not have an enviroment which will help to produce creativity. They do not have the day-to-day associations which will act as catalysts to the mind.

"BEAUTY IS ESSENTIAL"

"To believe that beauty is essential and that it will leave lasting impressions on the public mind and on the personalities of children and adults alike, to stop feeling apologetic about attempts to feed spiritual hunger, to stop trying by computers to justify every item of expenditure intended to add beauty to the city—these will be long steps toward releasing the creative powers of the architects and designers in the arts of landscape architecture, scultpure and urban design."

This is a remarkable statement, coming as it does from an official body in a city long noted for making unrelieved bleakness synonymous with industrialization.

For Detroit there is no uncertainty over image. This city has been, is and will continue to be known as "Motortown," the place where unending millions of automobiles are built. The motorcar has outsped the efforts of the city planners around the nation to cope with it, and has been a prime cause of many urban problems. The flight to the suburbs was made on rubber-tired wheels. Traffic congestion glutted downtown streets and helped pollute the air. The supposed remedies—land-devouring freeways and massive parking garages— sometimes were given overriding priority in renewal projects, to the detriment of the amenity of the overall plan.

Part of Detroit's restitution to the damaged design of urban life has been its demonstration that a city can be both automobile-oriented and a civilized place to live.

The ULI Central City Council panel which studied Detroit in 1955 found the expressway system design "remarkably well thought out." In use, the Detroit freeway system does an admirable job of linking the central business district with the widely-dispersed suburbs, and in recent years has provided mobility in both directions for residents of the new close-in neighborhoods in renewal areas. The routing of the expressways was carried out with consideration for the wishes of the downtown merchants, planners, redevelopers and suburban interests, which in Detroit include both residents and major industries.

Panelist Newton Farr of Chicago commented during the 1955 session that "Detroit is an automobile town," not only in its principal item of manufacture but in the travel habits of its populace. Renewal has been carried out within the pervasive influence of this fact, with no violence done to the principles of comfortable living. That alone, in Detroit's renewal efforts, would be distinction enough to merit recording in a place where other large cities might see it."

Urban renewal has been used to remold the style and substance of living in the core city. Nearly 10,000 acres have been redeveloped or rehabilitated through neighorhood conservation. Acquiring and clearing several blighted areas, twenty-nine in number, has cost $177-million. Official records indicate that "The value of redevelopment exceeds one billion dollars."

LAFAYETTE PARK—CLASSIC RENEWAL CLASH

One renewal project is particularly noteworthy—193-acre La-fayette Park lying just east of the central business district. What students of Detroit renewal call "a classic slum" was cleared during a long, continuing controversy over relocation of its 2,100 families and over plans for development. Lafayette Park also presents a classic study in the clash of renewal philosophies.

This slum clearance project was begun in 1946, before any federally assisted programs except public housing. It was 10 years before the area was completely cleared. At the heart of the controversy was the reuse issue—whether the area should be redeveloped to resume its old de facto role of containing a large part of the low-income Negro populace, or whether the former slum would be re-designed to attract middle and upper-income groups back to central city living.

At first, planning was built around a policy commitment to public and low-income housing. But in the end, Lafayette Park became a middle-to-upper-income neighborhood of apartments and townhouses, except for portions put to commercial, institutional, and park uses. The ULI panel's recommendation was a significant factor in the decisions which led to plan changes.

ULI said that the central city renewal effort "should be directed towards a step-up in accommodations, not downwards to the bottom of the income group. Detroit has a great mass of good workers able to pay economic prices. . . . These are the great, solid heart of your city's life. Orient your program accordingly."

The late Walter S. Schmidt, founder and first president of ULI, served on the Detroit panel and threw his experience and consider-

Lafayette Park, once termed a "classic slum," was rebuilt as a middle-to-upper-income neighborhood of apartments and townhouses with some space devoted to commercial, institutional and park uses.

able prestige behind the efforts of Detroiters favoring higher grade redevelopment.

Strangely, this initial and most significant of all Detroit renewal projects was not the subject of any of the questions posed by the sponsors to the ULI panel. However, the future of the "Gratiot Tract," as the Lafayette Park area was then known, was raised during the questions-from-the-floor period following the panel's presentation. Panel chairman Clarence Turley of St. Louis said, "I was hoping somebody would ask about that." On its own intiative the panel had studied the renewal project and had prepared a supplemental report. The dean of ULI panelists, Schmidt, made a presentation which had specific and general applications.

"It is the feeling of the panel," Schmidt said, "that as slums are wiped out, as they should be in increasing degree in your city, the land thus recovered should be put to its best use for the best benefit of the future city. We feel that such residential construction should not be in the form of the lowest-rent type of property, because that may become a slum again."

Schmidt continued, "We feel that this close-in construction should be attractive to persons who are able to pay an economic rent for modern apartments or for homes that would normally be constructed elsewhere in the region for your better paid workers. In other words, we feel that this close-in city, much of which will have to be rebuilt, should be stepped up instead of down in those whom it accommodates.

"That is only logical for the reason that homes are permanent wealth," Schmidt added. "They should last for 100 years or more. We feel that this central district is a convenient spot for living, and that accommodations can be provided there."

The Detroit panel was made up of men who appeared to share an antipathy for public housing, which at that time figured prominently in the city's redevelopment concepts. The earliest plan for the Gratiot area proposed 3,600 units of public housing. By the time of the ULI panel, the public housing allotment in the renewal project was down to 900 units. Panel members were critical but not unequivocally opposed to this much public housing.

"I don't think the 900 units would be too detrimental to the project if they were separated from the rest," Turley said. Schmidt said public housing would not be "too damaging" but still would be "detrimental" and "a discouragement to those that want to do something."

BY 1955, 8,000 PUBLIC HOUSING UNITS BUILT—NONE SINCE

In the end, no public housing went into the Gratiot-Lafayette Park area. In fact, Detroit, which had built 8,155 public housing units up to that time, has constructed no additional units since 1955. There are a number of reasons for this turn of events, but apparently these do not include lack of compassion for the plight of economically distressed families.

Tied as it is to the automobile industry, Detroit has shared its remarkably profitable growth period since World War II. For 1965 average weekly factory earnings in the metropolitan area were $151, and, gauged by wages and salaries paid to all persons covered by Social Security, Detroit ranked first nationally. During this period of affluence, the need for public housing diminished.

A diligent rehabilitation effort resulted in sufficient adequate low-rent private housing. Nearly 8,000 acres of the city have been upgraded by neighborhood conservation efforts. This form of renewal carried the strong recommendation of the ULI panel as the alternative to more public housing. The panel was not unfeeling in its regard for housing low-income families, as might appear from a reading of its public-housing comments alone, without reference to the further recommendation for extensive rehabilitation.

"It costs a lot of money to put brick and mortar together," said panel member Cyrus A. Hackstaff of Denver. "There are a great many dwellings within every city, especially older cities, which under an ordinance that insisted on safe and sanitary conditions could be made available for the type of people that would ordinarily go into public housing. They would not only have cheaper rent, but would get away from the ghetto living that public housing encourages."

Hackstaff pointed out that non-institutionalized housing "would integrate them (lower-income families) into the general population, where the finger of charity is not so easily pointed at them as it is while living in public housing."

The weight which the ULI panel's recommendations carried was enhanced by the fact that the sponsor was *The Detroit News,* the city's largest and most influential newspaper. *The News'* extensive coverage of the ULI report ànd its aftermath drilled the findings and recommendations into the public consciousness.

The panel's assignment from the sponsors was wide-ranged, covering such downtown essentials as parking, the promotion of the central business district's attractions for shoppers then being lured to suburban centers, and, of course, downtown renewal.

The panel found no major fault with the existing parking expansion plan, a $16-million development. ULI created a stir with its endorsement of two additional sites which long had been mired in controversy—municipal parking garages beneath Cadillac Square and Washington Boulevard. Also, the panel warned that without the transit system, the downtown parking demand would be twice as intense.

The city-owned bus system since has drawn patronage from the new, close-in residential areas. When the panel session was held, there was a stirring of interest in setting up a rail transit system linking the suburbs to downtown. ULI called this infeasible because of Detroit's automotive orientation, which soon would be abetted by the excellent freeway system.

The panel advised the city not to fret because General Motors, in the 1920's, elected to build 1.4-million square feet of office building space two and a half miles from downtown, or because attractive suburban shopping centers were under development.

Downtown could take up the slack by encouraging development of government buildings, banking and commercial services in the central city. The automobile companies' desertion of downtown was "regrettable," but could be overcome by the enthusiastic efforts of those interests with a continuing interest in downtown. The panel further advised that a CBD which is kept "healthy"—in terms of accessibility, parking, and vigorous merchandising—can survive the initial "tide flowing outward" toward shopping centers. Detroit was told that, in time, the situation stabilizes. "The development of shopping centers in itself does not, therefore, represent any flow from the central business district in total," the panel said. The central city is still dominant—"Without a strong parent city, the surrounding villages and towns would wither. The vigor of that parent city is the force that pulses life blood to a wide peripheral area."

The vitality of downtown, the panel said, can be insured by what was described as "a strong committee of top civic leaders, ready to invest not only their money, but their time and themselves in this cause."

"DETROIT OF TOMORROW COMMITTEE"— 230 MEMBERS

Mayor Albert E. Cobo had appointed the "Detroit of Tomorrow Committee" to marshal civic leadership in behalf of downtown. The Committee had 230 members. Panel Chairman Turley called a smaller committee "essential." He said, "We are simply endeavoring to point out the greater efficiency of a smaller group which would be constantly at work, rather than having a situation where everybody's business is nobody's business."

Detroit never did develop precisely the kind of committee the panel suggested. But its turmoil over renewal in the early stages did spur the evolution of a tight knit group which was dedicated and effective. This was the Citizens Redevelopment Corporation of Detroit, which began as an advisory body in the Lafayette Park controversy and ended up for a time as proprietor of the redevelopment.

The first offering in 1952 of cleared land in Detroit's first urban renewal project drew no bids from the builders and brokers present at the auction. In their book *"Profile of a Metropolis,"* two political science professors, Robert Mowitz of Wayne State and Deil S. Wright of Iowa State, offered reasons for the singular lack of interest in Detroit redevlopment. The writers reported that prospective bidders said that the density standards required by the Housing Commission were unreasonably low. Privately, doubts were rife over the feasibility of the low-and-middle-income housing mixture which was then official city policy.

"Doubt was expressed that middle-income whites would move into the project area," Wright and Mowitz wrote. "Therefore, to be realistic, construction had to be for the Negro market. To build for this market and still make a profit, it would be necessary to increase the density in order to reduce unit costs. None of the builders who were interviewed were optimistic about the chances of selling or renting to both Negroes and whites in the same area.

"One thing was clear from this first auction: selling the land was not going to be as easy as had been anticipated," the writers said.

A few months later, without altering the density requirements, but inserting a proviso for combining rental and cooperative units, the Housing Commission called for new bids, and this time found one taker. It was a Cincinnati group, the Housing Corporation of America. But two costly years passed while the principals wrangled over design, and finally in 1954 this agreement was cancelled. The cleared land became known derisively as "Ragweed Acres."

While the Housing Commission was considering the sole bid in the second round, a new element was injected into the public discussion of the renewal project. It was a pamphlet prepared by the late Walter Gessell, a mortgage broker who was then a member of the Housing Commission, and James W. Bell, an administrator who was formerly on the Plan Commission staff. Bell and Gessell proposed that a nonprofit corporation be formed locally to acquire and control the entire renewal area "in order to provide its redevelopment under highest standards of design and construction." This proposal was brushed aside by Mayor Cobo, but it survived as the origin of the idea which led to creation of the Citizens Redevelopment Committee.

About a week after the city's arrangement with the Cincinnati group faltered, *The Detroit News* revived interest in the Gessell-Bell plan for a citizens' group, dusting off the year-old idea and giving it prominent treatment in a feature story. The next morning, Walter Reuther, president of the United Auto Workers, sent a telegram to Mayor Cobo and the Common Council urging that they set up a citizens' committee to deal with the renewal crisis.

"It is economically stupid and morally wrong for an industrial community with the wealth, the power, and the know-how of Detroit to tolerate the social cesspool of our slums, which breed crime and disease," Reuther said in part. He pledged $10,000 in UAW funds to help finance the work of a citizens' committee which would explore the Gessell-Bell plan.

"Profile of a Metropolis" records that the Reuther intervention met with immediate objections from one of the most outspoken Common Council members, and placed the Mayor in an awkward position.

Cobo had recently appointed the Detroit of Tomorrow Committee, whose large membership "included the standard roster of distinguished citizens." This committee was "charged with the responsibility for saving the core city," the book says. The Gessell-Bell committee would undercut the position of the Mayor's blue-ribbon board.

CITIZEN'S REDEVELOPMENT COMMITTEE FORMED—11 MEMBERS

"Added to this," continues the book, "was the Cobo distaste for being pressured into anything, compounded by the fact that the pressure was being applied by Walter Reuther, for whom Cobo had little liking." Another complication for the mayor was the effect the committee would have on the status of his Housing Director and chief aide on renewal matters, Harry Durbin. Cobo saw a way around these tactical difficulties. With the backing of the Common Council, he named an 11-man citizens committee and made Durbin chairman.

However, it was obvious from the identity of the committee's membership that Cobo's action in creating the committee was much more than an insincere gesture to placate Gessell and Reuther. Both these men were placed on an "executive" inner group of the committee, along with the late Walter Gehrke, board chairman of the First Federal Savings and Loan Association of Detroit, and Foster Winter, vice president of Detroit's largest department store, the J. L. Hudson Company, and a trustee of ULI. James Bell was named director of the Citizens Redevelopment Committee, its only full-time staff member. The UAW's $10,000 starter fund was augmented by $50,000 more from bankers, merchants and other unions.

Bell told this reporter recently that "We were empowered by the city to recommend how the urban renewal area should be redeveloped.

"Where our approach differed from those that went before," he continued, "was in looking at the Lafayette area in terms of a total neighborhood, not with just a little part set aside for low-rent housing, another part for something else, and so on."

A system of checks and balances was created. Durbin's Housing Commission could not dispose of any renewal land without Citizens' Committee approval. Committee actions had to receive ratification by the Common Council. The elements of stalemate seemed to be present, but this evaluation does not take into account the determination of the ranking citizen members of the Citizens' Committee. They were wedded to the idea of a single developer for the area, and they were determined to succeed. The committee proceeded to have a comprehensive redevelopment plan drawn up by several noted architectural firms: Victor Gruen and Associates; Leinweber, Yamasaki and Hellmuth; and Oskar Stonorov.

A test of strength came quickly. Housing Director Durbin, nominal chairman of the committee, announced enthusiastically that he had an offer from a New York firm to develop part of the renewal area as apartments. The issue was joined on whether there was to be official or citizen control of the committee, and whether there was to be comphehensive or piecemeal redevelopment of Detroit's first renewal project. The outcome was that Durbin was pressured out as chairman, being succeeded by Gessell. Shortly afterward, HHFA Administrator Albert Cole gave informal approval and assurances of federal cooperation to the Gessell-led group's plans.

Mowitz and Wright say in their book that the Lafayette Park plans at that stage still included reference to "low-cost" housing, but with "a certain ambiguity." There were no specifics on how low the "low-cost" housing would be, and for whom it was intended. Nevertheless, the plans then extant were approved by all agencies concerned—the Plan Commission, Common Council and HHFA.

1955: CITIZENS REDEVELOPMENT CORPORATION

Execution of the plan was turned over to the citizens group which, on April 6, 1955, became chartered as the "Citizens Redevelopment Corporation." Bell explained how the corporation worked: It would purchase the land from the city agency. Builders would join the enterprise by purchasing nonvoting shares of the corporation, which would supervise and control the redevelopment. After satisfactory completion, land and buildings would be sold to the developer.

The two political scientists noted in their book that "with the incorporation of the Citizens Redevelopment Corporation of Detroit, the responsibility for the (renewal) site passed from the Local Public Agency (The Housing Commission) to a private nonprofit corporation."

The Redevelopment Corporation was funded with $450,000, including $180,000 from the three auto-makers, Ford, Chrysler and

General Motors; and $50,000 each from J. L. Hudson and the United Automobile Workers.

By late 1955, the Redevelopment Corporation had found a developer it considered suitable, a Chicago firm known as Cities Redevelopment, Inc., which brought in architect Ludwig Mies van der Rohe as chief designer. Without fanfare, the concept of low cost housing for low-income families was phased out of the plan. Lafayette Park would be apartment towers, townhouses and separated dwellings. The proposal for some public housing hung-fire until 1960, when it was dropped, and that portion of the project was given over to single dwellings in the $16,000-$18,000 price range.

The first occupancy of the renewal area came late in 1958, when a 22-story apartment tower opened. Lowest rent was $85 a month for an efficiency. A two-bedroom apartment cost $190 to $210. Lafayette Park was populated with a fair degree of economic homogeneity among its middle-class residents, and a racial mixture estimated at 12 to 15 per cent Negro.

Bell, who had become secretary of the Redevelopment Corporation, recently recounted some of its financial troubles. The accidental death of one of the developers from Chicago in 1959 triggered one crisis. "Funds required to meet debt obligations, plus maintenance and obligation costs, were not available," Bell said. "The properties were on the threshold of foreclosure." The Redevelopment Corporation was compelled to reacquire some of the existing rental properties, and to keep itself solvent brought in other developers to complete Lafayette Park.

"The cost to our Corporation of participating in this pioneer redevelopment program approximates $400,000," Bell said recently. "However, we feel this loss was more than justified in the light of the social, economic and architecural contribution that Lafayette Park has made to the City of Detroit."

Net cost to the City of Detroit was around $2.5-million. This cost is infinitesimal compared to the gain in tax revenues alone. Estimated total construction costs in Gratiot-Lafayette Park were about $65-million. City officials said that tax valuations were a little under $5-million before renewal, and something over $27-million for the fully redeveloped area.

"*Profile of a Metropolis*" gave an interesting summation of the Citizens Committee-Redevelopment Corporation's success. "Bell was careful to avoid stocking the committee with members who played the role of official ambassadors of various interests whenever citizens' committees were organized . . . (The committee) was composed of decision-makers, not mere representatives of interests, whose ability to act decisively contributed to their success. . . ."

The successful experience in Lafayette Park inevitably led to planning of other large-scale renewal projects. But the Lafayette formula was not reapplied, and Detroit's momentum in supplying new inner-city housing through urban renewal has slowed.

ELMWOOD PARK: PROPOSED 474-ACRE REDEVELOPMENT

Proposed for a 474-acre tract adjacent to Lafayette Park on the east is Elmwood Park, a three-stage development. No redevelopment corporation was created to assist this project. Moving through the labyrinth of city departments, Elmwood Park planning moved so slowly that, in 1965, Mayor Jerome P. Cavanaugh assigned his Community Renewal Project director, Harold Black, to make an investigation.

Black reported back that "The real problem is the same as in the conservation program, a variety of agencies each involved in a portion of the process." He cited the two key commissions, Planning and Housing, as chief offenders.

"The respective responsibilities of City Plan and the Housing Commission are not clearly defined, and the two agencies work at cross purposes with each other at various points," Black told the Mayor. "Each, for example, has at times initiated or attempted to initiate projects. Each works with the developers and quite often provides them with contradictory information. . . . In general, communication between the two agenices is very poor."

Black recommended that Cavanaugh put a "strong full-time urban renewal coordinator" on his staff "with power to cut across department lines and make decisions. He should be in charge of both redevelopment and conservation." If this move should fail to bring order out of "a somewhat chaotic situation," Black advised, "the only remaining solution would be the creation of a separate department of urban renewal."

Mayor Cavanaugh decided to give the coordinator suggestion a try, and in October, 1966, named Black to the post. Six months later Black told this reporter that "Internal slowdowns are no longer the case." He added that "There are still slowdowns in renewal here, but the cause lies with federal agencies and the money shortage."

"Slowdown" never meant stoppage in reconstructing the center of the city.

COBO HALL, MEDICAL CENTER AND OTHER RENEWAL PROJECTS

The 75-acre Civic Center, located between the CBD and the Detroit River, includes Cobo Hall, which Detroit claims is the world's largest convention and exhibit facility, attached to a 3,430-car garage. Several private office buildings and the elegant new Pontchartrain Hotel sit at the fringe of the Civic Center. A few minutes drive from downtown, by way of either of two freeways, is the 100-acre cultural center, now well under way as part of a 25-year development. Planned for a site just north of downtown is the 235-acre Medical Center, an urban renewal project with a net public cost of $13.7-million.

Three smaller urban renewal projects are located inside the CBD itself. One 59-acre tract, formerly housing skid row, is being occupied by a new federal office building and commercial structures. A 32-acre strip has been cleared on the east side of downtown. There is a pocket-sized but intriguing 5-acre urban renewal area in the heart of the retail district. Redevelopment proposals include one for a 76-story building, which would be Detroit's tallest.

Relieved now of some of the daily concerns with renewal preparation, Detroit's idealistic city planner, Charles Blessing, has turned toward the broad picture with refreshed vigor. "Just a few years ago we had 300,000 people living in the inner city, most of them living miserably. Many have gone. But when we are through we can have 300,000 people again in the inner city in a creatively planned environment.

"We needn't settle for less than a great city," Blessing said. "Is this unrealistic? I don't think so. Already we have worked 2,000 acres of the inner city into this concept. We've got 7,000 acres to go.

"The main job just ahead," Blessing continued, "is to settle the split between the two main groups here—those who want to see renewal creatively approached, and the spokesmen for low-income

Cobo Hall-Convention Arena, overlooking the Detroit River, is billed as the largest downtown convention facility in the world.

people who are tired of being pushed around and pushed out. I believe we can work it all out."

A dozen years before Blessing did his musing, the Urban Land Institute's Detroit panel engaged in some memorable generalizing which, to this observer, seems to apply to such scattered parts of urban America as Newark, Dallas, Denver, or Detroit.

"We are a nation of cities, all of which, in varying degree, we have permitted to become unsound for decent living in many respects. In different cities, this is because large portions of the residential quarters are unfit for human habitation, or because congestion is intolerable and bad traffic circulation causes irritating delays and time waste. Or it may be because health is affected by smog, or because of one or another weakness which goes uncorrected.

"We must make those cities wholesome, attractive and convenient places in which to earn a living and raise a family," ULI said in 1955, "since here live the majority of our people." In 1967, the problems and need for remedial action had intensified.

This reporter's investigation of renewal in nine cities has been intended to show, partly through the eyes of ULI Central City Council members and in part subjectively, the underlying reasons for success or failure in specific renewal efforts of all types. At the end of this effort, there is the hope that some good may come of it.

City leaders, official and civic, engaged in renewal work, tend to become excessively engrossed in local probems. A potential resource in overcoming difficulty is often overlooked—the case histories of struggles in other cities. Too much of the supposedly comprehensive writing on urban renewal is mired in pedanticisms. Or else an author sets out with a preconceived viewpoint on renewal philosophies, and he sifts and sorts the available facts and opinions, selecting those which sustain his thesis.

The author in this examination of city revitalization is pragmatic on the philosophy of renewal, urban renewal, federally assisted urban renewal, and all the possible combinations and variations. Whatever has worked is at least worth examining objectively. Again, there is the hope that some good may come of it.

The Medical Center, north of downtown Detroit, is a 235-acre urban renewal project with a net public cost of $13.7-million.

Detroit's central business district.

CENTRAL BUSINESS DISTRICT

THE CITY'S FUTURE

Profound changes in the style of urban living lie ahead. Population increases alone would guarantee that city life in 1980, for example, will be a far different affair than it was in 1967. Various governmental studies predict increases of between 35 and 45-million in the United States population by the end of the 1970's, about 85 per cent of the growth taking place in metropolitan areas. If nothing else changes substantially except the people count, if there are no dramatic improvements in city design during the next decade or two, Americans may find themselves looking back nostalgically at the relatively simple times which now appear so turbulent.

It is obvious that the pressures building up inside urban areas already are having effect, often in an undisciplined leap toward unpredictable consequences. But more and more frequently form and order are appearing within the confusion.

Federal civil rights legislation and the riots spawned by the "long hot summers" in the Negro ghettos are the extreme manifestations of pressures to correct one of the most critical imbalances in the national character. Clearly, the hoped for reversal of the exodus to suburbia by middle-class whites is not going to happen in a large way if the big city seems to be a place of peril. Just as clearly, there is not going to be any massive suburban-ward trek by Negroes anytime soon. Therefore, the city must become a place in which Negro families in large numbers have the freedom and economic power to live and work alongside a generally tolerant white population if they choose, or else to seek out voluntarily the benefits, political and cultural, of living in an ethnic enclave no longer stigmatized as a ghetto. All the lawmaking and lawlessness must be assumed to be leading toward a resolution of the "race problem." Or else the traditional assumption that the American democratic system can encounter no insoluble internal problems must be discarded. Certainly the latter is the more drastic assumption.

DIFFICULTIES MUST BE MET AND MASTERED

Other difficulties must be met and mastered simply because the failure to do so would be an admission that many national values have been spurious. Industrialization does not necessarily mean air and stream pollution. Intense urbanization does not necessarily mean overpowering congestion whenever people must move outside their homes. The existence of slums does not signal an inadequacy in national wealth or pride. All these problems are susceptible to the adequate applications of money, technology, and governmental direction.

Already a sufficient number of anti-pollution laws have been enacted to give some substance to the notion that the atmosphere and waterways are not unrestricted dumping grounds. On other fronts, there has been a dawning recognition that the suburbs and the automobile will not go away and stop causing so many problems. Automakers are planning electric cars which will take up less space and cause less pollution (but could give rise to other problems).

Private enterprise, without a doubt, helped make the nation great. Something more is needed in the effort to make the nation's cities great because "private enterprise" is in fact a proliferation of enterprises within the private sector of the economy, competitive and often contradictory forces. Private citizens unable to pay for what they need and sometimes unable to find what they want and can afford have given government its modern mandate. The federal government has become the direct ally of the cities because federal influence and taxing power are unimpeded by the maze of local political boundaries.

NEEDED: METROPOLITAN GOVERNMENT AND REGIONAL PLANNING

The 1966 study prepared for the House Government Operations Committee by the Advisory Committee on Intergovernmental Relations attempted to chart the maze. The report pointed out that, within the 212 metropolitan areas of the United States, there are more than 18,000 governmental units. Local government is so fragmented that frequently no agency has designated responsibility for handling some of the most common public problems. Townships, city halls, county boards, school boards, special districts, and state legislatures are under archaic restraints, and this apparently will be the case for generations to come. A more practical approach than overhaul of this politically entrenched system would be the fostering of a new concept, another layer in the local governmental sandwich, metropolitan government.

The pioneering effort at Metropolitan government in Dade County (Miami), Fla., has established a couple of points worth noting. One is that this new idea in local government can be "sold" to voters participating in a referendum. The other is Metro-Miami's record of consistently successful ventures into court. Local courts have ruled repeatedly that county-wide services should be performed by the county-wide government, Metro, since the voters had expressed their preference for the efficiency and economy inherent in the new system. The potential economies in an overlay of Metro government in places like Boston, St. Louis, and Newark are enormous.

Metropolitan and regional planning could be expected to place all due emphasis on the central city as the focus for commerce, entertainment, culture, and the most diversified modes of living available in the entire region.

Desire for something better is the triggering device for the changes which are well underway. The urban ideal attracted rural Americans by the millions and yet was found to provide far less than the ultimate in quality of living. Next the suburban ideal went through the same phases of acceptance and disillusionment. The new ideal is perhaps being developed from the realization that the nation can call upon an interaction of wealth, technology and maturity to make of itself whatever its combined citizens want it to be.

Index

Index :242

Index :244

Index :246

DATE DUE